THINKING FORWARD

Six Strategies for Highly Successful Organizations

D1506586

THINKING FORWARD

Six Strategies for Highly Successful Organizations

John R. Griffith

Kenneth R. White

with

Patricia A. Cahill

Health Administration Press
ACHE Management Series

Library of Congress Cataloging-in-Publication Data

Griffith, John R.
   Thinking forward : six strategies for highly successful organizations / John R. Griffith, Kenneth R. White.
      p.   cm.
   Includes bibliographical references.
   ISBN 1-56793-209-6 (alk. paper)
      1. Catholic health facilities—United States—Administration.   2. Catholic Health Initiatives.   3. Health services administration—United States—Planning.
   4. Integrated delivery of health care.   5. Strategic planning.   I. White, Kenneth R. (Kenneth Ray), 1956–   .   II. Title.
   RA975.C37G754   2003
   362.1'088'22—dc21   2003047783

The paper used in this publication meets the minimum requirements of American National Standard for Information Sciences—Permanence of Paper for Printed Library Materials, ANSI Z39.48–1984. ⊗ TM

Project manager: Jane Williams; Book designer: Matt Avery; Acquisition manager: Audrey Kaufman

Health Administration Press
A division of the Foundation of the
   American College of Healthcare Executives
1 North Franklin Street, Suite 1700
Chicago, IL 60606-3491
(312) 424-2800

Contents

Preface   vii

1 New Life, Energy, and Vitality: The Building Blocks
   of Catholic Health Initiatives   1

2 Governance: Sustaining Turnarounds at
   St. John's Regional Medical Center   19

3 Clinical Service Lines: Evolving Beyond Borders
   at Memorial Health Care System   57

4 Case Management: Optimizing Quality of Life
   at the Mercy Health Network   87

5 Prevention: Creating Healthy Communities at
   Good Samaritan Health System   119

6 Support Services: Surpassing Benchmarks at
   St. Elizabeth Health System   159

7 Service Excellence: Building the Future at
   Franciscan Health System   203

8 Thinking Forward: Completing the Transformation   237

   Index   257

   About the Authors   265

*Dedicated to the associates of Catholic Health Initiatives,
whose 24/7 efforts transform healthcare*

Preface

"Thinking forward" is the phrase used by Patricia Cahill, president and CEO of Catholic Health Initiatives (CHI), to describe the process that put CHI on the road to its current success. Thinking forward is the way CHI wants its associates to approach their work—not only to constantly look for ways to serve their patients and clients better but to enjoy that process and grow themselves. (CHI uses the term "associates" to include employees, affiliated physicians, and volunteers.)

This book is about the associates' successes, which have been dramatic in just a few short years. We believe it provides a model that any committed hospital or healthcare system can follow to achieve similar gains. The book arose from the research that supported the fifth edition of our textbook, *The Well-Managed Healthcare Organization*. In reviewing best practices and trends for managing acute care organizations, we noted that new positions had emerged on several issues.

- *Governance* has become stronger and more focused, using a balanced scorecard, or multidimensional measurements, to identify opportunities for improvement and stimulate management responses.
- *Patient care* has moved, not just to protocols but to a fundamental reorganization around patients with similar needs. Associates focus their efforts and their loyalty on the "microsystem," the small group of people who gives care. The microsystems range from primary care offices to hospices.
- *Measurement* and *evidence* have replaced guesswork, history, and authority as ways to understand and improve work processes. The

balanced scorecard has been successfully extended to all parts of the organization.

- *Prevention* and *wellness* have become both more important and more feasible. Successful programs are emerging, and acute care providers often play a leadership role.
- *Associate satisfaction* has risen in importance as healthcare organizations have recognized both the close relation between workers' and customers' sense of well-being and the long-term need to expand the associate pool.

We sought out CHI because of its impressive record of success. We asked them to identify their best practice sites related to each of these issues, and we visited those sites to learn what they are doing and how they are doing it. Pat Cahill worked with us closely on Chapters 1 and 8. She and others in the CHI corporate staff reviewed the chapters dealing with specific processes, but those chapters are essentially reports of what we were told by the associates on site.

This method describes, rather than tests, the CHI successes. We cannot claim that we have found the best solutions; indeed, the CHI associates or others may have invented several improvements since we talked with them in the summer of 2002. We can and do claim that the processes described in the book are effective, practical, and replicable. Based on the published work of others, these processes form a pattern of trends that any acute care organization can emulate, with similar success for similar diligence.

These six chief executives we visited opened their institutions to us:

- Gary L. Rowe, St. John's Regional Medical Center, Joplin, Missouri
- Ruth Brinkley, CHE, Memorial Health Care System, Chattanooga, Tennessee
- David Vellinga, Mercy Health Network, Des Moines, Iowa
- Kenneth Tomlon, CHE, Good Samaritan Health Systems, Kearney, Nebraska
- Robert Lanik, St. Elizabeth Health System, Lincoln, Nebraska
- Joseph Wilzcek, CHE, Franciscan Health System, Tacoma, Washington

These CEOs' style, implementing honesty, objectivity, empowerment, and encouragement, helped their institutions succeed and made writing the book a pleasure and a learning opportunity.

People who contributed to the book took pains to tell us their story accurately and thoroughly, and they usually backed their words with measured success. We have stressed the processes they used more than their results, but each chapter contains some summary measures of performance. We owe them a great debt, and we hope we have portrayed their situations fully and accurately.

Seven coordinators were essential to our success, including Debra R. Honey, R.N., CPHQ, vice president of clinical operations at CHI, who worked with the six site coordinators to bring the entire project to fruition. Her contribution was immense; without her, the book would not exist. The coordinators for each site are

- Cathy Wheeler, administrative assistant to the president and CEO of St. John's Regional Medical Center
- David H. Hickman, R.N., M.P.H., FACHE, director, Clinical Integration, Mercy Health Network
- Nan Payne, R.N., director, Medical Affairs and Performance Improvement, Memorial Hospital
- Lori Burkett, R.N., M.S.N., director, Performance Improvement, St. Elizabeth Health System
- Joan K. Lindenstein, M.H.A., FACHE, administrative director, Community Health Development, Good Samaritan Health Systems
- June Bowman, R.N., M.S.N., chief operating officer and chief nurse executive, Franciscan Health System

These coordinators worked long and hard to set up visits, check facts, and get approval for quotes. We are indebted to them.

John R. Griffith, M.B.A., FACHE
Andrew Pattullo Collegiate
  Professor
Department of Health
  Management and Policy
School of Public Health
The University of Michigan

Kenneth R. White, Ph.D., FACHE
Associate Professor and Director
Graduate Program in Health
  Administration
Virginia Commonwealth
  University

Chapter 1

New Life, Energy, and Vitality: The Building Blocks of Catholic Health Initiatives

INTRODUCTION

The coming decades will be demanding ones for hospitals and health-care systems in the United States. The pressures for cost reduction will not diminish. Caregivers will be scarcer, while patients will be more numerous and sicker. Patients will be more knowledgeable and more directly involved in their own care. They and their physicians will seek better health outcomes. Healthcare organizations will continue to compete for patients, for funds, and for caregivers of all kinds, and they will be held to standards far more rigorous than current performance levels. Taken together, these facts create a daunting challenge.

The good news is that the path to success is clearer now than ever. Some hospitals operate against benchmarks in clinical, operational, and financial areas. These hospitals create a culture that has two components—commitment to excellence and to collaborative teamwork. The world they create gives their patients better care and greater satisfaction. Simultaneously, it rewards caregivers and encourages them to grow professionally. The confusion, tension, and disputes that have frustrated so many in recent years are replaced with pride, collegiality, and shared accountability.

This book describes the efforts of one system, Catholic Health Initiatives (CHI), to meet the challenges posed by tomorrow's healthcare environment. CHI's effectiveness is demonstrated by a growing list of public awards and, even more clearly, by its standing on its own performance measures. We document some of CHI's strongest programs in detail to show how its approach plays out to the advantage of patients, caregivers, employees, and communities. We describe how CHI

1

hospitals reached their current levels, their difficulties and successes, and the "pressure points" for following their course.

The commitment to excellence has many parts. It is expressed in a realistic and universally accepted mission, vision, and core values and backed by comprehensive measures of performance. The measures are expressed as specific, achievable annual goals for improvement on each of the core strategy dimensions—operations, innovation, customers, and finance, or as CHI labels them, quality, people, growth, and performance. We describe how CHI has developed a balanced scorecard system of performance measurement and management and how its operating units translate its mission to local sites and services.

The commitment to collaborative teamwork is simpler. It begins with a broadly attractive vision—CHI emphasizes "human dignity and social justice as we move toward healthier communities"—that reminds people of their common values and mutual need, and then the vision is reinforced by daily practice. As a result, divisive argument becomes collegial debate. The energy once expended on injured feelings, mistrust, and self-protection becomes the energy that supports improved performance.

We have focused on six critical areas of operations where some hospitals are succeeding in the demanding environment. We believe these six areas will be the fundamentals for twenty-first-century success:

1. *Governance.* The leaders have made their governance more responsive to both customers and associates. The complexities of strategy get resolved carefully, effectively, and promptly.
2. *Service Lines.* The best clinical care is delivered through service lines that can focus on needs of similar patients. Accountability is delegated through patient-oriented work teams instead of through functional silos. Protocols have replaced independent, and too often uncoordinated, professional judgment.
3. *Complex Case Management.* Many cases require care beyond protocols. The leaders have found cost and quality opportunities in coordinating care for these cases, which are usually chronic and often involve multiple diseases.
4. *Prevention.* Clearly, the United States cannot afford to support the burden of disease that its aging population will generate, and changing disease risk is a major challenge. A few leading institu-

tions have stimulated promising activities and can demonstrate success.

5. *Support Services.* All those activities that do not directly manage care, including clinical support services like laboratory and operating rooms and managerial support like planning and supply management, have the potential to impair care or waste resources. The leaders have used customer focus and process improvement to make their support services more responsive and more effective.

6. *Service Excellence.* A few pioneering institutions are implementing the service value chain, moving to build new programs that attract and keep motivated workers and that rely on them to provide higher quality, more satisfactory patient service.

These areas are what many hospitals wrestle with. CHI's senior management identified the system's strongest sites for each area. In this book, we have tried to describe the activities of these best-practice sites in enough depth that others can learn from them.

The CHI national organization provides valuable support to its local units. We identify the contributions in each area and also suggest alternatives for freestanding hospitals. In this chapter, we describe how the national office is structured, how CHI perceives its role, how it supports its local organizations, and how it builds commitment and mission consensus. In Chapter 8, we discuss how CHI will implement its leading practices across its system, where we think the pitfalls lie, and how other systems and freestanding organizations can learn from CHI's experience.

ABOUT CATHOLIC HEALTH INITIATIVES
Ten Catholic congregations of women religious founded CHI in 1996 by merging three existing healthcare systems "to nurture the healing ministry of the Church by bringing it new life, energy, and vitality in the 21st century . . . by transforming traditional health care delivery and creating new ministries that promote healthy communities." That is to say, CHI was founded on the concept of change and continuous improvement.

CHI expanded in 1997, merging the healthcare ministries of two additional congregations of women religious, another large healthcare system and one freestanding facility. In 2002, CHI was a $6 billion corporation, operating in 64 communities in 19 states with 66,000 employees. Consistent with its vision, CHI provided more than $600 million in community benefits, 10 percent of its revenue that year and an average of nearly $10 million per community. CHI is larger than all but the *Fortune* 300 companies, all but two for-profit healthcare systems, and all but one not-for-profit healthcare system. It serves twice as many communities and operates in twice as many states as does Kaiser Permanente. Its community benefits are larger than the distributions of any charitable foundation, except the Gates Foundation and the Ford Foundation.

CHI's 64 communities are organized into 47 "market-based organizations" (MBOs). Several of these MBOs are large regional systems, but most have fewer than 100 beds. They are located in smaller cities and rural areas, although MBOs are located in Baltimore, Cincinnati, Denver, Omaha, and Tacoma. They have independent physician staffs, usually with a small percentage of employed physicians. Few are teaching hospitals, and none is an academic medical center. More than half of the MBOs operate a broad array of continuing care services. They are models for America's grassroots healthcare

CHI was formed as an equal "religious-lay partnership." It now has 12 participating congregations of women religious, and its Board of Stewardship Trustees is composed of 15 persons—seven of whom are religious trustees, seven are lay trustees, and the CEO serves *ex officio*. The system is committed to transforming healthcare by creating new models of healthcare delivery, based on collaborative relationships and partnerships with community groups, agencies, and other healthcare organizations.

DEVELOPING "SYSTEMNESS" AT CHI

Systems now constitute two-thirds of acute healthcare, but their performance has so far fallen short of many initial hopes. Friedman and Goes, surveying healthcare systems in 2001, said, "the enormous financial, human, and clinical resources devoted to integration have not borne much fruit. Evidence of quantifiable, sustained financial or clinical value is scant." However, CHI, which has focused on care delivery and worked to achieve a horizontal synergy, has a different story to tell.

The original regional structure of CHI presented a problem in building that synergy. The regions functioned more like separate, individual healthcare systems than parts of a larger, coordinated national system. The structure prevented the national office from seeing each MBO clearly and from developing and implementing national standards and accountability. CHI moved from six regions to three, and by 1999 it reorganized into a national organization with staff relating directly to MBOs, aligning the national organization more closely with local markets. Despite these changes, serious operational and financial problems were uncovered. In 1999, CHI lost $56 million on the bottom line, a far cry from "financial or clinical value." With board encouragement and support, CHI's management instituted a rigorous performance-improvement program for its most troubled MBOs and implemented a wide variety of financial planning and audit functions. In the words of many CHI associates, CHI became an operating company, not a holding company. The past three years have reflected improvement on a growing set of measures. Not only has CHI improved overall, but all of its 47 MBOs have improved as well. The record is summarized in Table 1.1.

CHI's operating model involves five elements:

1. *Commitment*—agreement that the MBO is a shared resource for the health of the community and is in the best position to understand and respond to the community's need
2. *Accountability*—mutually agreed-on goals and objectives between CHI's national office and the MBO that specify the desired performance
3. *Support*—standards and policies, procedures, training, information, and consultation that enable empowered physicians, management, employees, and volunteers to identify and implement opportunities for improvement
4. *Stewardship*—improving, transitioning, or closing services or facilities that fail to fulfill reasonable objectives; subsidizing operations related to specific mission objectives; and actively seeking new opportunities to serve
5. *Value*—making sure that all stakeholders' needs are met, including sharing in the gains for improved performance

The commitment was there from the start. The lessons CHI learned in 1999 were in recognizing that support, accountability, and stewardship must be balanced, that tough decisions cannot be evaded or postponed, and that value—material return for effort expended—must be delivered and explained to the MBO and its community. The stories

Table 1.1 Performance of Catholic Health Initiatives

	1998	1999	2000	2001	2002
People					
Employee satisfaction					
Turnover: organization				24.51%	19.77%
Turnover: RN only					16.34%
Growth					
Patient overall satisfaction[1]		4.21	4.19	4.20	4.18
ER patient satisfaction[2]		4.53	4.50	4.45	4.02
Patients rating care as "excellent"[3]		40%	40%	40%	38%
Performance					
Net patient revenue (millions)	$4,587	$4,756	$5,016	$5,399	$5,538
Operating margin	.5%	(3.8)%	(1.5)%	1.3%	3.7%
Total margin	4.6%	(1.0)%	1.7%	2.9%	4.4%
Days of total cash	145	120	142	164	171
Debt to capital ratio	34.6%	33.5%	36.7%	33.5%	35.5%
Expenses/adjusted income[4]	Not available	Not available	$4,928	$4,941	$5,273
Community benefit[5] (millions)	$415	$470	$549	$633	$601

Quality

Mean patient perceived quality[6]		4.42	4.43	4.43	4.18
Process and outcomes measures in use[7]	System approach for accreditation survey process pilot	System approach for accreditation survey process implementation	Pharmacy safety assessment process; systemwide DRG outcome report	Pharmacy safety assessment process continued; overall patient safety assessment process	Patient level outcome measures to include top system DRGs (i.e., CHF, AMI, CAP, vaginal delivery)

Notes: Measures were entered as they became available.

1. Inpatient survey results. These values were estimated from a regression equation using all original values and dummy variables for each quarter except from July to September 2002. The equation has excellent fit and significance. The parameters for the quarters prior to the current vendor are similar and highly significant. The adjustment model incorporates any time trend so that none can appear in the data above. However, inspection of the adjustment coefficients and original data suggest that there was no trend, either up or down, in these measures.

2. ER survey results; see note 1.

3. Percentage of inpatients surveyed rating quality as excellent.

4. Cost per case adjusted for severity using CMS's DRG index.

5. Community benefit is defined by Catholic Health Association and includes charity care, Medicare and Medicaid losses, education and research costs, and services or funds donated to community activities.

6. Inpatient survey results; see note 1.

7. Measures reported to the CHI board. In 2003, CHI will standardize many of these measures for comparative reporting.

from the six sites illustrate the model in action. The lessons were not easy; the migration to operating company was painful for many people. Sixty percent of CHI's MBO CEOs have turned over in the last three years, but 60 percent of their successors have come from within the system.

The model fits well with the approaches used by leading commercial corporations. It is similar to the management models of corporations like General Electric and Johnson & Johnson. The accountability model of CHI is deliberately designed to avoid illegal practices employed by commercial disasters like Enron and WorldCom. The model is supported by management research as well. Ram Charan, Harvard professor of strategy, says:

> [T]he inability to take decisive action is rooted in a company's culture . . . . [L]eaders create a culture of indecisiveness, and leaders can break it. Breaking it requires them to take three actions. First, they must engender intellectual honesty in the connections between people. Second, they must see to it that the organization's "social operating mechanisms"—the meetings, reviews, and other situations through which people in the corporation do business—have honest dialogue at their cores. And third, leaders must ensure that feedback and follow-through are used to reward high achievers, coach those who are struggling, and discourage those whose behaviors are blocking the organization's progress.

We believe CHI's model provides foundations that can assist in the management of the community hospital. Any other not-for-profit healthcare system that follows the approach can have similar success. Although not every freestanding hospital will have the resources to implement the model, many do and can. Like CHI, they should begin to see improved operation within a year or two. That is not to say that this is the last word in management. The model itself emphasizes continuous improvement. It will evolve and grow, and the details will be expanded and revised. But we believe the approach is permanent, and few of the major elements of the model will be radically changed.

Several other systems of varying sizes also push the benchmarks of excellence. One of the purposes of this book is to describe the CHI approach so that it can be compared with others. We believe most of these systems follow a similar model. Whether CHI is emulating them or they are emulating CHI, we cannot say. However, we know that if a better method emerges, CHI will move to implement it.

Commitment

CHI's evolution began when the founding congregations recognized the vulnerability of their respective systems to a takeover or failure because of inadequate size or poor performance. The founders wanted to ensure the existence of a strong, viable Catholic healthcare ministry in the twenty-first century, and they elected to address the issues by merging their efforts. Moving in that direction took courage and was ground-breaking in terms of collaborative spirit.

The first step was to form an irreversible equal partnership with the lay community. The founders brought Catholic values and Catholic structures to the table and asked for lay participation and commitment. CHI is a 501(c)(3) tax exempt, nonprofit corporation. As part of the offer to the lay community, the founding congregations prescribed the following mission and vision to which they aspired:

> Mission: The mission of Catholic Health Initiatives is to nurture the healing ministry of the Church by bringing it new life, energy and viability in the 21st century. Fidelity to the Gospel urges us to emphasize human dignity and social justice as we move toward the creation of healthier communities.

> Vision: Catholic Health Initiatives' vision is to create a national Catholic ministry that will live out its mission by transforming health care delivery and creating new ministries that promote healthy communities.

A very important first step in CHI's early history was the identification of the core values by which it would be defined as it sought to achieve the mission and fulfill the vision that the women religious had laid out for it. In 1997, more than 800 CHI employees, medical staff, and board members from both MBOs and the national office met in focus groups to identify the core values that they thought should be the hallmark of the fledgling organization.

> Core Values: Catholic Health Initiatives' core values define the organization and serve as its guiding principles. They are the roots or anchors from which all activities, decisions, and behaviors follow.

Reverence
Profound respect and awe for all of creation, the foundation
that shapes spirituality, our relationships with others, and our
journey to God.

Integrity
Moral wholeness, soundness, fidelity, trust, truthfulness in all
we do.

Compassion
Solidarity with one another, capacity to enter into another's joy
and sorrow.

Excellence
Preeminent performance, becoming the benchmark, putting
forth our personal and professional best.

These statements are guidelines for doing business and for building
healthier communities and are principles from which a commitment to
human dignity and social justice flow. CHI board members and senior
management consider themselves entrusted with the responsibility to
make this commitment live.

The healing and community health missions of community hospitals can differ from this only to the extent that special needs can be
documented in specific locations. For the vast majority of conditions—
childbirth, depression, heart attack, cancer, stroke, diabetes, trauma,
and joint disease—the goal, the method, and the standards of care are
no longer debatable. The need for prevention and efforts to reduce the
burden of disease is no longer debatable. Healing can be defined by the
goals the Institute of Medicine's report *Crossing the Quality Chasm*—
that is, safe, effective, patient-centered, timely, efficient, and equitable
care. Healthy communities require an emphasis on prevention and
health promotion that will be essential as the demographic and economic trends of this century evolve.

While some communities may choose different visions and values
from those identified by CHI, three issues are critical:

1. *The vision and values must be attractive to many different groups in
   the community.* CHI's vision and values, while based on its Catholic
   heritage, are universal enough to attract broad participation.

2. *These beliefs must be permanent.* For people to commit their health-care and, more important, for caregivers and other employees to commit their professional lives, the values must not change from year to year. A set of core values grounds the organization as it navigates the constant changes and demands of the healthcare environment.
3. *The concepts of Reverence, Integrity, Compassion, and Excellence are essential as guiding principles.* Without them, high-quality healthcare will be impossible.

Accountability

Accountability—which is clear statements of acceptable and unaccept-able behavior—must keep everyone oriented to the mission, vision, and values. CHI has developed a set of authorities to ensure that its publicly stated mission is fulfilled. These authorities can be grouped into three broad categories—reserved powers, audits, and oversight.

All large corporations with subsidiaries reserve certain powers to the parent organization. The usual reserved powers list for healthcare sub-sidiaries includes the appointment of trustees and the CEO; hiring of the external auditor; and approval of the strategic plan, annual budgets, large capital expenditures, issuance of debt, and real estate transactions. Reserved powers does not mean that local perspectives and needs are not considered; in most situations, proposals originate from the local MBO. CHI's expectations regarding reserved powers are clear in advance: pro-posals that will advance the mission and vision and that stay within the values will be approved, and dialog between MBO and national office's management is critical to ensuring that both local and national goals are congruent.

CHI also reserves the internal audit function to the national organi-zation. Each MBO has an internal audit team that is employed by an independent company, Catholic Healthcare Audit Network (CHAN). The auditor reports routinely to the MBO board's finance commit-tee and to senior management of both the MBO and national office. CHAN is a joint venture of CHI and Ascension Health, another large Catholic system, that provides audit services to numerous Catholic hos-pital and health systems.

In addition to the CHAN efforts, CHI uses national vendors to con-duct satisfaction surveys of patients, employees, and physicians (added in 2003). Through this, CHI gains sampling reliability, uniformity of reporting, and comparative data, including data from other organizations. CHI is developing standard definitions of quality measures, supplementing and moving in tandem with the core measurement program of the Joint Commission on Accreditation of Healthcare Organizations. It uses a single vendor for demographic data.

CHI uses two information platforms, tailored to the size and complexity of the MBOs. Both platforms are integrated to facilitate and enhance communication between units. The result is that nearly all the numbers used in the national and MBO balanced scorecards are precisely defined and routinely audited outside of the MBO. This series of actions makes it unnecessary to speculate about reliability of data and significantly reinforces the "integrity" value. It eliminates much discussion on "what are the facts?" and encourages debate about "how do we improve what we're doing?"

Finally, CHI maintains hands-on contact with its subsidiaries through the relationship between the MBO CEO and the CHI senior vice president of operations, who is an *ex officio* member of the MBO board. In addition, financial and other significant reports are submitted monthly by the MBO to the national office. The intent of this contact is to make it easy to follow the agreed-on plans, and this intent is facilitated through regular communication between national office and MBO functional personnel and through annual planning reviews involving MBO and national office staffs.

Support

To ensure the transformation of an organization, its governing structure must establish both support and accountability. Help—capital, consultants, performance standards and expectations, sufficient personnel, knowledge—must be available to support change.

CHI provides substantial support to its MBOs. Its array of national standards and services evolves as the organization matures and as MBOs participate in identifying and evaluating the need for these services. CHI encourages MBOs to share leading practices through formal and informal mechanisms. It purchases expertise in the form of consultants, software, and databases and shares that intellectual capital broadly. It standardizes data definition, facilitates comparisons, and seeks benchmarks.

The CHI national office, working collaboratively with MBO personnel, has developed a number of useful tools—processes or approaches that encourage continuing improvement, solve recurring problems, or promote sound decisions. Tools are typically piloted in one or two MBOs; reviewed by a task force crossing a broad spectrum of CHI; and, presuming success, made available to all. Examples include an integrated strategic, financial planning, and capital budget process; a mission and market assessment tool; and a regular mission assessment to evaluate mission achievement in areas such as ethics, spiritual care, advocacy, and diversity. Less universal tools are often shared throughout the organization in a variety of ways. In some cases, this sharing involves the use of intranet-based applications or the use of shared public folders within the CHI-wide messaging system. In other cases, they are shared through regular conference calls or regional meetings with particular affinity groups. Regardless of the mechanism used, the emphasis is on the sharing of meaningful information and experiences. Any MBO with a process or approach it feels worthy shares its experience with others who may want it.

One tool that contributes strongly to CHI's recent success is the MACBETH (Management Assistance Clinic Break Even Team) process, an approach to making employed-physician clinics more accountable financially. It was developed by physicians in one MBO, tailored in a multi-MBO task force, and now supports the efforts of several dozen MBOs. The model has significantly reduced losses on employed-physician practices. Although losses have not yet reached the goal of $40,000 per physician per year, they have come close. The continuing subsidy can be justified as support for CHI's mission of community service and care to underserved populations.

Each MBO is assigned national office advisers in operations, strategy, finance, human resources, advocacy, clinical management, information technology, communications, legal, mission services, and others. These internal consultants provide some oversight and are available to answer questions and to advise when needed at no charge to the MBO. Their service, as well as many others, are covered in an annual assessment fee—currently, it is 1.25 percent of an MBO's operating expenses.

It is important, in this context, to recognize the diversity of marketplaces within which CHI functions. Although CHI sponsors approximately one dozen large and complex organizations, its primary constituency is the smaller, sole community provider. Most MBOs, large or small, have benefited from assistance, but many of the smaller MBOs gain routine access to skills and knowledge they cannot otherwise afford. The diversity among MBOs also makes the cross-fertilization of ideas more valuable. Concepts can be copied, but they also can be tested and revised to fit different institutions.

Each MBO is encouraged to contact other MBOs that might have information to assist in improving performance. That contact might be from CEO to CEO, but it is as likely to occur between professionals from the same discipline (i.e., pharmacists, finance personnel, or human resources personnel) who are well networked across the organization through conference calls and e-mail. Thus, local performance-improvement teams can query colleagues in other MBOs, get consultation from national office leaders in key competency areas, and sometimes use processes formally developed and pretested by several MBOs.

The best way to understand support is through the specific areas of implementation, and we will show how CHI supports each of these areas. Taken in total, we believe the CHI support structure is a powerful competitive advantage and one that would be hard to replicate by a smaller organization. But the governing board of a freestanding facility can purchase many of these elements, and its first goal in demonstrating and implementing its commitment should be to strengthen the level of assistance it provides to its people as they aspire to excellence.

Stewardship

CHI, like any other organization, has come to realize that it cannot be all things to all people. There are places that, according to mission and market assessments, cannot sustain success. CHI must avoid those locations and implements an exit strategy if necessary. The CHI strategy reflects the realism of former GE CEO Jack Welch's dictum for GE subsidiaries, "If you are not number one or number two in your market, fix it, sell it, or close it." Few of the MBO markets have more than two competitors, thus Welch's ranking is not fully applicable. CHI's "watch list" MBOs are those that cannot meet agreed-on standards and measures for performance on the balanced scorecard. They lack sufficient market demand to make their services cost effective. They cannot recruit sufficient personnel or physicians to fulfill their mission. Their plant will not support modern clinical needs. Their cash flow, margin, and capital capacity are inadequate. Often, of course, these problems occur simultaneously.

The appropriate stewardship of resources comes in recognizing the problem and finding solutions. When CHI determines that an MBO must be fixed, divested, or closed, it still reserves the right to sustain its mission in truly unique circumstances to subsidize specific MBOs as an expression of social justice and compassion when warranted.

Since its founding, CHI has divested 11 MBOs, closed 2, and resolved serious problems in more than 12. Almost all of the divested MBOs had been substantially improved prior to divestiture. The problem was sustaining performance long term. CHI had six on its watch list in 2002 and expects to reduce that to three or four in 2003. Realism requires that progress be made and subsidies limited to truly deserving situations. But the mission requires that the problematic situations be approached carefully, with due regard for the community consequences. CHI has a mission and market assessment tool that evaluates alternatives and impacts from the perspective of patients (especially the poor and disadvantaged), associates, and its other MBOs. Each MBO self-assesses annually using this tool, which serves as one basis for determining needed performance improvement or potential transition. CHI's assessment of the impact of a decision on multiple constituencies echoes the priorities of the Johnson & Johnson Credo, which puts responsibility to "all who use our products and services" first and to its stockholders last.

The comparison and rank order of the MBOs on major balanced scorecard measures attests to CHI's realism. The ranks are widely circulated so that each MBO governance and leadership team knows not only where it stands but who is leading and who is in trouble. Given the rewards that are shared with success, MBO managers are strongly motivated to improve, and the leaders know that standing still will not be enough. Given the national office's demonstrated willingness to act, being at or near the bottom of a list is a powerful signal to local management, trustees, and physicians. However, wise managers recognize that CHI brings substantial resources to assist an MBO to improve and a source of best practices from the leading MBOs.

Value

Healthcare organizations are human service organizations that involve exchanges between people for both spiritual and material ends. CHI's patients expect service and improved health that are at least comparable to what they can get from other sources. The communities expect services that meet their needs and fulfill the mission. Physicians expect both a competitive income and an adequate supply of modern equipment and trained personnel. Associates expect fair compensation and recognition for successful extra effort. Part of CHI's improvement initiative in 1999 was its recognition that it needed to enhance the value it returned to its MBOs and other stakeholders. Because the national office does not generate care itself, this value must come from support and improved MBO performance. However noble its goals, CHI must improve performance by more than it costs.

In 1999, many MBOs were dissatisfied with the relationship with the national office. The regional organizational structure continued to impede a closer national office-MBO connection. Some troubled sites were absorbing more operational and financial assistance than seemed appropriate to more successful MBOs. Capital was short. A shaky CHI balance sheet impaired borrowing. At least one major strategy inherited from the predecessor systems—the purchase of physician practices—had gone sour. Regional inconsistencies created the impression that national office advice was either not helpful or was ignored.

A serious downturn in operating performance and cash and a large increase in the need for capital contributed to a 1999 crisis. A major performance-improvement initiative was implemented to address the problems identified and, in the process, helped to address the major concern raised about systems generally—that they did not add value. CHI took several different steps that allow it to say it has solved that problem:

1. *National office structures were simplified, connecting the national staff directly with the MBOs.* Office locations across the country were closed or consolidated. Communication to each MBO is focused through one senior vice president of operations, who is accountable for its performance.

2. *Services were substantially improved.* National office tools and support services were expanded and segmented into those that are required for use by the MBO and those that are optional for its use. Consultation capabilities, educational programs, and leadership-development efforts were also expanded. The system of shared resources was designed and implemented, and several specific

programs, such as the one to manage physician practices, were developed. The pattern of inter-MBO sharing was developed, and there emerged a greater organizational willingness to set systemwide standards and MBO performance expectations. A greater sense of systemness and interdependence was created.

3. *The problem sites were transitioned as necessary.* Losses were eliminated or brought under control. Balance sheets were cleaned of intangible and nonproducing assets. Cash flow was improved. A downgraded bond rating was returned to AA.

4. *Because of improved MBO performance, capital available for routine replacement and renewal of equipment and physical plant was increased.* Capital for master facility plans was made available.

5. *A consistent executive compensation program, including an annual incentive compensation component, was developed and implemented for all CHI executives, including MBO CEOs.* This program was initiated to ensure market competitiveness, internal consistency, and a consistent focus on national strategic and operational priorities by all CHI executive team members.

The result is that CHI can demonstrate value to any trustee, employee, physician, community group, or local media. The essence of the CHI argument is this:

- Your local hospital is improving and will continue to improve in performance, including patient satisfaction, quality of care, worker satisfaction, and finances.
- CHI offers a valuable package of systems and services to support this improvement that would cost significantly more to purchase on the open market. It brings the combined strength of committed and aligned organizations across the country.
- CHI helps your community to recruit and retain physicians and other scarce caregivers by providing attractive places to work with leading practices and technologies, assisting them to earn competitive incomes, and helping them to achieve professional excellence.
- CHI's commitment to healthy communities returns substantial value to your community and meets needs that would be unmet or could otherwise be a burden.

Communities seeking to partner with a healthcare organization that is committed to these promises can move to the forefront of healthcare in their locales, as the stories in the following chapters will demonstrate.

BIBLIOGRAPHY

Burns, L. R., and M. V. Pauly. 2002. "Integrated Delivery Networks: A Detour on the Road to Integrated Health Care." *Health Affairs* 21 (4): 128–43.

Catholic Health Initiatives. 2003. [Online information; retrieved 1/03.] *http://www.catholichealthinit.org/.*

Charan, R. 2001. "Conquering a Culture of Indecision." *Harvard Business Review* 79 (4): 74–82, 168.

Institute of Medicine Committee on Quality of Health Care in America. 2001. *Crossing the Quality Chasm: A New Health System for the 21st Century.* Washington, DC: National Academy Press.

Friedman, L., and J. Goes. 2001. "Why Integrated Health Networks Have Failed," (comments). *Frontiers of Health Services Management* 17 (4): 3–28.

Garvin, D. A., and M. A. Roberto. 2001. "What You Don't Know About Making Decisions." *Harvard Business Review* 79 (8): 108–16, 161.

Griffith, J. R., and K. R. White. 2002. *The Well-Managed Healthcare Organization,* 5th edition. Chicago: Health Administration Press.

Johnson & Johnson. 2003. "Credo" [Online information; retrieved 1/03.] *http://www.jnj.com/who_is_jnj/cr_usa.html.*

Shortell, S. M., R. R. Gillies, D. A. Anderson, K. M. Erickson, and J. B. Mitchell. 2000. *Remaking Health Care in America: The Evolution of Organized Delivery Systems,* 2nd edition. San Francisco: Jossey-Bass.

Chapter 2

Governance: Sustaining Turnarounds at St. John's Regional Medical Center

BACKGROUND

St. John's Regional Medical Center in Joplin, Missouri, is a tertiary provider serving a 17-county tri-state region of Missouri, Kansas, and Oklahoma. It has two inpatient sites, 367 beds in Joplin and a 25-bed critical-access hospital in Columbus, Kansas, with a total of 18,000 admissions. St. John's earns 23 percent of its revenue from ambulatory care. Its medical staff has 212 members, including 48 employed by St. John's, and joint ventures in ambulatory orthopedic surgery and occupational health. It operates a physician-hospital organization that helps coordinate 11 other hospitals and an additional 140 physicians in the outlying areas.

St. John's divides its primary market of 200,000 people with a similarly sized institution only a few hundred yards away. The two compete vigorously. St. John's had been accustomed to a 60 percent share until the competitor moved aggressively to attract patients, forcing the St. John's share to fall to 51 percent in 2000. St. John's recognized its crisis and began a turnaround in 1999, as Table 2.1 shows. Today, its revenue, market share, and net income are all up. Newly developed measures of customer and worker satisfaction are adequate (at or above CHI medians) and moving in the right direction.

Stephen Carlton, chair of the St. John's board; Gary L. Rowe, St. John's CEO; and CHI's senior management believe this turnaround is "sustainable." St. John's has not only recovered from its crisis, it has rebuilt itself so that it will improve over time. This is the story of "what's different" in St. John's governance and why those differences

Table 2.1 Major Performance Measures for St. John's Regional Medical Center

	1999	2000	2001	2002
People				
Employee satisfaction		3.59		3.69
Turnover: organization	37%	26%	22.35%	17.81%
Turnover: RN only	17%	17%	19%	17.7%
Organization vacancy rate	4%	4%	4%	4%
Growth				
Patient overall satisfaction[1]	4.21	4.19	4.20	4.18
ER patient satisfaction[2]	4.47	4.48	4.64	3.40
Market share	53.4%	54.3%	54.7%	55.0%
Performance				
Net patient revenue (thousands)	$157,128	$169,888	$197,252	$217,389
Operating Margin	(16.2%)	1.4%	5.8%	5.0%
Total margin	(14.0)%	3.8%	6.9%	5.5%
Days of total cash	102	166	170	164
Debt to capital ratio	37.3%	34.5%	29.5%	26.7%
Cost per discharge adjusted income[3]	$5,438	$4,352	$4,283	$4,999
Community benefit[4] (thousands)	$17,282	$18,101	$20,116	$25,346

Quality

Patient perceived quality[5]	4.42	4.43	4.43	4.18
Patients rating care as "excellent"[6]	44%	40%	42%	35%
Process and outcomes measures in use[7]	• C-section rates (primary and repeat) • Returns to OR • Medication errors • Falls • Blood stream infections • Urinary tract infections • Ventilator-related pneumonias • Patient satisfaction • Medication errors • Restraint utilization	• All previous focus areas plus: • Nursing core measures: advanced directives, Norton skin assessment, restraint documentation • Top 25 DRG: LOS, mortality, and charges • Medication-error severity	• All previous focus areas plus: • Transfusion product utilization • Same-day readmissions • Short-stay review	• All previous focus areas plus: • CHF patients receiving ACE inhibitors at discharge • Antibiotic timing for CAP • Aspirin for AMI patients within 24 hours • AMI patients receiving timely reperfusion (either PTCA or thrombolytics) • FMEA (pharmacy robotics) • Transfers

continued

Table **2.1** *continued*

	1999	2000	2001	2002
	• Mortality • SF 36: total joint population			• Patient-safety initiatives • ED documentation
Quality improvement focus areas[8]	• All previous focus areas plus: • Restraints • Nursing documentation revision	• All previous focus areas plus: • Overall documentation	• All previous focus areas plus: • Correct admission status (inpatient versus observation)	• All previous focus areas plus: • Correct physician census • Ankle/arm indices

Notes: Measures were entered as they became available.

1. Inpatient survey results. These values were estimated from a regression equation using all original values and dummy variables for each quarter except from July to September 2002. The equation has excellent fit and significance. The parameters for the quarters prior to the current vendor are similar and highly significant. The adjustment model incorporates any time trend so that none can appear in the data above. However, inspection of the adjustment coefficients and original data suggest that there was no trend, either up or down, in these measures.

2. ER patient survey results; see note 1.

3. Cost per case adjusted for severity using CMS's DRG index.

4. Community benefit is defined by Catholic Health Association and includes charity care, Medicare and Medicaid losses, education and research costs, and services or funds donated to community activities.

5. Inpatient survey results; see note 1.

6. Percentage of inpatients surveyed rating quality as excellent.

7. Measures reported to the MBO board. In 2003, CHI will standardize many of these measures for comparative reporting.

8. Areas selected for intensive study by the MBO.

might support similar achievements in other community healthcare organizations.

Governance at St. John's

Governance is the strategic positioning of the organization, the management of all matters that transcend the components of the organization. That includes many of the relationships with the outside world and all of the elements that participants in the organization share. Governance is the Achilles' heel of organizations of all kinds. Not surprisingly, governance is the weakness and the downfall of a great many hospitals.

Governance was the downfall of St. John's. Mike Pence, the past chair of the board, says:

> I wanted to serve, but when I started, I was confused. It's not a typical kind of business. As I began to get my feet on the ground and understand the issues and the structure, I began to get the feeling that things weren't right. The financial reporting was inadequate and inaccurate. Management was not united at all levels. They weren't singing out of the same hymnbook, let alone the same page. There were signs of discord—infighting, no real strategic direction, no shared vision that everybody understood. It took me a year and a half to come to this awareness.

Carlton, who joined the board in 1995, adds:

> The hospital had always been profitable and the biggest in town. Our two competitors merged, and they became much more aggressive. We had maybe a little bit become a sleeping giant, not paying attention to our competition, believing we had the market cornered. It became obvious to our board that we needed to take steps.

Dr. R. Robert Hatlelid, a nephrologist who has served in most of the offices of the medical staff and is now a board member, states:

> Suddenly, we discovered that we were in serious trouble, and the physicians on the board became strong leaders in putting management's feet to the fire. When we hired Gary [Rowe], the board was suddenly energized. In the transition the real energy was from the

physician side of the board. We learned that we had to make our expectations very clear and to be very critical of the information we received.

By 1999, St. John's market share was declining, revenue was plummeting, and costs were out of control. The hospital lost $23.5 million, 16 percent of its net revenue. By 2000, all of these trends were reversed. By 2002, receivables and cost were in competitive ranges and the margin was 5 percent. Financial ratios had recovered. Debt to assets dropped to 36 percent, and the hospital had 164 days cash and liquid assets.

What makes this turnaround sustainable is that it was done while improving the critical relationships with patients, insurance companies, physicians, and employees. Patients and families still choose the hospital despite cost reductions. Physician recruitments are up, and physician leaders report greater satisfaction. Quality of care has become a focus of attention. Newly added measures of patient and worker satisfaction showed acceptable, although not excellent, levels. James Kaskie, FACHE, senior vice president of operations at CHI and liaison to St. John's, talks about the changes:

> I was way too benevolent in continuing to support the management team, letting it go way too long. Never will I be that tolerant and open on the time frame. Our intervention now is much quicker and much clearer. We have more process in place to audit performance. We have more benchmarking and checks and balances with more people interacting with the MBOs. When we start seeing patterns of problems, we gather quickly and create an intervention plan. If the management team does not respond, we take action. I've had to replace more CEOs than I'd like. I'm hoping that more can avoid problems in the future.

Many of the actions St. John's took were typical of turnarounds, but four key values placed the organization on a growth path that it can sustain:

1. Transparent honesty
2. Measured accountability
3. Managed delegation
4. Motivated executive team

As the St. John's board and executive office applied these values, they moved their organization from loser to leader. As the details described below suggest, this change can be replicated by any institution that has the will.

TRANSPARENT HONESTY

Honesty is essential in today's healthcare. Evidence-based decisions, continuous improvement of quality and service, and an increasingly informed and critical public demand honesty. CHI emphasizes honesty in all its activities, for all its sites. It reinforces its policy with frequent review of performance measures and systemwide control over both the internal and external audits.

St. John's now goes beyond that. It strives to make every decision clear to those it affects and to answer every question to the satisfaction of the asker. That is the transparent part—there are no secrets at St. John's.

It was not always so. According to Pence:

We've been successful in bringing some really outstanding people to the board. We now have retreats that are very effective. We start each meeting with a 45-minute educational session. These sessions were rarely held before, and they have been very beneficial in helping board members understand how they fit in and what's expected of them.

The board room is now a free and open environment where all members are comfortable in questioning management. That's compared to a room where people who came to the board got the impression that they were not expected to challenge management. The environment now is much more fruitful and productive. The board is stimulated and challenged by management. Management expects them to contribute. The benefits that can come from good governance come much more abundantly in this kind of environment.

Most boards give management the benefit of the doubt, and go too long before they make the changes they know have to be made. We were guilty of that. Once we made the change, however, it was the key to unlocking the boardroom, letting it blossom, and bringing forth its full potential.

Carlton elaborates on this new honesty:

> I wish we would have done the board self-assessment a few years ago. We've become more serious about doing it within the last couple of years. We have to be self-critical. I was on the nominating committee, and "being involved" is a criterion; we aren't interested in window dressing. We have found that when we approach people and tell them how much time is involved, they decline if they can't do that. Our members must attend the meetings, sit on committees that will take two to four hours a month, and review the agenda packet. The chair must spend a half-day a week, plus attending functions as a representative of the hospital.

The emphasis on candor and accuracy is carried through the organization. Gary L. Rowe, St. John's CEO, explains his philosophy of honest management:

> There is a difference in the core of this institution. There's a spirit, and it's real. If you try to violate it, people raise an uproar. That sets us apart. Our success depends upon our willingness to change and take risks. If we err, we admit it, fix the problem, and move on.
>
> It would have been harder without the crisis. In a turnaround, crisis is your friend. In a good program that just needs to adjust its focus, crisis is your enemy. I've learned that crisis lets you make very tough decisions fast. Everything bottoms out, but it comes back fast. In a good situation, you have to move slower, a degree or two at a time. It takes more preparation.
>
> You can't go slow in a crisis and be honest. You'll be asked, "Will we have layoffs?" The answer is "Yes." If you say yes, morale immediately declines. If you say "No," you've lied to them. I like to get the layoffs done, so I can say, "Yes, but from now on there will be no more." That way you build credibility and trust.

Dr. Dean Backstrom, vice president for medical affairs:

> The physicians appreciate the change. There is a lot of comfort about performance that wasn't present in the former administration.

Beth Eagleton, Ph.D., chief nursing officer:

> In our board orientation, Gary makes it clear: This is what you should expect from me and the leadership team. If you aren't getting that, you should be asking these kinds of questions. That combination of education and structure wasn't here before.

Dean DeHaven, Jr., FACHE, vice president for human resources:

> It's more than fact-based management; I think it's the way the facts are delivered. I remember one of the early decisions was to meet every member of the organization about our core values. We said if you want to leave, then leave, but if you want to stay and be part of this staff, we are going to give you credit. I don't think people were resistant, but they were suspicious. It took us about a year to convince people.

CHI reinforces honesty in several ways. "Integrity" is a value. The internal audit is conducted by Catholic Healthcare Audit Network (CHAN), outside contractors rather than local hospital employees. CHI selects and supervises the external auditor. A compliance program reports directly to the central offices, and CHI has policies protecting whistleblowers at all levels.

Sister Geraldine Hoyer, CSC, chief financial officer at CHI, describes the CHAN system:

> CHAN audits every area—operations, finances, and compliance. Any of those areas could address revenue issues, expense issues, or both. Balance sheet auditing is common. The auditors are strictly internal; they do not render opinions.
>
> The CHAN auditor has reporting relationships that guarantee the independence of the auditor. One of the criticisms of the internal auditors is that they are dependent for their livelihood on the company that they are auditing. In CHAN, that's not true. If there's a conflict of either values or personality, then CHAN can handle it. CHAN auditors do not report directly to me, but the summary reports go to our board. The CHAN supervision can contact anybody in CHI if there's a problem, and they would.

CHI leaders support candor in all relationships. CHI is not the only company to make this commitment. Johnson & Johnson is famous for its Credo, which states "We must provide competent management and their actions must be just and ethical." The company believes the Credo, which also emphasizes product users as "our first responsibility" and stresses respect for workers, contributes to its exceptional financial record. (View the Credo on the Johnson & Johnson web site, *http://www.jnj.com/who_is_jnj/cr_usa.html*). St. John's transparent honesty is the fullest implementation of CHI's policy.

Transparent honesty means both a reliance on empirical truth and a commitment to promise keeping. It means a fundamental change in organization culture and behavior. In a transparently honest organization,

- *facts decide questions.* "evidence-based medicine," the approach endorsed by the American Medical Association and consistent with scientific progress, becomes "evidence-based management." The opinions of senior people are respected, but they do not automatically determine the outcome.
- *dialog and debate are welcome.* People at St. John's know that by listening to one another, they will learn and grow. People can debate the implications and the interpretations, and those debates can be resolved by discussion and negotiation.
- *neither good news nor bad news can be concealed.* The balanced scorecard approach, reflected in Table 2.1 and used throughout St. John's to measure achievement, means that each worker sees what her or his boss sees, and vice versa. There are no secret decisions. If you do not know, you can ask and expect a straight answer.
- *contracts and other promises are carefully made and fully honored.* At St. John's, the atmosphere of trust that results allows everyone to focus on their job, confident that St. John's will support them in their efforts.
- *rewards are dispensed fairly, without favoritism.* There is no "in crowd" or "favorites" at St. John's. St. John's will not tolerate gender, ethnic, or religious discrimination. St. John's is careful to keep its religious commitment, which is strong and visible, framed in terms that will not offend non-Catholics.

Augusto (Tony) Noronha, Sr., vice president and chief financial officer:

> It's pretty uncomfortable for me to sit in the finance committee
> meeting and talk about my dirty linen. The committee has a very
> practical sense. They don't beat me on the head for not achieving
> the goals. They are more like a group of counselors who under-
> stand that things are not perfect. They want an open dialogue and
> a receptiveness to change. I used to rely on presentation. Here, it's
> all discussion, with everybody participating.

Rowe:

> CHI protects our hospital. For example, they insist on 100 percent
> review of physician contracts. They do compliance audits that pro-
> tect me and the board. Sometimes CEOs don't feel the need for
> this, but the truth of the matter is the top admitters can put a
> lot of pressure on management. The compliance audit stops the
> temptation. Because it's there, I can say to the doctor, "This isn't
> going to fly."

MEASURED ACCOUNTABILITY

St. John's mission, vision, and values are shown in Table 2.2. They
closely parallel CHI's, as they must. Much of the wording is similar
to thousands of other hospitals. What makes the values real, rather
than window dressing, is quantifying mission achievement. Being able
to measure accountability, and using the measures to focus on mission achievement, is the second key to making the St. John's effort
sustainable.

The commitment to quantification, combined with the commitment to transparent honesty, transforms the governing board activities. It

- clarifies the reality of the mission for all who participate in St.
  John's;
- allows faster, broader, and more effective review of progress so that
  both board and management have enhanced control; and
- identifies the opportunities for improvement, allows them to be
  prioritized, and aids in improvement design.

Table 2.2 St. John's Mission, Vision, and Values

Mission:	To nurture the healing ministry of the Church by bringing it new life, energy, and viability in the 21st century.
	Fidelity to the Gospel urges us to emphasize human dignity and social justice as we move toward the creation of healthier communities.
Vision:	St. John's Regional Medical Center, guided by our Values and Mission, will continue to be the preferred health care provider, promoting healthier lives, and being the recognized leader in providing quality, cost-effective care for the people and communities in the Four State region we serve.
Values:	Reverence
	Integrity
	Compassion
	Excellence
	Healing Ministry
	Human Dignity
	Social Justice
	Healthier Communities

Reprinted with permission from St. John's Regional Medical Center, Joplin, Missouri.

The balanced scorecard (St. John's board routinely receives everything on Table 2.1 and more) means that the board can be assured that basic goals are met and can focus its attention on the areas where its advice is essential. Rowe talks about St. John's effort at choosing, using, and following the right measures:

> We asked people, "What should the board look at?" and "When they look at something, how do they know it's accurate?" We started with 10 or 12 strategic indicators. Many of them were financial. Each year, we modify the indicators based on our needs. That led the board to focus on important issues, and they had the auditors telling them that what we presented was accurate.
>
> I think our board wants the hospital and medical staff to give them more on outcomes measures and benchmarks. A year and a half ago, I told the management team that it was time to turn our attention to quality. I couldn't defend our quality management program objectively. Most of what's been done is smoke and

mirrors. We don't even know ourselves. So we want to determine what we'll measure, how we'll measure, and how we'll benchmark. Trends are important, but I want to know what is best practice. We talked about it at the board retreat. Our board is now demanding this. I told the board that, if possible, within two years I'd like to be able to publish our clinical outcomes data. That doesn't mean we'll be perfect in every measure, but we'd be very good, and we could say we have a plan to improve our weaker results.

We had some help from CHI, but the number one catalyst was a physician consultant on clinical measurement. He's helping us select quality measures—identify what the definitions, calculations, and benchmarks are—and how best to present the data to management, medical staff, and board. We want to integrate this data into our decision making and market our quality performance.

To move to a measured environment, a hospital must both collect the measures and establish the ways they will be used. Both problems have been solved in many different institutions, and St. John's used this knowledge to build its turnaround.

What to Measure

The goal of measurement is to have sensitive indicators of all activities that affect the enterprise. Two Harvard Business School professors, R. S. Kaplan and D. P. Norton, articulated the balanced scorecard (BSC) concept a decade ago, and it quickly became routine in leading commercial companies. Kaplan and Norton argue that four dimensions measure long-run success in achieving any organization's mission and vision. With modest variations, this concept has held up in many different industries. By 2000, its popularity had spread to hospitals and healthcare institutions. In healthcare much of the learning/change dimension assesses worker availability and satisfaction. CHI has labeled its BSC variables to match its corporate strategies, but the crosswalk is not difficult:

Kaplan and Norton's BSC Dimension	CHI Corporate Strategy Dimension
Finance	Performance
Markets	Growth
Operations	Quality
Learning/Change	People

Specific measures must be identified within each of these dimensions. What to measure is an evolution. Measures are added as they are demonstrated to be reliable, valid, and cost effective, building a much larger set than presented in Table 2.1. Hospitals that are committed to measurement build a large archive of measures, a "source of truth" about various aspects of mission achievement. Any measure in the archive is accessible to the board; enough measures are routinely reported on each dimension to assure the board of continued progress. The "transparent honesty" rule means that the measures are actually accessible to anyone in the organization and that all concerns about the reliability and validity of the measure are fully discussed. People who oppose measured performance often argue that the measures are not sufficiently reliable. St. John's experience shows that measures can be used effectively; the danger of misuse is overrated.

Nationally defined measures permit comparison to other similar institutions and best practice identification as well as local trend analysis. All three are useful in identifying targets for improvement. St. John's used this process to get its operations under control. It looked to comparative data to identify areas of overstaffing. It copied processes that were both more efficient and higher quality. For each area where major reductions occurred, St. John's found similar institutions that provided safe, high-quality service at the new staffing levels. According to Pence, past chair of the board:

> The internal management statements drive the business. Understanding those statements, and getting good information in them is essential. In the previous management, people weren't putting them together and using them to manage.

Kaplan and Norton's learning/change dimension is the organization's ability to keep up with its markets. Recognizing the importance of people in healthcare, CHI has focused its fourth measure on people, but it does not ignore change. CHI identifies and measures change by specific project. For example, St. John's recently targeted a new surgical joint venture, expanded its insurance contracts, assisted its cardiovascular group, and reported progress on these as they developed. The business plan for these projects specifies the desired effects on all the BSC measures and the timetable for that impact.

What Goal to Set

St. John's governing board uses the BSC measures as the core of a dialog in which the community stakeholders state what they would like and the operators state what they can achieve. The agreements that result from these negotiations shape what happens at St. John's. They created the turnaround, and they impel its continuity and sustainability.

Effective goal setting begins with governance. The board must set specific realistic targets on the most global measures in each of the BSC dimensions. That is to say, St. John's has a 2003 target for each of the measures reported in Table 2.1. According to Rowe:

> Our strategy was to pick realistic targets that are strong challenges, and exceed those. If we know we have someone monitoring our work, we are a little more motivated. I tried to create a model where we were challenged and where I was personally challenged. I think that's the right thing for an organization to do.

Setting these targets is one of the most critical actions for governing boards. St. John's and most successful organizations tie the goal-setting exercise to an annual retreat that allows the board to review and discuss all the major trends in its environment. St. John's board gains a powerful advantage from CHI's comparative data and CHI's advice, but the decisions are local. Competitors must be evaluated. Alternative strategies such as acquisition, merger, joint venture, and closure must be reviewed. The local board must find the configuration most valuable to the community.

Rowe describes the process where it begins, setting the basic directions for St. John's:

> We give our board a set of planning assumptions, and they act on those. They know we are working with CHI. We really don't have a lot of difficulty. Management comes up with what we think we can do, based on trends and benchmarks. The CHI board sets corporate objectives, and CHI management pushes us toward those goals. Our role is not to agree to something we can't deliver.

The board moves on to approve specific goals that every part of the organization sets for itself, within the overall direction. Rowe continues:

Our annual business plan specifies the capital and operating budgets and the initiatives necessary to accomplish them. Each of our managers needs to set his or her own goals within the business plan. We track progress every month. We assess patient and employee satisfaction and satisfaction of referring doctors. We will start assessing medical staff satisfaction this year. I've done it before, and it's very useful.

At St. John's, the board monitors progress closely through the finance committee. The monitoring helps motivate the work groups to achieve, and, as Noronha explains, it helps the board grasp the reality of the operations:

The finance committee schedule has a special focus on specific reports each month. For example, in July we do profit and loss, cash flow, and managed care performance; in August, the balance sheet and physician financial performance. The finance chair constantly asks, "What should we be focusing on?" "What are the core issues?" As we discuss these things, what really is happening is that we are educating the board so they can contribute to the strategy. They are helping us identify the opportunities. They are challenging because they understand. The participation of our physician board members has been valuable.

Rowe describes how the board's actions are implemented by management:

Once the board has set global targets for the institution, management works with every work group to set targets for the groups that aggregate to the global targets. Again, the process is one of comparing actuals against history, budget, competition, and benchmarks.

The targets guide management's negotiations and commitment with each work group. The board is only occasionally involved in these discussions, when management feels an issue is important enough for their participation. The individual work group commitments are summarized in the annual budget. The budget is returned to the board for approval. When the process is successful, the board's global targets accurately reflect community needs, and the proposed budget meets those targets. Then the board can accept the proposed budget with a minimum of debate.

The implementation process is not painless, but it is effective. Noronha notes that Rowe has a central leadership role, helping his team accept both the limitations and the reality of the numbers:

> Labor accounts for 50 percent of our expenses. We set a goal of being in the best productivity quartile in three years. We achieved that. Invariably, questions will come about the validity of the benchmark a department is being compared to. To Gary's credit, he stands up and says, "Everybody can pick at the numbers, but this is the best information we have. So understand where the numbers are coming from and then move on to improving your operations."

The operating managers find the process tolerable. Eagleton concedes that not everyone liked it: "As we moved to more measured care in nursing, there was minimal resistance. Even if people did not like the improvement goal that had been set, everybody knew what it was." Marshall Smith, vice president of professional services, is more positive:

> When I was hired as executive director of oncology, it was evident that there had been lots of talk but very little planning and very little sharing, no inclusiveness as an organization. Now we are goal directed—we know where we are going at CHI and how we will bring that down to the local level and move forward. Now we have more open and honest communication. We focus on evaluating our performance.

St. John's demonstrates that this process works and that it can drive sustainable turnarounds. It results in BSC goals negotiated with each work group in the hospital and accepted by them as reasonable and attainable. St. John's usually meets the goals it sets; in fact, exceptions are rare. So the process overall balances two strategy questions:

1. What kind of institution do we want?
2. What kind of institution can we realistically become?

Using the measures to negotiate goals is very different from using them to find fault. It is proactive, not reactive. It opens the possibility of rewards, not blame. Most importantly, it allows the whole organization to examine and improve processes, to build new ways to solve recurring problems. It is a central part of sustainability.

How Much to Measure

St. John's and CHI's commitment to measurement is dynamic, not static. Some measures will be dropped, and some improved. The available information will expand each year, and the cost of information collection may go up. Two questions must be answered at St. John's each year:

1. What specific areas of measurement should we expand?
2. What measures are to be reported routinely to the governing board?

The answer to the first is conceptually simple. An expanded or improved measure is justified whenever the value of actual mission achievement will exceed the cost of the improvement. Implementing the answer requires a solid management team that can see where the greatest value opportunities lie and how difficult they will be to achieve. When management can present a convincing plan that improves an important aspect of mission achievement, the board should approve the measures necessary to track that improvement. Conversely, proposals that lack measured achievement should probably be returned for further study.

The answer to the second is more difficult. St. John's reports voluminously to its board. A conscientious board member can easily spend as much time preparing for board and committee meetings as attending them. The theory is that too much information is better than too little, and the extensive reporting reinforces the transparent honesty. But for the board members pressed for time, certain specifics should be emphasized:

- *Finance*—any material departure from operating, cash, or capital budgets
- *Markets*—any unexpected shift in satisfaction or demand
- *Operations*—any departure from approved budget goals on cost and quality
- *Learning/Change*—any unexpected shift in skilled caregiver availability, in overall worker satisfaction, or the satisfaction of criti-

cal skill groups, or any major departure from scheduled renewal activities

A board member's fiduciary duty begins with these specifics. All four dimensions are essential for sustainability. The one that is not monitored is the one that will bring the turnaround and improvement to a halt.

MANAGED DELEGATION
Managed delegation is the process that empowers workers and teams while retaining overall control. Boards achieve it by negotiating the goals carefully, providing the resources, and staying out of the details.

Any hospital governing board faces a number of complex strategic questions that require trade-offs between competing goals and interests. Here is St. John's current agenda:

- *Ensure safe, effective, comprehensive, efficient care.* St. John's has quality initiatives in several areas, including congestive heart failure, community-acquired pneumonia, and acute myocardial infarction. It is expanding its overall quality measurement system and moving from a retrospective peer review to routine performance reporting. Its Healthy Community activities include $20 million of free care, educational expenses, and outreach activity in rural care, domestic violence, teen pregnancy, end-of-life care, screening, immunization, and counseling.
- *Expand its referral centers.* St. John's added obstetric services and is working closely with its cardiovascular team.
- *Manage its physician relations.* St. John's operates a physician-hospital organization that includes many rural physicians, provides medical office services, and has an employed physician group that is expanding even as it wrestles with cost control.
- *Support the small communities in its referral area.* St. John's operates a Critical Access hospital in Columbus, Kansas. It operates an expanding Med-Mobile program for primary care serving five rural communities.
- *Sustain the supply of caregivers.* St. John's has recruitment needs in primary care and several referral specialties and continuing need for professional nurses.
- *Relate to its competitor.* St. John's leadership hopes for continued competition to achieve benefits for the service area that might

not occur in a monopoly situation. How to reach this goal and sustain a constructive competition is problematic. Preventive and community outreach activities might benefit from a collaborative approach, and a few services might require centralized management to ensure adequate volume of work. The competitor might face a crisis ironically like the one St. John's had in 1999.

This agenda, like the St. John's mission, is not substantially different from those of thousands of American hospitals. St. John's differs principally in its programs to answer the issues. Almost all the issues in the agenda have successful responses; the few that do not are receiving intensive attention. Many hospitals cannot make that claim.

From the perspective of a community member of the governing board, the agenda represents a complex net of risky decisions in specialized fields well beyond most people's experience. The board members at St. John's are prominent, successful, dedicated people, but people like them serve on a thousand boards. What is it that makes serving on the St. John's board different? The answer is the services of the parent company, Catholic Health Initiatives. CHI provides

- a "ministry/business model" that establishes unequivocally the mission, values, and long-term objectives under which the local institution must operate;
- the CEO and formal evaluation of his or her performance;
- a professional senior vice president of operation and group leader of several hospitals who is an active board member. Most boards have only one professional manager, the CEO, but St. John's has two. The second brings perspective from several similar institutions;
- an off-site orientation session for new board members;
- a specific timetable for board actions; the timetable is an essential component of the expectation-setting process, and CHI enforcement makes it impossible for any specific stakeholder group to use delay as a tactic;
- an integrated, consistent set of internal consulting services that identify best practices and shared experiences; and
- coaching and learning opportunities for the St. John's senior executives.

When these benefits are added to transparent honesty and measured performance, they provide St. John's with a major competitive advantage. Whatever the decision at hand, members of the board approach it with a stronger grasp of fundamentals, a clear and powerful set of values, and the assurance that they have accurate and complete information about the alternatives. Carlton:

> Prior to CHI, St. Johns was involved in another group [national system], but with no real reporting requirements to anybody and no upper level of governance. CHI has been beneficial in cost control, quality, and customer satisfaction. If we have a problem in any of those areas we can call on somebody there to learn how others have dealt with it. You have a sounding board out there. You don't feel like you are the only fish in the sea.
>
> [CHI] certainly helped us through a major management problem. They have given us guidance on purchasing and cost control. We can now measure ourselves on quality issues and patient satisfaction against other hospitals we know are giving us accurate data. It's kind of nice to see how you stand up against a hospital from Philadelphia and one from California.

Pence:

> We could not have turned things around without CHI. Today, CHI is an extremely valuable resource to any MBO. If you don't use that resource, you are just not managing to your full potential. In any area of the hospital—management, finance, you name it— the experts are there. They've done it right.

Several of the CHI services deserve elaboration.

Ministry/Business Model
CHI's business model:

> reaffirms the role of the market based organization (MBO) as its fundamental operating unit responsible for configuring CHI resources in relation to market needs and opportunities and effectively managing the performance of those resources with appropriate accountability and mutual interdependence as part of CHI.

It identifies the CHI role "to advance the mission, vision and values of CHI as a national Catholic health care ministry." It states that CHI will implement its role by pursuing strategies and establishing functions at the corporate level which create significant advantage or value for its key stakeholders—its [religious] sponsors and MBOs.

This business plan clarifies the role of the CHI parent and MBO subsidiaries, makes clear the accountability of MBO boards, and gives the criteria for CHI support. An MBO, as opposed to a freestanding local hospital, is accountable to an attentive higher authority, and it can turn to that authority for support that an independent hospital might not be able to get at all or would purchase at a substantially higher price.

The structure inherent in the business plan means the MBO mission can be shaped to local needs but must fit within the parent's. Pence comments:

> Things are drastically different from the prior system. There wasn't much communication; now there's plenty, the channels are wide open. Middle management is encouraged to communicate with CHI. Good things don't happen in a vacuum. They happen when people are communicating.

According to Mark Tozzio, FACHE, senior vice president for marketing and business development:

> Three years ago we set three critical success factors [organizational performance, organizational aggressiveness, and physician strategy] and eight strategies. The management team identified the risk factors for each strategy and the board accepted the strategies. The strategies have been the driving force. Everything we do relates to them. The department level goals must feed into these strategies.
>
> The second year we showed how we did against the risk factors, and we offered new risk factors. We presented detailed plans for the service lines to the board. We proposed expansion for our four best performing service lines. That led to agreement on capital priorities. The third year we offered plans to improve our weakest performers. We said, "How can we make it better or get rid of it?" It was really tough. We identified critical success factors.

Training for Board Members

Rowe notes that CHI can reject local board nominees:

> When that happens there's conflict. It's never happened to me. My job is to identify potential conflict and work it out quickly.

The training provided to new board members is more critical. CHI offers three board-orientation programs a year for new local board members. They are two days in length, presented by CHI senior managers, and cover an impressive amount of material:

- the CHI mission, vision, and values;
- CHI structure and reserved powers;
- local board member obligations, including an explicit review of duties and conflicts;
- the healthcare market and national drivers of change;
- CHI's "ministry/business model";
- local board member responsibilities for quality of care;
- the role of the finance committee and income targets;
- the role of the audit committee and internal audits;
- opportunities in community health and social justice;
- the importance of worker satisfaction and a supportive organization culture;
- a case study of failed governance with CHI responses; and
- a list of CHI's value-added services available to local institutions.

These sessions accomplish four goals. First, they make clear that board service can be a source of personal satisfaction. Second, they introduce board members to many like-minded people and develop a spirit of commitment to shared goals. Third, they give every board member a common understanding of the complexities of healthcare and the elements of the "ministry/business model." Fourth, they show the resources that CHI has to help local institutions. Carlton states:

> Some board members had doubts about what we were really going to get from CHI. They attended some of the CHI informational sessions and learned how they should be hand-in-glove. They saw results of bringing Gary on board, and how the new people are

indoctrinated into CHI. The people who were somewhat doubters cycled off the board.

Audit Services

CHAN assigns an internal audit manager to each institution. CHI also hires the external auditor. Noronha explains the audit function at St. John's:

> The CHAN auditor reports to the chair of the finance committee on audit related issues and to the chair of the corporate responsibility committee on matters of compliance. Gary moved the auditor's office so the auditor is closer to the CEO's office than [the CFO's office]. The message is that internal audit and compliance are important. I have often reached out for help from CHI and CHAN for assistance in areas such as compliance, internal controls, coding, and financial reviews.

Rowe:

> Trust must be earned every day. I think we all need to be monitored. That's the reason you audit. The CHAN auditor is as close to me as he is to the CFO, and we make it very clear that that he does not report to the CFO. He is directly accountable to our finance committee chair, and they meet without us.

The result is that it is substantially harder to mislead the St. John's board than that of a freestanding hospital because a hierarchy of financially skilled people supplements the local CFO. The board can increase its trust in the financial reports.

Medical Staff Support

About 90 percent of St. John's doctors are in fee-for-service practice, mostly in small single-specialty groups. The traditional support issues are the supply of capital for new equipment, the maintenance of patient volumes, recruitment of new physicians, and credentialing. The development of protocols and service lines to achieve quality and economy has expanded the agenda.

An important part of governance is maintaining relations with physicians. According to Carlton:

The medical staff saw that [the layoffs] went all the way up to the top. Gary took enough time to distinguish fat from muscle. It was a clear message that waste would not be tolerated. We heard through the grapevine that people thought it should have been done years ago. We have doctors in board meetings; we have them on every committee. When we did the changeover, [the medical staff] recognized the need.

Gary has a strong opinion about issues. The medical staff felt that he was a person they would be butting heads with—and they have butted heads. I don't know that that's a bad thing. What's good for doctor is not necessarily good for the hospital. I've heard medical staff people say, "I don't like what he did, but I'd have done the same thing if I had been the CEO." That's a fair comment.

When we can hold hands and pull in the same direction, it's the best of both worlds; but we need to recognize that cannot always be the case. The medical staff members on our board can have a difference of opinion—that's healthy. From talking to the doctors, my opinion is [Gary] has the support of the vast majority of the medical staff.

Dr. Hatlelid comments on the evolution of the medical staff's involvement:

Few specialists or primary care doctors practice at both hospitals. The staff that was tied to this hospital realized they had lost alternative options; they must make this hospital work. You can see the change. It used to be physicians got what they wanted because they could leave if they didn't. The medical staff now understands that our job is to ensure quality and take an active role in making the hospital financially viable. So our doctors are actively involved in service line development.

Rowe describes how he has dealt with the medical staff:

We inherited physician involvement, and I expanded it. We have four voting doctors and a nonvoting president of the medical staff. The board nominating committee looks for clinically sound, reputable, independent-thinking doctors who will contribute and participate objectively.

The doctors on the board opposed giving the president voting rights. They said the president should represent the medical staff [and] the voting doctors must represent St. John's. The other board members agreed. It works well. The one difficulty is that these doctors can bring personal issues into the board room. I tell them, or another board member tells them, that that's inappropriate.

I had to leave the medical staff alone for my first year and a half. They were mad at management. We worked with them on projects. On overall strategy, I would tell them our problems but they weren't buying. I shared what the problems were, what we were doing, and what would happen. They'd see that same style—very direct, very open honesty, and a willingness to challenge. They saw the changes. After a while, they started to believe and became more open. The staff would say I'm too hard nosed because I set firm parameters.

We had a debate last night with a group of doctors who feel that asking for their input means accepting what they want. We need their participation, but we need to be objective. We can't buy Brand A, because it's one doctor's opinion it's better, if other doctors feel Brand B is better. We have other medical centers in CHI, and we draw on their expertise as well. We look for the objective evidence.

Dr. Backstrom:

The impression the staff had of the former CEO was that he was a very nice person who wasn't very effective. When Gary came, he came with a definitive action plan. He has now educated the staff so that the physicians understand the management issues. In the past, all they had to do was glad hand the CEO. Now there are a lot more straightforward moves and conversations. Gary has trained the board to hold management accountable, and the staff respects him for that.

Service lines started under the former CEO. What we have now includes cardiovascular care, which was started by two superb physicians trained by Cooley and DeBakey. It still contributes over 40 percent of our revenue. Three years ago, we added our other service lines—neuro, rehab, trauma, ortho, and women's health. We're a Level 2 trauma center with a helicopter. Oncology is an area of keen interest to us. We are working with a local group.

We have a linear accelerator and two medical oncologists. We are trying to attract a general cardiologist who will circuit ride and do noninterventional work in our rural communities. We have a hospitalist program, and many of our primary care offices have contracts with the hospitalists.

The hospital recruits for both independent and employed physicians. Our recruitment team brings in pretty much all the doctors who come to our area. We have pressing needs in radiology, cardiology, anesthesia, general internal medicine, and primary care in general.

Tozzio:

We developed a very sophisticated set of measurements to monitor progress in the service lines. They are related to goals in the strategic plan. We have them on the computer. Anybody in the organization can pull this up and see where we are.

Internal Consulting Services

CHI offers a comprehensive package of internal consulting services. The list of services is shown in Table 2.3. Many of these services use teams from the MBOs themselves, offering consultants with unimpeachable "in the trenches" credentials, recognizing exceptional work by MBO managers, and building a network across CHI.

These services provide substantial support to management. There is help available on more than 45 different topics, covering every major area that is likely to reach board attention. Furthermore, the senior management team has a coach—CHI's senior vice president—who can encourage use of these services. Noronha states:

CHI attitude is one of assistance. When I started at St. John's, my inventory expense was high. We brought in a CHI expert who helped us recruit a new director and developed a plan to reduce inventory and supplies expense. He calls me every once in a while to see how we are progressing.

The key to our relationship is that we are not dinged for their finding out that we're not doing the right thing. As a result, we've had numerous process audits that have improved our operations. Gary encourages us to tap all the resources in CHI. When there

Table 2.3 Programs and Services Available Through CHI to Its Market-Based Organizations

Strategic Planning
- Mission and Ministry Fund
- Mission and Ministry Fund grant workshop
- Core values assessment process
- Long-range strategic and financial planning process

Governance
- Mission/Vision/Values
- Community benefit reporting manual
- MBO Board Development Resources
- Onsite orientation presentation
- Shared service organizations (two) that are governed by their participants
- Values-based decision-making manual

Finance and Accounting
- Balance sheet management advice
- Capital planning and allocation process
- Cash management program
- Centralized investment program
- CHI debt capability
- Corporate responsibility program (compliance)
- National liability, property, and D&O insurance programs
- Inventory and assessment of all noncore real estate
- Internal audit

Human Resources and Workforce Development
- CEO recruitment
- 360-degree leadership assessment tool
- Affinity groups in professional disciplines (e.g., human resources, finance, mission)
- Employee satisfaction survey
- Employee savings program
- Employee health insurance, pension plan, life insurance, and disability insurance plans
- Incentive compensation program
- Coaching resources
- Turnover and retention action plans

Clinical Management
- Ethics consultation (clinical, organizational, and social)
- Clinical affinity groups
- Integrative Health Manual
- JCAHO preparation and support program
- Best practices dissemination
- Performance management process manual
- Physician clinic management program
- Physician satisfaction survey
- Pharmacy standardization and safety practices
- Standardized measures of quality care
- Performance-based development systems

continued

Information Systems
- Single IT contract
- Uniform IT platforms (three to accommodate diverse MBO structures)
- Patient Archiving Communication Systems

Materials Management
- Bundled equipment purchases
- Clinical engineering support
- Standardized purchasing programs
- Required purchasing programs management and procedural advice

Educational Activities
- Biennial national leadership conference
- Education for physicians on end-of-life care
- Education program for chaplains
- End-of-life nursing education consortium
- Ethics associate training program
- Executive orientation program
- Leadership development program
- MBO board orientation
- Middle management development program (pilot in the fall of 2002)
- Mission leadership competency program
- Physician leadership program

---

are major changes in Medicare billing, CHI puts together a task force that identifies all the necessary changes and builds an action plan. This has been an invaluable tool. I don't have to reinvent the wheel.

Dr. Backstrom:

CHI helps more each year. Around 1999, it transformed itself to an operating mentality and to have corporate be a true resource. One of the ways they do that is to recognize the expertise of the MBOs. They put resource groups together, so we are helping ourselves. I've felt the heavy hand of corporate before, but I don't feel it here. The meetings I go to are helpful, useful; there's plenty of time for networking. I get the feeling that all the way to Pat Cahill, corporate is there to serve our patients and to be useful to us. They have four or five physicians advisers divided among the MBOs. I can call them any time, and they will be helpful. I have used CHI for individual physician peer review. I got a well-known specialist to review one of our physicians.

DeHaven:

> The more I asked for help, the more I laid out our problems, the more they responded. We don't treat CHI as the regulators or bad guys, we treat them as people who have resources.

Tozzio:

> CHI's vice president of communications did an analysis of our promotional needs and structure. The previous strategy spent a lot of money and did not do the job. We selected a national company to plan our campaign. We spent $1.3 million, focused on our key service lines of heart, cancer, and trauma. We focused on electrophysiology and women's heart issues. We had our female cardiovascular surgeon on TV. We based our campaign on our slogan, "Exceptional doctors; exceptional care." Our competitor never mentions their doctors in its promotion. We had 19 percent growth in cardiology that year, and 18 percent growth in total discharges.

What this means to the governing board is that almost every issue will reach the board properly developed. The board will not have to invent or define. The obvious opportunities will have been explored. The proper data will have been collected and properly analyzed. Along the way, of course, a number of issues that might have consumed board energies will have been resolved. The board agenda is reduced to the critical issues.

With transparent honesty, the limitations and potential errors in the factual situation can be openly and fully discussed. According to Carlton:

> We've streamlined some things about the board meeting. They are only every other month, but they run from 7:30 to 1:00. We are mindful of the timeline. We streamlined to keep things moving along, to keep people's attention. All the board members have the opportunity to review the minutes in the consent agenda, but we don't rehash the work of the committees.
>
> It was such a breath of fresh air the first time Tony Noronha, the new CFO, gave a report, to listen to him not just about the positive things, but also the negatives and suggestions and directions.

Straightforward answers to questions about how he envisioned the problems being corrected. We put those folks to the task of doing what they said they could do.

Tozzio:

When we presented the strategic plan to the board at their retreat, we got a standing ovation. I was very surprised. Most people don't want to plan. Here, it's a process they enjoy. A lot of the work is given to them, structured enough to give them something to work with, but flexible enough to tweak.

This management style has been proven to work in the long run by some of the nation's finest companies. It does not make board decisions easier; the issues are still complex and challenging. But it provides a major competitive advantage.

MOTIVATED EXECUTIVE TEAM

Executives make the programs happen. They deal directly with the needs of patients, caregivers, and other workers. They find measures, implement them, set up "sources of truth," report to the board on the environment, propose global expectations, and negotiate specific ones. Executives also enforce the transparent honesty rule on which the whole approach rests. Their effectiveness and commitment determine success as much as or more than the board's decisions. The CEO and his or her team must have both the skills and the will to carry out the board's intent.

Building the Skills

The skills to implement measured performance and a massive shift in direction can be bought from consulting houses, but sustainability is difficult because there is no plan for strengthening relationships with customers, physicians, and workers afterwards. The newly planted measures fail to thrive after the consultant leaves. St. John's chose a permanent CEO instead of a turnaround consultant.

CHI provides CEOs. It can draw on a pool of promotable people within its system, and it can offer attractive terms to recruit from outside. It can counsel the MBO board much as an independent executive search firm can. Beyond the usual search firm services, CHI works to develop its managers, preparing them for greater responsibility. Carlton explains:

> CHI told us we were in trouble. They let us know we had a problem. CHI helped us find the person and get the person here quickly. That's where they helped us the best. I first met Gary at a CHI function. CHI had told us we should spend some time with him. The people who were on his board [at another CHI MBO] were very positive about him as a CEO and disappointed that they would be losing him. They would have told me if we were making the wrong choice.
>
> Jim Kaskie was our CHI liaison. He had worked closely with the problems we'd been having and the then CEO. He gave us good guidance quickly. We were pleased that Kaskie took the steps to discharge the CEO. Not a person on the board at that time opposed his decision.

Creating the Will

Will must balance skill. The executive team must be committed to the management style. As it implements the style, most of the managers and many of workers will become committed to it as well. Commitment is gained by

- an understanding of, and sympathy with, the mission, vision, and values;
- a faith in the consistency of board commitment; and
- a system of rewards that reinforces the initial commitment.

Good companies use their mission, vision, and values to recruit and help select their workers. Disney World, for example, explains its values in a video that discourages applications from people who might hold other views. At Johnson & Johnson, it is clear that if you do not like the Credo, you would not be happy working at J&J. Similarly, all the MBOs share the CHI values of Reverence, Integrity, Compassion, and Excellence. You should not work at St. John's, let alone be a manager or an executive, if you do not believe those values.

To keep managers who are both skilled and sympathetic, the board and senior management must consistently show their dedication resisting short-term expediencies that impair future performance. The values-driven structure that CHI has built steadily reinforces dedication. Peers support one another, superiors encourage commitment, and superficial and incomplete work is challenged. "Living the Mission: Key Indicators," is a new scoring tool developed by CHI that assesses implementation of its core values, culture, ethics, spirituality, diversity, healthy communities, and service to the poor. The tool will be used every three years at each MBO to affirm areas of accomplishment and identify areas for growth and development.

The reality of the mission makes the difference for transparent honesty. Cynicism is to be expected; too many organizations profess these values without implementing them effectively. Overcoming cynicism means a zero tolerance for dishonesty. As conviction about the policy grows, it becomes an asset in recruiting people. It is, after all, a pleasure to work in an organization where nobody lies—not behind your back or to your face.

Measured performance provides a score, and few people can resist the challenge of improving the score. CHI uses this dynamic daily. Terry Wachter, vice president for mission, ministry, and advocacy at St. John's, comments:

> I'd like to be in CHI's top five. Fortunately, we're in the top 15, but there isn't anyone on the management team who wouldn't want to be on the top five. Two of the top five are part of the same Chattanooga system. They provided a very successful training program for their employees. The challenge is for us to replicate this at St. John's.

Finally, compensation must be tied to performance. St. John's has incentive payment for its vice presidents and directors, and Rowe wants to make it universal:

> Next year, we hope to extend incentive payment down to every employee. This year we are including all managers. Senior management can earn a bonus of 20 percent on very measurable criteria. Department directors can earn up to 15 percent, managers up to 7 percent. We are thinking in the range of 3 to 5 percent for employees. The bonus is based on the team effort toward four sets of targets—financial performance, patient satisfaction, employee retention, and social accountability. Next year, we'll include quality.

Financial incentive programs are an added layer of complexity on an already complex system; they supplement, rather than supplant. Managers and workers rank nonfinancial incentives—like the satisfaction of carrying out the mission, of working with like-minded people, and of making a real difference in people's lives—more important. Because financial incentives can put stress on important but fragile parts of the mission and culture—Integrity and Compassion, for example—they must be used with care.

The incentive program for Rowe and his annual evaluation are administered by CHI through the senior vice president. David Goode, FACHE, senior vice president of operations at CHI, explains:

> I ask Gary to make his own evaluation of the year, dealing with his accomplishments with the MBO, his scores on the four incentive compensation goals, and some specific goals established with the board evaluation committee at the beginning of the year. We then meet with the board evaluation committee and discuss the year past. Gary presents his goals for the coming year. The incentive compensation goals are set at the system level, not the local level. There's a personal development goal. We try to tie that to findings in his 360. Our system policy is to do 360 on MBO CEOs and senior system executives about every three years. We've just finished the first round of 360s, and we are starting the second. In most of my MBOs, the board sits as a whole as the evaluation committee.

The "360s" that Goode refers to are formal performance reviews by those who associate with an executive, such as superiors, subordinates, customers, and peers. The results are summarized anonymously by an independent review administrator to encourage candor.

WHY THE ST. JOHN'S TURNAROUND IS SUSTAINABLE
Several elements of the new governance at St. John's reinforce the organization's commitment to improved performance. These include

1. *the balanced scorecard,* with the increasing array of measures and the "source of truth." It is difficult to ignore quantitative measures once they are installed. Evidence-based management is so consistent with basic values of modern society that a motion to abandon the scorecard would be unthinkable.

2. *the system of transparent honesty.* The system reflects the most admired virtues of Western thought, and achieving it becomes a reward in itself. Distorting or destroying it is strongly discouraged by the group commitment, the active use of the data, the formal incentive structure for management, and the extensive audit and compliance procedures. The 360-degree review process used in management evaluation and the protection for whistleblowers support an environment where people keep each other honest.
3. *the reinforcement from CHI.* CHI deliberately reinforces the supportive environment with its training and consultative services and by encouraging the MBOs to learn from one another.
4. *the record of success.* It is easier to support any organizational culture when the organization is winning.

Kaskie:

> The transformation gave CHI an operating model that made the reporting relationship between the MBOs and the parent much cleaner, much more definitive. It was based less on a persuasion model and more on a management model. We got clear about CHI priorities, our senior management structure, and each of our assignments. To get there was very difficult, but we blew up the old model of regional management.

Carlton:

> I believe we are in a much better, fail-safe system now than we were then. We got our shins kicked for not having that overview that's now in place. That's the benefit we've gotten from CHI. The board is comfortable with CHI involvement. CHI is over our shoulder, but they recognize that each of us must be independent. It has to be community involved and community minded.

The greatest risk to St. John's in the future is that its overall strategy could fail, either as a result of misjudgment like a rash overexpansion or because the environment simply will not support two excellent centers in Joplin. This risk is inherent in the environment itself—that is, it is a risk faced by all similar institutions. The steps St. John's has taken have reduced this risk. It is prepared for the world ahead, turbulent or calm.

KEY LESSONS

St. John's started with a crisis, which it turned to advantage. Other organizations with a strong board and a knowledgeable CEO can create a pattern of growth and improvement without a crisis. Here are the steps St. John's and CHI took:

1. *They recognized the market-driven nature of modern healthcare.* They accepted that patients, physicians, workers, and payment agencies all have the right to make demands on their organization. They realized that success lies in meeting as many of these demands as possible. Each group wants something at the expense of the others, but at the same time each group needs the others. So the resolution will be based on compromise, and the organization that forges the most acceptable compromise will succeed. Although the demands are rarely realistic, the solutions must be.

2. *They reaffirmed their commitment to mission.* The mission is the core statement of the stakeholders' shared values. CHI draws its mission largely from religious commitment, but many of the religious elements are desirable in secular terms. Mutual respect, integrity, compassion, and excellence make this world a better place.

3. *They began to think in terms of the balanced scorecard, even before they had a balanced scorecard.* The concept of balance across the organization and between the various elements of the mission can be introduced with only rudimentary measures of some dimensions. The insight itself is critical to sustainability. It improved the board's understanding of its environment and its ability to formulate successful strategy. Improving the measures is inevitably an evolutionary process, and waiting for better measures is self-defeating.

4. *They began the process of building "transparent honesty" with a reconstruction of the accounting system.* It may be possible to commit fraud or deceit at St. John's, but it is certainly harder now than it used to be.

5. *They increased the accountability of the CEO, insisted on a benchmarking process to identify areas where performance was unacceptable, and rewarded prompt improvement.* St. John's found it necessary to

replace the CEO and most of the senior management team. Such replacements are common in major restructurings. They should not be automatic, and they may not be inevitable. The CEO can lead the transition and build it in both the board and the senior management team. Doing so requires a thorough knowledge of the desired transition (probably from prior experience), unshakeable commitment, and unwavering board support.

6. *They restructured their board meetings and board member preparation.* The meetings are now focused on questions that only the trustees can answer because they deal with marketplace conflicts. The board pays more attention to critical matters, more attention to the calendar, and less attention to matters that are proceeding as expected or are peripheral to success.

7. *They installed ongoing process analysis and improvement as a part of the St. John's culture.* Most of the major operations processes at St. John's have been revised in the past three years. Clinical care has moved strongly toward service lines. Performance improvement teams seek better ways of doing things. The business office, planning, and human resources programs have been substantially strengthened.

8. *They supported continuous improvement of their knowledge base.* The board benefits from improved environmental scanning, expansion of the performance measures themselves, and ongoing education for its members. Each of these is the result of increased management attention. The management team is both better trained and better motivated, and there is a development program for managers. The result is that everyone enters the room better equipped to address the issues of the day.

BIBLIOGRAPHY

Catholic Health Initiatives. 2003. [Online information; retrieved 1/03.] *http://www.catholichealthinit.org/*.

Collins, J. C., and J. I. Porras. 1994. *Built to Last: Successful Habits of Visionary Companies.* New York: HarperBusiness.

Kaplan, R. S., and D. P. Norton. 1992. "The Balanced Scorecard—Measures that Drive Performance." *Harvard Business Review* 72 (1): 71–79.

Chapter 3

Clinical Service Lines: Evolving Beyond Borders at Memorial Health Care System

BACKGROUND

Built in 1952 by concerned citizens who raised money for a faith-based hospital to be operated by the Sisters of Charity of Nazareth, Memorial Hospital is the flagship hospital of Memorial Health Care System, one of three acute care systems in Chattanooga, Tennessee, that serves an area of about 425,000 people. In the 1990s, Memorial Hospital acquired North Park Hospital and opened other satellite facilities through partnerships and joint ventures with physicians and various community organizations. In 1998, it was renamed Memorial Health Care System.

Memorial is licensed for 422 beds, and its medical staff consists of more than 700 physicians, nearly 500 of whom are active physicians. Memorial is the area's leading provider of cardiac care, cancer care, orthopedic surgery, and many other surgical services. It provides an extensive network of outpatient, home care, wellness, and physician care and emergency services throughout Chattanooga and surrounding areas. Historically, Memorial emphasized tertiary care, but in recent years it focused its efforts on building five centers of clinical excellence or service lines: cardiac, cancer, orthopedics, medical, and surgical services. Memorial Home Health has been strengthened to provide needed continuity of care; as a result, it is now the leading provider of home care in the Chattanooga service area. Obstetric services were discontinued in 1981, and inpatient pediatric services were discontinued in 2001. Table 3.1 displays key performance indicator outcomes.

To provide clinical excellence and patient service, Memorial adopted the strategy of restructuring services around "like" patient populations

Table 3.1 Major Performance Measures for Memorial Health Care System

People			
Employee satisfaction			3.70
Physician satisfaction		7.53 (scale of 1–10)	
Turnover: organization		28.24%	21.66%
Turnover: RN only			27.1%
Growth			
Patient overall satisfaction[1]	4.32	4.23	4.25	4.34
Patient perceived quality[2]	4.51	4.35	4.35	4.11
Market share	37.5%	36.2%	35.3%	
Performance			
Net patient revenue (thousands)	$242,460	$262,281	$271,514	$294,253
Operating margin	4.5%	1.4%	3.1%	5.1%
Total margin	4.8%	1.8%	3.5%	5.2%
Days of total cash	26	30	73	86
Debt to capital ratio	44.6%	42.3%	39.9%	35.0%
Cost per adjusted discharge[3]	$3,605	$3,960	$4,269	$4,346
Community benefit[4] (thousands)	$15,531	$16,008	$17,981	$12,730

Quality

ER patient satisfaction[5]	4.68	4.57	4.53	4.1
Patients rating care as "excellent"[6]	49%	44%	44%	51%
Process and outcomes measures in use[7]	• Patient satisfaction • Restraint utilization • Medication errors	• Patient satisfaction • Restraint utilization • Falls resulting in injury • Medication errors • Care of the AMI patient • Care of the community-acquired pneumonia patient • Wrong side/site surgery/procedure	• Patient satisfaction • Falls resulting in injury • Medication errors • Antibiotic timing in community-acquired pneumonia • Care of the AMI patient • Care of the CHF patient • Restraint utilization	• Patient satisfaction • Falls resulting in injuries • Medication errors • Adverse drug events • CHF patients receiving ACEI at discharge • Antibiotic timing for community-acquired pneumonia • Aspirin for AI patients within 24 hours of arrival • AMI patients receiving timely PTCA • AMI patients receiving timely reperfusion therapy • AMI patients receiving prescription for Beta Blocker at discharge • AMI patients with LVSD receiving prescription for ACEI at discharge

continued

Table 3.1 *continued*

	1999	2000	2001	2002
Quality improvement focus areas[8]	• Patient satisfaction • Restraint utilization • Medication errors	• Patient satisfaction • Restraint utilization • Falls resulting in injury • Medication errors • Care of the AMI patient • Care of the community-acquired pneumonia patient • Wrong side/site surgery/procedure	• Patient satisfaction • Falls resulting in injury • Medication errors • Antibiotic timing in community-acquired pneumonia • Care of the AMI patient • Care of the CHF patient • Restraint utilization	• Patient satisfaction • All the above items noted

Notes: Measures were entered as they became available.

1. Inpatient survey results. These values were estimated from a regression equation using all original values and dummy variables for each quarter except from July to September 2002. The equation has excellent fit and significance. The parameters for the quarters prior to the current vendor are similar and highly significant. The adjustment model incorporates any time trend so that none can appear in the data above. However, inspection of the adjustment coefficients and original data suggest that there was no trend, either up or down, in these measures.

2. Inpatient survey results; see note 1.

3. Cost per case adjusted for severity using CMS's DRG index.

4. Community benefit is defined by Catholic Health Association and includes charity care, Medicare and Medicaid losses, education and research costs, and services or funds donated to community activities.

5. ER patient results; see note 1.

6. Percentage of inpatients surveyed rating quality as excellent.

7. Measures reported to the MBO board. In 2003, CHI will standardize many of these measures for comparative reporting.

8. Areas selected for intensive study by the MBO.

or service lines. Clinical excellence is described by Ruth Brinkley, R.N., CHE, president and CEO at Memorial, as:

> . . . providing the best possible care for the spiritual, emotional, and physical needs of patients. The service line approach allows us to do this in a seamless manner that is convenient and comforting to the patient. This is essential to keep Memorial as the hospital of choice among patients. Grouping services also allows for efficient and effective use of resources, including the specialized skills of staff and physicians, thereby increasing their job satisfaction.

By 2002, Memorial and its five service lines achieved rising trends in most balanced scorecard measures, and it had risen to top quartile and better where comparisons with other CHI systems were available. In 2002, Memorial was the top hospital in the CHI system for patient satisfaction. Its success allows Brinkley to say:

> We are blessed at Memorial to have high levels of patient satisfaction as well as employee satisfaction. We also operate at lower costs per case as compared to our CHI peer group. This level of performance helps us to continue the growth of our ministry of healing.

Memorial's focus has evolved since the mid-1980s. Cardiac services were the first to become a clinical service line. Sister Thomas de Sales Bailey, the hospital's administrator at the time, began developing strong relationships with physicians in cardiac care when Dr. Malcolm Daniell, who had assisted with Memorial's first open-heart surgery in 1972, came to Chattanooga in 1975. Dr. Daniell encouraged cardiologist Dr. Kinsman Wright to join him. These two physician champions worked with Sister Thomas de Sales to establish the cardiac service line. According to Dr. Wright:

> In the mid-1980s there was no cardiologist devoted to just one hospital in Chattanooga. Cardiologists worked at three different hospitals and care was event-oriented. It was inefficient, and it did not contribute to optimal patient outcomes. Physicians often had to intervene late in the disease progression, after a precipitating event had damaged systems beyond repair. Physicians were not

happy with the fragmentation of services among the different hospitals and the lack of depth of programmatic focus for a continuum of care.

By the mid-1990s, the cardiac service line had exploded in popularity in the community and with physicians, and profitability and patient outcomes had significantly improved.

A BLUEPRINT FOR CLINICAL EXCELLENCE

By 1995, the initial cardiac service line vision had been realized, and it was time to set new goals to accommodate the rapid growth of the service and its popularity with patients and physicians. The cardiac service line was fine tuned organizationally, and new space was created to house the growth in cardiac services.

Designing

Sister Thomas felt that it was important to work with Memorial's physicians to consolidate certain services. She charged the nurse director at the time, Jill Aplin, to "build a cardiac program out of the disjointed services Memorial had for heart patients." Working with Sister Thomas and champions like Dr. Daniell and Dr. Wright, Aplin propelled the cardiac program forward. The vision of the group was to be a regional and national leader in standards of cardiac practice, patient care, and clinical outcomes.

Over time the reporting relationships of the existing organizational elements of the cardiac program were shifted to Aplin, as the first service line administrator; she says:

> Even without the formal reporting relationships, it was possible to work effectively because of strong preexisting relationships throughout the organization. As I built the leadership group for the service line, I was able to develop or attract and retain people with "good people skills" who shared in the vision and had passion for what we were striving to become. They each had a strong sense of pride in what they were a part of and a loyalty to each other and the team. My philosophy has always been to create a positive supportive work environment for the leaders and staff and get out of their way once they demonstrate their competence and loyalty to

the strategic plan. I focused on taking care of them so they could take care of patients, families, and physicians.

The physician champions of the program were willing to work with nurses and administrators, as Aplin adds:

> I can't underestimate the value of respect and trust to the ultimate success of the program. The relationships between physicians and nurses existed before the formation of the service line so it made it easier to go forward with a shared vision rather than consuming time and energy in building relationships.

Dr. Wright describes Aplin as a champion of the development of the cardiac service line in this way:

> Jill Aplin was a successful change agent because she went out on a limb to try new and different things. She had credibility with physicians, nurses, and administration; she was a good nurse; and she valued depth in training successors. She brought everyone along slowly to see that new ways of taking care of patients was needed.

Working largely behind the scenes, Aplin began to collect information about clinical service lines, clinical pathways, best practices, and ways to organize for clinical excellence. Aplin herself notes that she is not an abrasive change agent and that the early success of the cardiac service line involved a tremendous amount of work in the background:

> First, I had to formulate a clearly articulated vision. Then I had to learn as much as I could about improving patient outcomes. It involved visiting other organizations that were providing top-notch cardiovascular care, attending conferences, and conducting library searches. It took some time to map out an infrastructure that was needed to support a clinical service line approach to cardiac care. Once it was finalized, it was presented to senior management and to the governing board.

My job is to solve problems for physicians and staff so they can do their jobs better. The key to building credibility is to build trust, communicate honestly, develop staff, and plan for succession.

One of Aplin's nurses in the 1980s was Deb Moore, now the interim administrator at Memorial North Park Hospital. On the success of the cardiac service line, Moore comments:

The cardiac service line works because it had a champion in the beginning. Aplin had a vision, but it was important that she had good followers. Aplin encouraged others to take risks, she respected others' opinions, and gave her support for others to try new things. Aplin was quick to say, "You can do this."

Building

Cardiovascular services were centralized at Memorial, and physicians located their offices at the hospital. The cardiovascular volume grew exponentially, but the physical capacity of the hospital in the late 1980s was not able to support expansion. Aplin and the physician champions visited a number of high-profile cardiac facilities. They conducted focus groups with patients and families to gather information on what they did and did not like about access, flow, and the care environment. Based on that information, plans were developed and implemented to upgrade and expand the physical structure and equipment of the hospital and to establish an integrated outpatient facility.

Out of this vision came the Chattanooga Heart Institute, a joint venture between physicians and the hospital. Built adjacent to the hospital in 1992, the Chattanooga Heart Institute facility promotes a seamless flow between inpatient and outpatient cardiac services. The building houses cardiac physicians' offices and outpatient preventive, diagnostic, and treatment services for cardiac patients in one convenient setting. Aplin began a system infrastructure by working with information systems to develop databases for physicians and nursing leadership. According to Aplin:

A key to the success of this program is the use of data. I had to translate the data into useable information for doctors and administrators. Measures and goals were designed around where we were when we started. We were not afraid of our data looking bad because we knew the numbers would improve and because we knew our customers well, and we had the support of administration to do what was necessary to improve patient care.

The current coadministrators of the cardiac service line are Diona Brown and Melissa Roden. Roden has responsibility for strategy, planning, marketing, and clinical program development, while Brown is responsible for operations of all cardiac services, including inpatient nursing units. Designated physicians participate in the leadership of the cardiac service line using a "clinical comanagement model." Physicians are compensated for their service with a base salary and incentives. By 2002, 16 full-time cardiologists and 6 cardiovascular surgeons served an inpatient volume of 20,595, which makes up 53 percent of the Chattanooga market share.

REPLICATING THE BLUEPRINT
The initial success of the cardiac service line prompted Memorial's administration to examine existing areas that would benefit from a service line management concept. The service line concept was applied to additional patient populations.

Organizing
Once the cardiac service line had taken off as a successful model for clinical excellence, Memorial's administration identified four additional patient populations to create service lines. The first decision was the organizational design of the service lines. The administrative team, with support from the quality improvement department and physician leaders, decided to gradually organize service lines around functional departments and units for a "whole systems" clinical service line structure. This plan challenged the traditional nursing organization.

Service line administrators have complete authority and responsibility for inpatient and outpatient nursing units assigned to the service line. The chief nursing officer (CNO) focuses on standards of nursing practice, performance improvement, training and development, and clinical problem solving. The service line administrator reports to the chief operating officer and is accountable for all management and clinical performance outcomes. The interface between the service lines and nursing is as follows:

- *The CNO is responsible for the nursing practice.* This responsibility includes developing standards of care, staffing guidelines, and staffing resources; patient bed assignment; initial and ongoing training and development programs; recruitment and retention; and coordinating performance improvement teams. The CNO chairs the nursing practice council composed of nurse leaders throughout the organization.
- *The nursing practice council brings nursing together with service line administrators and the CNO.* The CNO participates in goal setting and performance evaluation relating to clinical responsibility of nurse leaders who report to service line administrators.

This organizational structure was difficult at first. Several of the service line administrators comment on this structure. Vance Freeman, service line administrator of Memorial's medicine service line:

We had to continually remind ourselves that we shared a vision for clinical excellence and we could not be mired in territorial disputes.

Diona Brown, service line coadministrator of Memorial's cardiac service line:

At first we had to adjust to having different people to report to for different things. We worked out ways to integrate clinical care across traditional functional lines by trying different things, such as cross-functional performance improvement teams, and including service line administrators in the nursing council membership.

Melissa Roden, service line coadministrator of Memorial's cardiac service line:

Our nurses continue to work on fine-tuning service line and traditional hierarchical nursing issues. For example, solutions to nursing management functions such as staffing and scheduling are being negotiated in nursing practice council meetings.

The service line management structure is accountable through several organizational mechanisms. The nursing practice council brings all of nursing management and service line administrators together to work on nursing practice issues. The leadership council is composed of all of Memorial's top management. Service line working groups include clinical, support, finance, and human resources members, and they work on process improvement. The quality councils for each service line are physician-driven groups that evaluate, develop, adopt, and implement performance-improvement standards and protocols to measure clinical outcomes.

Expanding

Sister Thomas had begun to unify Memorial's cancer services (the second service line) when the H. Clay Evans Johnson Cancer Center was built on the hospital campus. This facility provided the most technologically advanced diagnostic and treatment options for radiation therapy. It also incorporated more spiritual and emotional support of patients and families. But other cancer services were scattered throughout the hospital. Cancer services were organized as a service line in 1995. The cancer service line was expanded in 2001 to increase space for diagnosis, treatment, and patient and family education. The service line administrator, Judy Dierkhising, Ph.D., says:

> Our patients not only have physicians and nurses that are specialty trained in cancer diagnosis and treatment, we have a team of social workers, chaplains, clinical dietitians, educators, and volunteers who work together as a multidisciplinary team. My background as a clinical social worker and administrator helps me to pull together a shared vision, facilities, and programs that support the patient and frontline caregivers.

When the third service line—orthopedics, neurology, imaging— was formed, Memorial was already the leading provider of orthopedic surgery. Highly skilled staff in surgery, recovery, nursing, and physical therapy had gained the respect of several orthopedic groups. Service line administrator of orthopedics, Shawn Morrow, CHE, says:

> The service line concept is like running a business within a business. Memorial has the right environment for organizational changes like this to occur. For example, if there is one physician

with a cost per case that is significantly higher than other physicians', a focused assessment occurs with the service line management team and physician director that allows for changes to take place. This results in improved patient care and decreased cost. I am held accountable for bottom-line performance and quality outcomes.

The fourth service line—medicine—is directed by Vance Freeman, a registered respiratory therapist. This service line brings together patients with medical diagnoses that do not usually involve surgical interventions. The medicine service line has standardized care, with standing orders and care paths for approximately 50 diagnosis-related group (DRG) diagnoses. Case management is used for patients with chronic conditions to decrease hospital inpatient stays and emergency department visits. An innovation from a manager that is used extensively in this service line is the use of assessment nurses. Freeman describes the role of the assessment nurse:

> One of the basic nursing functions is patient assessment on admission. This is a nursing activity that takes time. To allow staff nurses more time to be with individual patients, roles were created for assessment nurses. The assessment nurses go where the patients are. Patient care is standardized as assessments are done consistently and completely, giving staff nurses more time to interact with assigned patients.

The fifth service line consists of inpatient and outpatient surgical services. Dedicated in 1983 to provide innovative, responsive, and continually advancing resources for all specialties, Memorial's 75,000 square-foot surgery center supports all surgical service lines. The service line includes the preadmission, diagnostic and educational process, and pain management procedures. The newest addition to the service line is the Weight Management Center, which provides a multidisciplinary approach for the patient undergoing surgical intervention for weight loss.

Memorial recognizes that healthcare requires a multidisciplinary team, where every player must succeed for the team to succeed and any individual failure can cause the team to fail. Behind clinical service line organization are processes for accountability, which Mark O'Bryant, CHE, chief operating officer at Memorial, explains:

The service line programs are like spokes of a wheel with the patient at the center. Service line administrators are accountable for coordinating care around the needs of patients. Accountability is measured by performance in market share, profitability, quality, service, productivity, physician loyalty, and recruitment and retention of physicians and staff.

Clinical service lines are ultimately very effective in controlling resources and setting policies, standards, and performance measures. To maintain the market-leader position in the clinical service lines, Brinkley says:

We continue to strengthen our core mission of nurturing the healing ministry of Christ. We will

1. maintain and build on the quest for excellence in quality;
2. remain focused on the physical, emotional, and spiritual needs of patients and their families to provide excellent service and patient care;
3. focus on recruiting, developing, and retaining excellent people who share our core values of excellent service and patient care;
4. partner with internal and external champions for excellence in leadership (physicians, nurses, board members, other organizations); and
5. balance quality, service, and cost measured with multiple dimensions to ensure performance accountability.

THE ARCHITECTURE OF CLINICAL SERVICE LINES

The team at Memorial deliberately implements the concepts in this section in its service lines.

Quality

Quality excellence means going beyond what is required. Achieving quality means benchmarking with other organizations that have the best outcomes and asking the question, "How can we continually improve our processes to improve our clinical outcomes?" The use of evidence-based protocols and electronic data must support clinical decisions. Achieving quality also means having systems in place to measure clinical outcomes and to be able to retrieve data quickly and efficiently that can be easily translated into usable information for the benefit of patients and bedside clinicians.

Memorial's initial vision for designing clinical services around its cardiac patient population focused on improving quality. In researching best practices for cardiac care, clinical pathways and evidence-based protocols were developed and implemented through a multidisciplinary team approach. Since then, other service lines have been organized and evidence-based protocols have been established and implemented to guide patient care. The question of how quality can be improved at Memorial is asked by anyone on the care team, from staff nurses to physicians to managers. Clinical outcome indicators are continually canvassed for ways to improve care.

Answers to clinical questions are determined by available evidence. At Memorial, the most common conditions are treated according to protocols derived from national and international sites and approved by a hospital's medical staff. Benchmarking and best practices are determined formally and informally. Formally, Memorial compares itself to other hospitals locally and within the CHI system. Informally, the service line administrators and physicians canvass other organizations and professional networks that have leading practices nationally.

The service line administrators and their teams collect protocols. In conjunction with physicians, the protocols are tailored for Memorial, approved by physicians, and implemented. The individual physician's role is to interpret evidence in light of the patient's unique needs. Departure from the protocol for individual patients is expected, although the patient record is reviewed for the reason and the result. When departure from the approved protocol is not documented adequately or deemed inappropriate by a physician's peers, then action is taken to monitor and change the physician's practice patterns to better reflect current standards of care.

Memorial's performance improvement department works closely with the service line administrators and aligned physician to implement evidence-based protocols. Nan Payne, R.N., director of performance improvement and medical staff services at Memorial, oversees the performance improvement function to ensure that it is coordinated among physicians, nurses, and other caregivers and is consistent across service lines. Patti Spangler, R.N., quality services coordinator at Memorial, and Roden comment on this coordination.

Spangler:

> For most diagnoses or DRGs, we benchmark outcomes with state and national data. We have physician-approved admission orders, outcome measures, and goals for the next level of care, whether it is self-care, home care, or discharge to a subacute care organization.

Roden:

> We call our clinical guidelines "Caretracs." They are guidelines for consideration, and they may be modified according to individual patient needs. This is a way for physicians, nurses, and other care-givers to work together to make sure that all expected outcomes are being considered in the same manner for each patient.

Memorial uses an electronic patient record (EPR) that supports safe and timely care for inpatients. Radiology images and radiologists' reports are digitalized and stored with patients' records. The record can be retrieved easily for subsequent encounters. The EPR is also tied into management and clinical databases so that performance is measured quickly, results are analyzed, and improvements are implemented as necessary. To improve integration of inpatient and outpatient care and to increase the speed of measuring outcomes, Memorial is extending the EPR from discharged records to all records. Measures are selected by service line teams, and data are collected and analyzed by the quality improvement department and service line administrators and referred to the councils for improvement.

Service

Memorial's faith-based tradition is rooted in the Sisters of Charity of Nazareth, whose motto is, "The love of Christ impels us." This tradition continues through CHI's mission and core values of Reverence, Integrity, Compassion, and Excellence. Memorial uses its faith-based tradition to support a patient-focused culture. Service encompasses not only excellent care as perceived by the patient, but a culture that sets service standards and provides the people to support a patient-focused culture. At Memorial, all employees are expected to put the patient first, as interim administrator Moore states: "Everything that is done in this organization is patient-oriented. If it is not, then we ask ourselves the question, why are we doing it?"

Another expectation at Memorial is that colleagues will work together in a collegial manner for the benefit of the patient and the patient's family. The culture and values of the organization are continually reinforced through the techniques of service excellence (see Chapter 7), including the following:

- prominent display of the values (Reverence, Integrity, Compassion, Excellence) using posters, newsletters, and other visual devices;
- promotion of culture and values through internal and external publications, newsletters, and educational materials;
- promotion of individual accounts of "lived values" across the CHI system. CHI publishes *Sacred Stories* (now in its fourth edition), in which employees articulate their lived spirituality and the sacred environment of their workplace. These stories are included in prayers, during orientation for new employees, and on Memorial's web site;
- attracting like-minded applicants through description of the work environment in recruitment efforts;
- careful description and explanation of culture and values during formal orientation and training programs. Telling the story of the founding religious sponsors keeps the history of Memorial and the vision of its founding sponsors alive. Incorporation of the CHI story focuses on the future;
- use of extensive mentoring to provide one-on-one guidance to new workers and new managers;
- conducting worker-satisfaction surveys to measure loyalty to the organization and to indicate retention trends;
- use of both recognition and tangible rewards to reinforce the values; and
- rewarding longevity with incentive payment and personal development programs.

In addition, Memorial has been able to completely avoid using external contract temporary or agency workers who are not employees of Memorial's registry.

People

Memorial has had exceptional success in retaining and promoting employees and maintaining the quality of its nursing and clinical staff. Memorial has a 5 percent vacancy rate for nurses, although this number is expected to increase. Turnover rates are low overall—15 percent per year. In-house educational programs are numerous, and opportunities for training and development within Memorial and throughout the CHI system are made available. According to Payne:

> I was a staff nurse in the operating room for many years. Leaders in the nursing organization at Memorial were interested in my development within the system, and I was approached about applying for a job in the quality improvement department. Since then, I have been given added responsibility in the area of medical staff development and initiatives that improve accountability for patient outcomes.

Moore:

> As a staff nurse working with Jill Aplin in the 1980s, I was given the tools needed to do my job. Aplin was there to teach and empower staff nurses the many concepts that were important to improve patient care. From that experience, I was encouraged to move up the ranks within the nursing organization.

Payne:

> Memorial has committees and task forces that look at recruitment, retention, and training needs for staff. It is important to look within the organization for people who possess the values and clinical competence to move into management roles.

Chattanooga has several nursing schools at various levels, and Memorial affiliates with them for clinical practicum sites. This affiliation has lead to attracting new nurse graduates. But recruitment is only a part of the program. Retention may actually be more important, as emphasized by Payne:

Memorial has always been able to attract and retain nurses without using agency or temporary workers. Recently, nurses that have left Memorial are generally the ones that have been employed for a shorter time. A performance improvement work group is investigating ways to reduce turnover.

Brinkley:

We maintain an in-house registry of nurses who are Memorial employees who have been oriented to our mission and values. They are cross-trained in several areas of nursing. This in-house registry, along with a pool of part-time nurses, helps us to staff for high census and regular staff leave time. We have not used outside contract nursing labor at Memorial since 1990!

Memorial focuses on in-house training for its clinical employees. The CNO oversees the nursing education program. A program designed to assess and develop clinical competency for clinical staff is underway at CHI's national office; this program is headed by Debbi Honey, R.N., vice president for clinical operations at CHI. Payne describes the nursing education program at Memorial:

Memorial employs four full-time clinical educators. In addition to general orientation and annual training sessions, the clinical educators design mentoring programs for newly hired nurses. A nurse new to Memorial is assigned a mentor who oversees the orientation process. The mentor also is available after the initial orientation to assist with skills development and other nursing questions.

Honey explains the importance CHI places on continuing training for its clinical employees:

CHI sees the need to standardize the development of standards for measuring clinical competency of its nurses and other clinical staff. We are designing a system that will interface with all CHI hospitals to ensure that our workforce is continually trained for new and changing standards of practice.

To allow staff nurses to have more time in direct patient care activities and to standardize routine procedures, a nursing pool is available for specialized functions such as patient assessment and intravenous therapy. The staff nurses are cross-trained to be able to work across units within a service line. Employee satisfaction is very high at Memorial. In the most recent survey, Memorial scored in the 78th percentile among all of its clients.

Leadership Partners

A focus on leadership permeates CHI. Leadership development programs are provided at the national and MBO levels. The important role of champions was iterated over and over by physicians, administrators, managers, and staff as a key to clinical excellence. In the case of Memorial, certain individuals were thinking forward and committed to a vision for improved patient care.

The key to successes at Memorial is the involvement of physicians as partners, not only in the formulation of a vision but also in the day-to-day management of operations relating to patient care. When asked to comment on the key to the success of the cardiac service line, Dr. Wright stated:

> One of the accomplishments that I am most proud of is the physician-hospital partnership that has formed the backbone of the Chattanooga Heart Institute. Related to this is the amount of collaboration between the medical staff and the hospital in recruiting good physicians and other members of the care team.

Cancer service line administrator Dierkhising echoed the comments of Dr. Wright:

> Physicians are our partners in the treatment of people living with a cancer diagnosis. And so are nurses, social workers, chaplains, and others who have much to offer in the way of psychosocial and spiritual support.

PERFORMANCE ACCOUNTABILITY

To achieve performance-improvement goals, Memorial's leadership developed an organizational framework for implementing a performance-improvement plan. Expectations—from the board, medical staff, senior management, and service line administrators to department and clinical leaders—have been defined in job descriptions and performance goals.

Setting Improvement Goals

The operations council uses two major devices to keep the culture focused on clinical service and improvement. First, they have rigorous accountability standards, as many measures as they can, and a procedure to set annual goals on important measures. That process creates balanced scorecard goals not only for every work group and service line but also for every new program or capital investment. Second, they use performance-improvement teams extensively to develop ways the measures can be improved.

Every service line administrator and director has written accountability standards, including the following:

- mission integration (with emphasis on community service),
- cost management,
- quality of service,
- human resources management,
- medical staff relations (if applicable),
- strategic plan implementation, and
- situational leadership ("responds to changing circumstances . . . cooperates harmoniously . . . completes staff assignments . . . .").

The accountability standards are the foundation for negotiating the annual budget and other annual goals. Memorial's budgeting and financial accountability processes are described below. Carol Newton, chief financial officer at Memorial:

> Memorial's financial staff—including cost and reimbursement, fiscal services, and budgeting associates—become financial representatives. Their role as financial representatives is to develop an understanding of how the service line operates and to assist with financial issues and decisions. Budgeting procedures, financial policies, and reporting ratios are standardized. Each service line is accountable for its profitability. Some service lines are not as profitable as others by the nature of the service. The mission of the organization is taken into consideration in these instances.

Sean Donohoe, from health information services:

> The traditional medical records function is expanded at Memorial to include collaboration with service line administrators on the role of coding and particular diagnoses that form trends.

David Winchester, financial consultant for Memorial:

> Finance works from the beginning of a new program or service line to get plans, systems, and capital needs included, analyzed, and funded. A service line administrator prepares a business plan, and the finance department checks projections and the financial impact. The plan then is submitted to administration for approval and consideration for funding in the next budget cycle.

Measuring Performance

Memorial builds its strategy around its balanced scorecard measures— quality, people, growth, and performance. Its strategic plan specifies four or five goals under each of these measures but does not describe specific initiatives. Instead, a set of initiatives is selected, developed, prioritized, and presented to the hospital CEO and board and CHI's senior vice president and her team for review and approval.

GETTING RESULTS

Processes must be in place to set new, continually improving targets. Memorial has built a results-oriented culture that makes it hard not to improve. Its service line administrators and managers have measures and rewards to encourage them; they can document some impressive improvements. Newton describes one such improvement:

> One example of a positive result achieved at Memorial is in the area of joint replacement surgery costs. First, analyses were performed to determine the reasons for unfavorable financial performance. It was determined that the primary contributor was the cost of the prosthetic device itself. A multidisciplinary team (surgeons, service line administrator, surgery personnel, materials management, finance staff, and chief operating officer) worked together to negotiate a better price with vendors. Memorial determined the need for a cap on the amount paid for the devices. This strategy carried

a high degree of risk that physicians would not be willing to make the standardization necessary for the hospital to receive a desirable price. The risks were communicated to the board.

The collaboration demonstrated the high degree of commitment of the organization to this strategy and facilitated a favorable outcome. Memorial also negotiated with the two major insurance payors in its market for additional reimbursement to cover the prostethic device costs. The resulting combination of cost reduction and reimbursement led to an improvement of approximately $2.5 million without compromising the quality of care.

An advantage of clinical service lines is that outcomes of care are the focus rather than the impact of a particular department or function. Freeman works with physicians and other service line administrators to improve patient outcomes:

Twenty-four percent of our inpatients have diabetes. Although it is seldom the primary reason for admission, it greatly impacts the expected outcomes for other comorbid conditions. Several years ago, our average length of stay for patients with diabetes as a comorbid condition was 1.5 days longer than patients without diabetes. We have decreased this to .76 days due to the following:

- education sessions for physicians,
- use of a nurse to see any inpatient with a new diagnosis or others that may need education about their condition,
- use of intraoperative protocols to control glucose levels resulting in decreased postoperative wound infections,
- an education center utilized by 3,000 outpatients a year,
- free glucose monitors provided on discharge, and
- increased awareness among all service lines about the relationship of diabetes to all diseases and conditions.

Progress Reports

The system of setting goals on measured performance is a powerful incentive in itself. As of 2002, Memorial's service line administrators and managers received the following measures for their areas of responsibility:

- *An accounting report similar to that generated by most commercial accounting systems.* It shows full detail of costs and revenues and counts of service and case-mix adjustment and is available within ten days after the end of month. Memorial constructs the report to show each item's status for the accounting period and year to date and compared to budget. Productivity measures, such as "cost per adjusted discharge," are calculated. The manager can specify measures of particular interest to be displayed at the start of the report.
- *Employee-satisfaction surveys.* Action plans based on survey results are developed, and progress toward these plans is tracked. Service line administrator goals are tied to outcomes.
- *Market share and demand information,* which is given at annual budget briefings to assist in devising new targets.
- *Access to specific information as needed,* which is available through support services in planning, marketing, and finance.

Incentives

Memorial's culture provides a strong incentive to record actual improvement with these measures; this incentive is reinforced by an extensive program of recognition and tangible rewards. Assistance is available internally if performance does not meet expectations. CHI also offers help in the way of consulting services for certain issues related to quality and performance improvement.

Memorial's incentive plan ties managers' annual wage and salary adjustment to goal achievement. Goals are negotiated annually. Performance accountability measures are weighted accordingly: 25 percent for retention; 25 percent for financial performance; and 50 percent for department-specific goals, including patient satisfaction and quality. For a 100 percent share payout to occur, financial performance and service indicators as measured by patient-satisfaction targets must be met. All service line administrators' bonuses and half of individual merit increases depend on the overall service line and hospital performance. The balance is earned through individual unit performance.

CHALLENGES

Memorial faces three challenges it must overcome to sustain and build its service line program.

Balancing the Service Line Portfolio

Several service line administrators state that "the value of a service line is the revenue it generates and its fidelity to Memorial's mission." Some service lines are inherently more profitable than others. A challenge for Memorial is how to improve or maintain profitability of all service lines. Memorial's senior management team and governing board must be alert for opportunities to reduce costs. This can be done by streamlining current service lines for greater efficiency; collaborating with other organizations to provide Chattanooga with increased access to specialized care; or discontinuing a service, as it did some years ago with obstetrics and pediatrics. In other cases, new service lines may be started, such as Memorial's nonsurgical services that include stroke, diabetes, and depression, which are groups that are often identified as service lines in their own right. Ultimately, the most appropriate group of service lines that provide care to the community may have to be subsidized to fulfill achievement of the overall mission.

Blurring of Traditional Professional Boundaries

The professional boundaries of nursing and medicine are facing profound challenges. For clinical service lines to be successful, it is necessary to build cross-functional multidisciplinary teams for a more seamless continuum of care.

Traditional views of nursing promote insularity and organization of nursing services along a hierarchical structure. Implementing a service line organization challenges this traditional view. Memorial must continue to refine ways that help the nursing organization and the service line administrators work collaboratively for continuous improvement. Similarly, the physician role is changing to emphasize teamwork. The silos of functional care activities—medicine, nursing, laboratory, pharmacy—are disappearing, as service lines create teams that are focused on patient needs. As that occurs, all the professions must learn new habits. Memorial's emphasis on measured outcomes and evidence-based protocols provides the foundation for this transition.

Making Changes Quickly

Organizations must proactively engineer changes that correspond to pressures such as decreasing reimbursement, new and changing regulatory standards, and disruptive innovations or new discoveries in medical diagnosis and treatment. Scenario planning must be promoted and systematized with management practices and rewards. Memorial has done this effectively by improving quality and reducing costs. Morrow, the service line administrator for orthopedics, references a quote he enjoys when talking about Memorial's data-driven decisions:

> "Trying to manage an organization by variance is like driving a car by looking in the rear-view mirror" [according to D. J. Wheeler in *Understanding Variation: The Key to Managing Chaos*]. Memorial has made huge leaps forward by providing data and information that are useful in making changes to patient care prospectively, so we don't have to manage from variance reports.

Making decisions quickly to change systems and practices are key when potential problems and ways to improve care are identified in advance. This is the true meaning of thinking forward. Memorial does not wait for problems to occur; it identifies potential problems and makes changes early to improve clinical outcomes.

KEY LESSONS

Organizing care around patient populations is easier said than done. Although the task seems simple, it is not easy in reality. Memorial has learned some lessons as it evolved into a champion of clinical excellence. It constantly manages and shifts its successes and challenges according to demands and changing scenarios.

1. *The support of the governing board and top administration is essential to moving forward with clinical service lines.* Top leadership must advocate and support clinical initiatives. Through its committee structure, the board should be given information about clinical and quality outcomes and about ways that the mission is measured and benchmarked against other leading practices in the region and nation. In addition, the board should be informed about ways other organizations are achieving results and should be given a vision on how those efforts can be done locally. The vision of Sister Thomas was shared with others in the organization, allowing for champions to emerge with creative and innovative service line programs. According to Brinkley:

> We have made tough decisions about changing from a traditional functional and hierarchical organization to one that is

organized around patient populations. We shifted accountabilities to service line administrators and rewarded excellence in clinical and financial performance. We must maintain a steady and relentless pursuit of excellence.

2. *Outline a structure for a service line organization. Delineate authority
   and responsibility for patient care services, clinical outcomes, and
   bottom-line performance.* Decisions need to be made about how to
   organize along service lines. A matrix organizational design would
   retain traditional nursing and clinical services within functional
   units, with "dotted-line" responsibility to service line administrators. A pure service line design would organize similar nursing,
   clinical, and support functions under a service line administrator.
   This approach redefines the traditional role of the CNO. Organizations that implement service lines must decide whether to
   adopt a matrix management style and retain the traditional nursing
   organization structure or to emulate the Memorial model.

   Appoint service line administrators, identify physician champions, and give them the tools to do the job. Provide resources for
   them to see how the leading practices nationally are organized and
   systematized. Assign individuals throughout the organization the
   responsibility of working with specified service line administrators.

3. *Affirm the mission to put the patient at the center and organize
   services around patient populations.* Core values of an organization
   set the expected level of performance. What is valued on paper
   must be valued in individual actions. Memorial has a long history
   of communicating its faith-based values to all employees and
   reinforcing them in policies, services, and employee recognition
   and reward. The culture must also support innovation and risk
   taking, which are rooted in the pioneering tradition of the Sisters of
   Charity of Nazareth. When something is tried and does not work
   the way it was anticipated, it should be analyzed. "Organizational
   learning" would indicate ways to build, change, adapt, or rethink
   the concept. In many instances, however, innovation and risk
   taking are rewarded with unimaginable positive outcomes.

   Another important aspect of culture is the focus on processes
   and clinical performance rather than on traditional professional
   roles. Redistribution of work is inherent in a service line organiza-

tion. Difficult decisions need to be made that inevitably challenge functional and professional territories.

Service line administrators need to be given full authority to make decisions about service line operations within mission, strategic plan, and budgetary guidelines. Having the respect of and access to senior management is important. Building a culture of excellence in patient care is essential for great performance. O'Bryant adds:

> The culture also needs to be built on a strong foundation of strategic planning and problem resolution. Service line administrators need to be a cohesive group that shares common successes and problems. It is only through replication of what works at Memorial that we will be able to sustain a competitive advantage in the marketplace.

4. *Develop and promote a culture of clinical excellence. Find the best physicians, nurses, and other clinicians and give them exposure to leading practices.* A culture of excellence in clinical care attracts people who want to practice in a high-performing, mission-driven organization. The key is to recruit, continually educate, and retain and reward top performers—from frontline employees to top administrators. At the same time, individuals with leadership talent must be identified, developed, and placed in positions of increasing responsibility. Succession planning is important for the continuity of leadership. Brinkley supports this concept:

> Memorial is blessed with many capable leaders. When given the right tools, they are able to take the ball and run with it. We continually stress the value of selection, development, and empowerment throughout the organization.

Selecting service line administrators is a carefully orchestrated process. Memorial looks to its own champions to assume service line leadership positions first. If the person is not identified in-house, then a national search is conducted. Service line administrators must have a demonstrated understanding of and a proven track record for managing the multiple demands of the business. They must possess knowledge of clinical operations and the ability to work collaboratively with physicians, the CNO, and other organizational managers.

5. *Identify champions in the organization. Reward leaders who have vision and are willing to take risks to improve quality and service and decrease costs.* Champions may be physicians, nurses, or other key players. They know how to plan, organize, and set high expectations. Administration must support them with resources and give them ample time to research best practices in the service specialty. An empowered environment is a fertile ground for identifying champions. Champions rise to the surface with new ideas and ways to make vision a reality. They are "can do" people. They may or may not be formal leaders of the organization, but they will grasp the mission and vision and embody them in their professional lives.

Every member of the service line team has an important role. When selecting team members, it is important to identify people not only in clinical services as team members but those in support services such as environmental services, human resources, finance, building maintenance, pastoral care, and the like.

6. *Identify physician partners and bring physicians into the planning stage early.* Include other hospitals or physicians in the area as possible partners. When planning for service line care that is seamless, organizational partners (such as hospice and home health organizations, rehabilitation facilities, continuing care retirement centers, fitness centers, and other organizational providers) enhance services and programs.

7. *Develop an expectation-setting process that makes service line administrators accountable.* Service line administrators should be supported by all functions in the organization. They need information on competitors, market demographics, financial performance, comparative standings, benchmarks, patient satisfaction, and employee and physician satisfaction. Consistent with the overall organizational mission and goals, service line administrators establish goals for performance improvement and are evaluated and compensated according to outcomes measures.

8. *Install or upgrade information systems appropriate to the size and scope of the organization.* Performance improvement requires decisions based on information. The accuracy, speed, and ease of recovery of data all contribute to performance improvement. Patient care practices need to be modified based on outcomes that are measured. Computerized standing orders, care paths, and ongoing measures of results have contributed substantially to Memorial's success. Other systems and freestanding hospitals have similar needs for information systems and technology support. A key to having a system that works well is careful planning and input from all clinicians who will use the system.

9. *Identify leading practices and use them as benchmarks.* Although Memorial had implemented a service line organization before becoming part of the CHI system, several systemwide initiatives have aided Memorial's service line progress. CHI holds regional and national best practices conferences where member organizations share information about programs and outcomes. Policies, protocols, systems, and measures are made available as well as information on standard definitions, reporting of key measures, and ways to compare organizational performance to other MBOs. CHI has established a culture of information exchange among its MBOs that encourages both formal and informal transfer of processes. For widespread opportunities, task forces and internal consulting knowledge are assembled to reach a consensus on best practice. Other well-managed systems offer similar advantages. Hospitals that are not members of systems can purchase much of what is needed from consultants, information services, and alliances.

BIBLIOGRAPHY

Wheeler, D. J. 1999. *Understanding Variation: The Key to Managing Chaos*, 2nd Edition. Knoxville, TN: SPC Press.

Chapter 4

Case Management: Optimizing Quality of Life at the Mercy Health Network

BACKGROUND

Mercy Health Network (MHN) is a joint operating agreement between Catholic Health Initiatives and Trinity Health in Novi, Michigan, that combines member healthcare provider organizations to form a unique, integrated regional delivery network. MHN consists of 9 owned hospitals, 26 managed hospitals, and 104 clinic sites in Iowa and surrounding states, as shown in Figure 4.1. Mercy Medical Center-Des Moines is a tertiary medical center that provides acute and chronic care services across the continuum for its service area and for other hospitals across Iowa.

MHN provides a comprehensive array of services through its 1,792 staffed beds of owned hospitals, 668 staffed beds of managed hospitals, outpatient clinics, home health and hospice services, the Iowa Heart Hospital at Mercy, long-term care and retirement centers, and senior housing.

MHN's 1,637 affiliated physicians and extended role providers are in independent practices, physician-hospital networks, and staff/employee arrangements. The network receives 1.9 million emergency and outpatient visits a year from a secondary service population of more than 1.2 million people. Approximately 40 percent of MHN revenues come from outpatient services. Managed care penetration for Iowa is low—about 13 to 21 percent—depending on the definition used.

Since the founding of MHN in 1998, its net revenues have grown steadily from $823 million in 2000 to $941 million in 2002. MHN earned positive margins in 2000 at 1.9 percent and in 2001 at 2.8 percent. Regarding patient satisfaction, 85 percent of MHN's patients

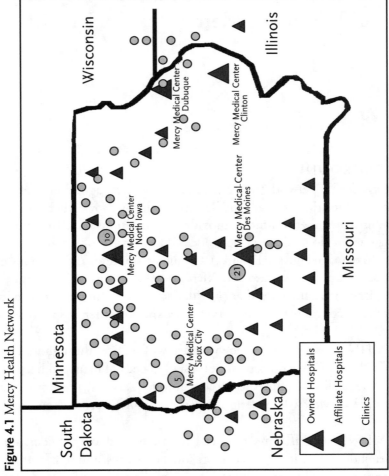

Figure 4.1 Mercy Health Network

would recommend their hospital for healthcare services. Nearly 30 percent of MHN's employees indicate they have the highest level of satisfaction with their employing entity in the network. Key operating and financial indicators are reported for Mercy-Des Moines in Table 4.1.

MHN achieved its growth and successes with case management gradually. In 1993, case management action plans were written by Larry Schumacher, the chief nursing officer at the time, and Jane Brokel, the nursing director, both of whom are from Mercy Medical Center-North Iowa. The case management program was implemented through a grant funding to Trinity Health (then called Mercy Health Services) from the Robert Wood Johnson/Pew Foundations' "Strengthening Hospital Nursing Programs" initiative. The grant funds were used to organize case management for chronic and episodic diseases and conditions. The outpatient or community-based case management program to aid patients with chronic diseases was implemented first, and episodic or acute case management was implemented in 1996. Of this effort, Schumacher says:

> We knew there were several core concepts that work in managing a patient's care throughout the continuum of services. This grant allowed us to take these concepts and organize them into a structure with processes that focus on the relationship with the patient and the patient's physician. The case manager assumes the role of advocate to assist with coordination and navigation through the system. The core concepts are the same, but the processes are different.

In 2000, the Centers for Medicare and Medicaid Services (CMS) identified Mercy-North Iowa as a "best practice in coordinated care" site (Chen et al. 2000). Since case management was implemented in Mason City, it has been replicated in other MHN locations. David Vellinga, CEO of Mercy-Des Moines and CEO of the MHN Management Council, describes how MHN contributes to the diffusion of services like case management:

> MHN was founded in order to take advantage of synergies of people and practices in the system. MHN's staff . . . are available to guide and facilitate change and performance improvement with

Table 4.1 Major Performance Measures for Mercy Medical Center-Des Moines

	1999	2000	2001	2002
People				
Employee satisfaction			3.64	3.91
Turnover: organization			17.80%	15.78%
Turnover: RN only			15.0%	13.9%
Organization vacancy rate			9.8%	3.9%
Growth				
Patient overall satisfaction[1]	4.22	4.19	4.14	4.05*
ER patient satisfaction[2]	4.56	4.46	4.34	4.06*
Market share	43.9%	44.2%	45.2%	
Performance				
Net patient revenue (thousands)	$343,418	$355,694	$388,923	$447,155
Operating margin	5.2%	0.1%	2.5%	2.8%
Total margin	6.7%	2.0%	3.5%	2.8%

Days of total cash	105	113	131	105
Debt to capital ratio	19.3%	18.3%	16.4%	15.0%
Cost per adjusted discharge[3]	$5,107	$5,351	$5,421	$5,691
Community benefit[4] (thousands)	$30,051	$36,802	$33,897	$41,084
Quality				
Patient perceived quality[5]	4.40	4.40	4.36	4.05
Patients rating care as "excellent"[6]	41%	38%	38%	36%
Process and outcomes measures in use[7]	• Customer satisfaction • Employee injuries, specifically latex allergies	• Antibiotic administration delay intervals • Incidence of nosocomial decubitis	• ACE inhibitors at discharge for CHF patients • LOS for pneumonia patients	• Medication-error reduction • Narcotics • Insulin

continued

Table 4.1 *continued*

	1999	2000	2001	2002
Quality improvement focus areas[8]	• Full-time patient advocate • Reduction of wait times in ED • Latex-exposure-reduction team	• Reduction of antibiotic-administration delays in ED • Identification of "at-risk" patients for skin breakdown; staff education and early referrals to Wound Care Team	• Development and implementation of order sets, information, and education to physicians; monitoring and follow-up of processes	• Automation of medication processes • Identification of high-risk (sound alike, look alike, spelled alike) medication to formulary using Failure Mode Analysis

Notes: Measures were entered as they became available.

1. Inpatient survey results. These values were estimated from a regression equation using all original values and dummy variables for each quarter except from July to September 2002. The equation has excellent fit and significance. The parameters for the quarters prior to the current vendor are similar and highly significant. The adjustment model incorporates any time trend so that none can appear in the data above. However, inspection of the adjustment coefficients and original data suggest that there was no trend, either up or down, in these measures.

2. ER patient survey results; see note 1.

3. Cost per case adjusted for severity using CMS's DRG index.

4. Community benefit is defined by Catholic Health Association and includes charity care, Medicare and Medicaid losses, education and research costs, and services or funds donated to community activities.

5. Inpatient survey results; see note 1.

6. Percentage of inpatients surveyed rating quality as excellent.

7. Measures reported to the MBO board. In 2003, CHI will standardize many of these measures for comparative reporting.

8. Areas selected for intensive study by the MBO.

our medical centers and physicians in accordance with our strategic and quality plans. Additionally, the support and resources from our parent organizations is tremendous.

Schumacher is now the COO at Mercy-Des Moines, and he has implemented case management there. He also serves in an advisory role to other hospitals within MHN that are in various stages of implementing case management. Schumacher and David Hickman, FACHE, director of clinical integration at MHN's system office, discuss their respective roles in case management leadership.

Schumacher:

My role is to support a culture where people are allowed to take risks and experiment with improving processes. The processes are different according to local market situations. For example, in Mason City and Clinton the hospitals are the sole community providers. This contributes to case management success because there is less competition and the patients and physicians are affiliated with Mercy.

Hickman:

I help to identify clinical needs and outstanding clinical practices within MHN. I also assist with the assessment and implementation of key clinical improvement projects within our parent organizations. We bring people together to better understand their successes and facilitate replication. We used this process with case management and learned that different locations needed different models.

WHAT IS CASE MANAGEMENT?

The term "case management" came into common use during the 1980s as hospitals and health systems began to feel the impact of Medicare's prospective payment system (Cudney 2002). In 1994, 44.4 percent of the hospitals that responded to the American Hospital Association's Annual Survey of Hospitals indicated they had adopted case management services. By 2000, 71.2 percent of these respondents said they provided case management services. Because various models of case management exist, what type of case management these hospitals are providing is not known.

There are many definitions for case management. Case management generally refers to the coordination of health and human services for improved quality, patient satisfaction, and cost effectiveness. Case management has long been an implicit activity of nurses. With the growing complexity of our healthcare system and with increasing pressures to conserve precious clinical resources, case management has become a formal discipline, complete with professional associations and a body of professional standards. A commonly accepted definition of case management is by Powell and Ignatavicius (2001):

> A collaborative process that assesses, plans, implements, coordinates, monitors, and evaluates the options and services required to meet an individual's health needs, using communication and available resources to promote quality and cost-effective outcomes.

MHN expands that concept with its own definition. This definition was developed by Mercy Health Services (now called Trinity Health) with input from the Center for Case Management:

> Case management is a value-driven clinical system and process that focuses on the coordination of care across an episode or the continuum for selected patients with exceptional social and health problems. Case managers intervene at key points to negotiate, procure, and coordinate resources to achieve clinical, financial, and quality outcomes. Case managers collaborate with physicians, nurses, and other clinicians as a healthcare team. This service may be provided in the acute care setting to influence the course of an illness from acute to chronic, or the service may be provided as community-based care to address the chronic and complex needs of certain patients.

MHN emphasizes "value-driven" in its definition, which is consistent with the mission of CHI (as discussed in Chapter 1). Case management at MHN includes episodic and chronic care delivered in inpatient and outpatient settings. Because social problems often contribute to a person's health status, they are included in MHN's definition. To implement these distinctions, MHN has formal organizational mechanisms to provide integration of clinical services throughout the system. Clinical integration is in the form of providing information on best practices, benchmarking, standards of care, continuity of care, people skills, and ways to improve quality and decrease cost. Hickman adds:

> Our job is to find the best way of doing things to improve patient care quality and decrease cost. Sometimes it means I find the best practice within MHN or within the CHI or Trinity Health Systems. For case management, the best practice was started in our hospital in Mason City and has been replicated in other MHN medical centers. We present a general framework of what works, and then we provide assistance to . . . make it happen. However, each organization has the autonomy to develop a model that fits its organization and patient populations.

The majority of the studies that have analyzed the effectiveness of case management used an inpatient delivery model. MHN, being a network of providers in a largely rural state, has the challenge of providing access to healthcare in the communities being served, some of which are at a distance from an acute care hospital. The inpatient model of case management services does not fit all of the providers and consumers of healthcare services. Therefore, MHN's case management definition reflects a broad spectrum of case management needs, from episodic care to care across the continuum to care that is provided in inpatient and outpatient settings.

The Advantages

The goal of case management is to handle an acute or chronic illness by offering alternatives to costly hospital stays while increasing the quality of life. Case management is a way to decrease the fragmentation of healthcare along the continuum of services. For example, a person who is in an acute phase of illness will need plans for the next level of care, whether it is at home or in a subacute facility. For persons with chronic conditions, case management is appropriate for teaching the patient how to live with an illness or how to access services outside of acute care hospitalization.

Studies have shown that case management decreases cost and improves quality (Zander 1988), although the majority of the reports are anecdotal rather than evidence based (Cook 1998). Cook analyzed 18 research studies prior to 1995 that measured inpatient case management and outcomes such as patient satisfaction, provider satisfaction, quality, costs, and length of stay. Although the studies indicated that measures were varied and outcomes were mixed, several of the studies showed positive correlations between case management and the outcomes (Cook 1998). More recent studies have measured quantitative effects of case management, such as reduction in payer denials (Daniels 1999); decreased length of stay, critical care utilization, and mortality in patients with coronary artery bypass graft (Walters et al. 1998); decreased average length of stay for specific physicians (*Hospital Case Management* 2000a); decreased cost and limited readmissions (*Hospital Case Management* 2000b); and market and organizational factors associated with case management adoption (Roggenkamp, White, and Bazzoli [unpublished]).

As healthcare has become more complex, the coordination of care has gottten more fragmented. According to Mary Ellen Speck, a 30-year nurse and a heart failure case manager at Mercy-Sioux City:

> Thirty years ago, there was more coordination of care by physicians and the nurses had more time to educate patients and families about their illness or condition. As healthcare grew in complexity, coordination of care was left behind. There is little or no time for teaching. Managing care is still fragmented, but case management is a way to focus on education with the patient and family.

For patients with chronic conditions, case management is especially useful in improving quality of life and decreasing cost associated with frequent utilization of provider services. Sharon Blanche, director of cardiovascular services, and Lori Swanson, clinical patient case manager, started a case management program at Mercy-Sioux City because of the need for improvements in the nontechnical aspects of care. According to Blanche:

> Our case management program grew out of a cardiovascular leadership group that identified ways we could do better with nontech-

nical care and guest services. We knew that patients and families were not well-informed about their clinical conditions.

Swanson:

> With our patients that had chronic diseases, we were seeing caregiver strain, frequent trips to the emergency department, a decreased quality of life for the patient, and high usage of costly inpatient services.

Blanche:

> At first it was difficult to quantify the benefits of case management in financial terms. Now we can show that it decreases costs, but measuring quality of life is more qualitative than quantitative. We measure quality of life by our patient's stories, satisfaction surveys, and feedback from patients and their physicians.

The Types

There are two types of case management: hospital based and community based.

Hospital-Based Case Management

The inpatient or hospital-based case management type is designed for the short-term, episodic, acute care conditions of hospitalized patients. The focus of this type is the control of resources while the patient is hospitalized. Across MHN facilities, the hospital-based case management grew from nurses not being able to provide effective discharge planning. Patients were ready to be discharged, but they were not ready to leave the hospital for the following reasons:

- the patient and family needed education on the disease or condition or assistance in assembling essential resources for continuity of care,
- there was fragmented patient advocacy because of discontinuity between the clinical caregivers on different shifts and various physicians within the organization, or
- facilitation for the next level of care (home health, hospice, or subacute facility) had not been arranged and coordinated.

At Mercy-Dubuque, discharge planning prior to 2000 was the primary responsibility of each staff nurse. Breakdowns in communication between shifts at times contributed to discontinuity of discharge planning. Kay Takes, vice president of patient care services, and Ann Burds, director of quality improvement and social services, worked together with a multidisciplinary task force to improve patient readiness for discharge. They implemented a system of case management, designed after the Vanderbilt triad model (see *Hospital Case Management* 1999), on three large inpatient units: medicine, surgery, and skilled/rehabilitation. This triad model uses an integrated approach to case management, incorporating the functions of the clinical nurse, utilization review nurse, and social worker who work with the primary nurses on each unit. The case manager is responsible for coordinating discharge planning, including patient teaching, facilitation of transfers, and communication with caregivers at home or in referral facilities for about 80 percent of the patients in these areas. The benefits of this model are described by Takes and Burds.

Takes:

> Our patients are better prepared for discharge, satisfaction scores have increased, and the patients are more empowered to make decisions about postdischarge care because they know more about their options.

Burds:

> Using social worker and registered nurse case managers gives more flexibility in staffing and it also helps to bring different disciplines together for solving problems. The case managers aid the staff nurses in planning care and teaching the patient about their illness or condition, and this contributes to increased satisfaction among staff nurses.

In planning for implementation of hospital-based case management, certain challenges must be expected and carefully considered. Takes and Burds believe that buy-in from staff nurses, physicians, and patients is crucial for success. Staff nurses need to see the case manager as an internal consultant rather than someone who is taking away a nursing function. A way to avoid this is to have explicit role definitions for case managers and staff nurses.

Community-Based Case Management

The outpatient or community-based case management type is designed to help patients manage their disease or condition and its trajectory, with education and outpatient services facilitated by a case manager. The purpose of community-based case management is to establish long-term relationships with patients, to manage patients' disease with help from their physicians, to prevent or minimize inpatient hospitalizations, and to improve patients' quality of life.

In preparing to write the grant for the initial funding of Mercy-North Iowa's case management program, Schumacher identified a case management best practice after which to model his program. The best practice was developed at Carondelet St. Mary's Hospital in Tucson, Arizona (see Cook 1998). The St. Mary's model focuses on chronic disease management beyond the hospital environment. Baccalaureate-prepared nurses or nurse practitioner case managers are employed to work with patients in their homes with the following goals:

- build relationships with patients, their physicians, and their family members to increase everyone's confidence and comfort in dealing with the patient and his or her disease;
- teach patients and families skills for navigating the healthcare system;
- facilitate access to services and care when increased levels of care are warranted;
- identify problem areas, such as financial and psychosocial issues, that relate to the patient's disease process; and
- ensure that patients and families understand the disease trajectory and know what to expect and how to respond during times of exacerbation.

At Mercy-North Iowa, community-based case management policies and procedures are designed collaboratively between the organization's nursing and medical staffs and are approved by the organization's administration. Patients are accepted as a case management client based on utilization history of system services and disease state. Inclusion criteria specify certain chronic diagnoses and conditions that are suitable for case management. Physicians approve a medical plan of care, and the case managers devise a plan to manage the patient's care. In addition to case management services, some patients also receive home care. The case manager serves as a consultant to patients, their families, and MHN's home care team to augment services that keep patients from seeking more costly care. Most patients who consume community-based case management services are enrolled long term or until end-of-life services, such as hospice, are needed. An information system is in place to provide daily and monthly reports. In 1994, a data set was designed and pilot tested. In 1995, the information system was implemented to track utilization of health system services, such as emergency department visits, and contractual losses.

The benefits of community-based case management are partially attributed to a shared governance (Porter-O'Grady 1992) model of nursing practice as described below. According to Jane Brokel, who was involved in writing the grant requests for funding the case management program in 1993 and 2000:

> Mercy-North Iowa in Mason City adopted a shared governance model of nursing practice in 1989. This nursing model empowers clinical caregivers to develop ways to improve patient care. Early on, . . . our nurses . . . were instrumental in implementing our case management program. They saw that certain patients had repeat emergency department visits and hospitalizations and were not able to manage their disease process effectively. Now, our patients are better able to cope with their disease or condition, patient satisfaction and employee and physician satisfaction scores are high, and patients have a . . . nurse case manager . . . that they can contact for any problems.

Marie Cole, a case management nurse practitioner at Mercy-North Iowa:

> I was one of the original case managers based in the community in North Iowa. Administration was supportive of our initial shared governance model of community-based case management practice. We were given space in a building in the community and administrative support, and we were requested to keep good records. After we had some history, and with our excellent information systems

database, we were able to show how we added value to the organization and to the patients.

Brenda Kern, a case management nurse practitioner at Mercy-Algona:

> Six years ago I started as a nurse case manager. Since then, I have been supported by Mercy to receive additional education and now I am one of the nurse practitioner case managers in the group practice. I maintain a small satellite office in a rural location, serving a client base within 35 miles of Algona, Iowa. Being a part of a shared governance model of community-based case management allows me to work directly with patients in remote areas. The patients either come to the office for routine visits or I go where they are to make sure they are adhering to medication regimes, controlling diet and exercise, and preventing exacerbations.

A goal of community-based care is to keep patients from seeking more expensive hospital services during times of disease exacerbation or when the patient or caregiver is strained from psychosocial issues that accompany a person who lives with a chronic condition. Cole reflects on her hospital's success with this goal:

> George was our first patient. George visited the emergency department 21 times in the previous year. More out of loneliness than disease exacerbation, he would go to the Mercy emergency department. We picked him up one day and took him to get ice cream. George knew he had someone to call when he was having problems dealing with his illness. After we picked him up as a client, his emergency department visits decreased to two in that year.

Representatives from nursing, education, social services, finance, home care, human resources, administration, and senior services developed case management at Mercy-Clinton. Using Mercy-North Iowa's program as a resource, the hospital introduced community case management in 1996; within that first year, two nurse case managers enrolled 36 patients in the program. Mercy-Clinton's hospital-based case management program started in 1997, bringing on two additional case managers. A social worker joined the program in 1998.

The benefits of the program are shown through reduced admissions and a better quality of life for patients with many healthcare needs, and as a result referrals have steadily grown. Eighty-three people are being served in the program in 2002, and many of these people are part of the 170 patients the program has served since its inception. Case managers Chinma Nnanji and Marilyn Hamilton speak of the success of the program.

Nnanji:

> Our patients are happier because they feel better. I can tell they are happier by the way they look and the way they are dressed—not in hospital gowns! Our physicians are pleased because their patients have someone who can help them understand their disease and take action to prevent more costly care in a hospital. Even though this is a free service, we have decreased hospital admissions and emergency room visits, so the service more than pays for itself.

Hamilton:

> Each day I work through problems with patients that can be solved relatively easily but could be impossible for the patient to solve alone. Helping patients solve problems through early recognition of symptoms, accessing appropriate healthcare, and utilizing available resources provides a fuller and more independent life for the patient, builds their confidence in navigating the healthcare system, and benefits the hospital through appropriate utilization of services. This win-win situation gives the case manager satisfaction as well.

TWO CASE MANAGEMENT MODELS

Case management programs can be built around inpatient or outpatient care and can be disease specific (e.g., heart failure) or continuum-of-care specific (e.g., end of life). The scope of case management services within MHN varies depending on the patient population, degree of competition and collaboration within the local communities, and level of services provided along the continuum of care. Where sufficient volume can be attained, it is often fruitful to organize case management around patients with similar clinical needs. MHN uses this model for heart failure case management.

The disease-specific model often incorporates both inpatient and outpatient approaches, but MHN adapts the model to the resources and needs of the local organization. Palliative care is a case management model that is general in nature, and it is used to decrease costs and improve quality of life for patients who have chosen to forego expensive technological interventions or patients who are living at the end of life.

Disease-Specific Case Management for Heart Failure

One of the top discharge diagnoses in the United States is congestive heart failure, and heart failure hospitalizations are increasing in both men and women (American Heart Association 2003). The majority (79 percent) of emergency department presentations of people with a heart failure diagnosis are repeat visits (Cardiovascular Roundtable 1998). Moreover, approximately 80 percent of emergency department visits for congestive heart failure result in hospitalizations. National rates of hospital readmission are 2 percent within two days, 20 percent within one month, and 50 percent within six months (Cardiovascular Roundtable 1998). The causes of hospital readmission for congestive heart failure are diet noncompliance (24 percent), medication noncompliance (24 percent), inappropriate medication (16 percent), failure to seek care (19 percent), and other (17 percent) (Vinson et al. 1990).

Persons with a heart failure diagnosis have a disease progression that worsens as the heart muscles weaken. The person must learn to monitor fluid intake and urine output, body weight, and food selections. When the weakened heart muscles are strained by too much volume to pump or decreased contractility of the heart muscles themselves, a patient may experience an acute episode of shortness of breath and weakness requiring medical intervention. When presented with this disease exacerbation, a patient will likely go to an emergency department or a physician's office for relief. Case management is used to educate patients about heart failure and to provide services to reduce the incidence of exacerbation and, therefore, more costly emergency and inpatient hospital services.

The genesis of the heart failure case management program at the Iowa Heart Hospital at Mercy was a vision of Dr. William Wickemeyer, a cardiologist. Dr. Wickemeyer's specialty is care of persons with heart failure, from initial diagnosis to end-stage disease, including those who may be suitable for a heart transplant. Dr. Wickemeyer knew that if his patients had more education on how to avoid an exacerbation and on ways to increase adherence to accepted protocols, they would have a decreased need for hospitalization. In his private practice, Dr. Wickemeyer began using nurses to help educate his patients about heart failure. By using nurse case managers in the outpatient setting as well as following patients when they were admitted to the hospital, Dr. Wickemeyer was able to show that patients were decreasing their utilization of the emergency department and that hospitalizations were fewer. If admitted, lengths of stay were decreased. The result for the hospital was a decrease in costs because heart failure diagnoses generally result in financial losses. The result for the patient was an increase in quality of life. According to Dr. Wickemeyer:

> I wasn't the only physician admitting patients with heart failure diagnoses. In order to maximize outcomes, I knew we, as a medical staff, had to agree on a standard set of treatment protocols. I also knew that we needed to work with the hospital to establish outpatient services to stay in touch with our patients and to relieve periodic discomforts related to their disease.

The adoption of standing orders and treatment protocols by all physicians has been gradual. As the medical director for heart failure services, Dr. Wickemeyer routinely meets with individual physicians to give them updates on treatment protocols and to describe ways to improve patient care. As the heart failure case management program grew under the direction of Dr. Wickemeyer, the Heart Hospital formalized its hospital-based heart failure program under the direction of Deb Willyard, a heart failure nurse case manager. Willyard's charge in 1998 was to reduce hospital stays and improve quality of life for patients with a heart failure diagnosis and who were being attended by physicians other than Dr. Wickemeyer or his group. The Heart Hospital physicians and administration jointly compensate a nurse to work in the hospital to follow hospitalized patients of the Heart Hospital. The original Heart Hospital case manager was then able to focus solely on community-based heart failure case management.

For persons living with heart failure, education is not enough. The hospital-based and community-based case managers need to alert patients to programs, in addition to home care and case manager education services, that can assist them in adhering to accepted protocols for treating heart failure. Two programs that contribute to quality of life for patients and that decrease emergency department visits and inpatient admissions are the telemanagement and infusion clinic services.

Telemanagement Program

The telemanagement program is a free outpatient service for MHN patients with heart failure that was started in 2000 with grant funding from the National Retirement Foundation. Purchase of the telemanagement product license, a computer and printer, and five telephone lines was the major start-up expense. Telemanagement allows heart failure case managers to gather symptom data of heart failure patients at home. MHN has used the program to decrease exacerbations and hospital readmissions.

Each day, a client phones a toll-free number to reach an interactive voice response system with prompts. The client is instructed to enter his or her daily weight, fluid intake, and output and to answer other questions. By 1:00 p.m. that day, heart failure case managers receive a report. For clients who have variances from preestablished clinical parameters, case managers implement standing orders that are tailored to individual needs, such as adjusting medication dosages or reviewing dietary restrictions.

Infusion Services

To improve quality of life for persons with severe failure, Dr. Wickemeyer is using a medication called inotropes. Inotropes are a type of drug that improves the contractility of the heart muscle, thereby decreasing the energy that the heart must expend. Dr. Wickemeyer started an outpatient clinic in 1998 for the purpose of administering inotropes by intravenous infusion. Dr. Wickemeyer and Kim Carlberg, infusion nurse, comment on the success of this service.

Dr. Wickemeyer:

> Although treatment with inotropes is controversial, our patients have responded with incredible results. We have medical staff-approved criteria that to be a candidate for the infusion clinic, a person must have a Class III or IV heart failure diagnosis, must be ambulatory, and must have been seen by a cardiologist.

Carlberg:

> Our results are astonishing. Although the cost to run the clinic is subsidized by Mercy, the foregone cost by keeping patients out of the more costly emergency or inpatient care more than pays for the

service. We have witnessed an 84 percent decrease in admissions due to heart failure complications. The most overwhelming results, though, are personal testimonials of our patients. For some, the quality of life has improved dramatically.

The decreased costs of medical and hospital care and increased quality of life are made possible by the integrated approach used by the Heart Hospital. A successful service like this is a product of several elements— hospital-based and community-based case management, telemanagement, and outpatient infusion clinic services—working simultaneously to improve clinical outcomes. For overall system performance improvement, it is necessary to have mechanisms that support replication of best practices, like the heart failure case management program at the Heart Hospital, in other organizations within the system; this is where MHN plays a pivotal role. MHN identified heart failure case management as a best practice and brought the people from various network hospitals together in the form of a best-practices symposium. Not only are case management processes being replicated, but certain services (like telemanagement and infusion clinics) are being shared by several hospitals. This decreases the costs associated with running multiple automated disease-management systems.

End-of-Life Case Management for Palliative Care

Persons living with advanced chronic diseases have multiple needs and face many challenges, including pain, anxiety, and disabling symptoms. These challenges severely distress patients and caregivers long before what is typically considered the patient's "end of life." Too often, the care given to these patients is episodic and fragmented, focused only on treating their diseases. Palliative care services are provided by an interdisciplinary team and offers physical, emotional, social, and spiritual care that focuses on relieving suffering and improving quality of life regardless of life expectancy or treatment measures. This is a service that may be integrated into a community-based or hospital-based case management program.

At Mercy-Sioux City, a community-based palliative care program was developed with Hospice of Siouxland. A collaborative effort was initiated to support persons living with heart failure. In 2002, ten patients with heart failure diagnoses were selected for a palliative care pilot study. The objective of this program is to provide community-based support to alleviate recurring emergency department visits and hospitalizations. The palliative care team coordinates care with Mercy-Sioux City to manage pain and symptoms, decrease the emotional distress experienced by patients and caregivers, provide 24-hour on-call availability to respond to changes prior to a crisis situation, and coordinate community resources. The palliative care team consists of a registered nurse, a social worker, clergy, and volunteers with specialized training in palliative care.

Admission criteria for palliative care include the following:

- presence of an advanced/chronic illness regardless of diagnosis, treatment choices, or life expectancy;
- physician referral (required);
- physicians or office staff have deemed the patient and family are experiencing distress from physical, psychological, social, or spiritual issues that are affecting their level of suffering or quality of life; and
- patients and family members identify the need for palliative care services.

In addition, palliative services are provided without regard to the patient's age, cultural background, or religious affiliation.

This program is financially self-sustaining through grants, donations, and private funding. This model of community partnership has the capability of being replicated in other communities, and plans by MHN's hospice directors are underway to adopt standardized screening tools, data collection, and educational programs involving physicians, nurses, and hospice leaders in each location.

Linda Todd, director of Hospice of Siouxland and Siouxland Palliative Care, and Blanche believe this program adds to the quality of life by giving patients more options at the end-of-life stage.

Todd:

> When a person has lived with a chronic disease that is worsening and nothing can be done to improve that person's situation in an acute care setting, we can help ease the pain and suffering in his or her own environment. We have been able to demonstrate high

patient/caregiver satisfaction and decreased the high cost of emergency department and hospitalizations with the community-based palliative care services.

Blanche:

> Our partnership with Hospice of Siouxland has been a godsend for our patients with end-stage heart failure. Not only is the team experienced at giving care, it also focuses on the needs of the caregivers, and when the time is appropriate the team can facilitate end-of-life discussions, including referrals to hospice.

The palliative care program is new and faces certain issues. Financing palliative and end-of-life care is fragmented and inconsistent among third-party payers. Many people who choose palliative care are not in the stage of illness that qualifies for hospice care and reimbursement, and palliative care is not a covered service. There are opportunities for educating employers, insurance companies, health policymakers, community agencies, and providers on the value of palliative care and when and how to talk with a patient about the palliative care option.

Mercy-Des Moines has developed a program that uses hospital-based case managers to assess and collaborate with physicians in improving acute and chronic pain. In the early 1990s, Joan Beard, director of pain management services at Mercy-Des Moines, reported that the hospital's physicians, nurses, and administrators recognized that a more organized and focused approach to pain management was needed in response to an organizational value that pain management is a basic human right. Today, each registered nurse in a direct patient care role is required to complete classes on pain management during orientation and then repeat them each year. One-and-a-half full-time equivalent nurses who specialize in pain management function as case managers. Physicians also receive ongoing education and information about pain management.

Pain management services may be requested by physicians, other clinicians, or patients themselves. The pain case manager assesses the patient's level of pain and then consults with individual physicians to discuss a plan of care. Including assessments and follow-up care, an average of 460 patient visits are conducted monthly in inpatient, subacute, long-term care, and outpatient settings.

Mercy-Des Moines's pain management program was implemented throughout the organization by educating clinicians and students and collaborating with physicians and other caregivers. Pain management services are available to patients with acute or chronic illnesses that involve the control of pain. Beard is a champion for pain management; she says:

> The patient is at the center of everything we do. Our pain management team consists of physicians, pharmacists, physical therapists, staff nurses, anesthesiologists, and chaplains, and pain management includes such things as pet therapy and other complementary medicine modalities. I am a proponent of finding pain champions within the organization and partnering with them to improve care for our patients. We form lifetime relationships with our patients.

Beard believes that administrative and medical staff support is crucial to the success of a pain management program. But perhaps the most significant predictor of success is organizational culture:

> Mercy's culture allows unique visions to be put into practice. Our values of compassion and reverence have helped form the culture. Champions are in every organization, but they must be supported and allowed to put their visions into practice and take risks

CASE MANAGEMENT RESULTS

MHN has found that case management services improve quality of life and that they can be provided without impairing the institution's overall financial performance. Integrating inpatient and outpatient programs produce the best results for patients with heart failure diagnoses.

At the Heart Hospital, heart failure is the number three admitting diagnosis for all ages and the number two admission diagnosis for persons over age 65. In fiscal year 2001, the average Medicare reimbursement for a congestive heart failure (DRG 127) admission was $4,138. The average cost was $5,167, for a loss of $1,029 for each heart failure admission within MHN facilities. The Heart Hospital implemented a telemanagement program in 2000 to enable patients with heart failure at home to stay in touch with their case managers daily. By May 2001, analysis of data showed an 84.4 percent reduction in heart failure readmissions.

When the Heart Hospital reported its results to MHN's heart failure improvement team, other hospitals in the network wanted to adopt telemanagement. Education for all program site case managers and demonstrations by the vendor were completed. Telemanagement was expanded to three additional MHN facilities by early 2002. The heart failure case managers across MHN hold bimonthly conference calls to analyze telemanagement outcomes, review case studies, and discuss promotion success stories. Plans for expansion to remaining MHN facilities are underway.

The funding of telemanagement is primarily from cost avoidance. For every readmission that is foregone, the hospital is able to save the $1,029 loss that would have occurred in variable costs. In addition, MHN receives funding from the Trinity Community Health Fund grant to partially offset technical and administrative costs through 2004.

Measuring Outcomes

To measure the effectiveness of telemanagement, several outcomes are measured and benchmarked with the initial successes at Mercy-Des Moines. Clinical, financial, process, and patient satisfaction outcomes are measured for the patients enrolled in the telemanagement program. Using nine months of data from 2002, the outcomes are detailed in Figure 4.2

On satisfaction surveys, the following are patients' comments about telemanagement:

- They remind you if you forget to call.
- It gives me peace of mind.
- I know there is someone caring for me every day.
- I like being able to call in from anywhere.

Goals have been established to increase the number of patients enrolled in the telemanagement program—to 15 percent of heart failure acute admissions in 2003, 20 percent in 2004, and 25 percent in 2005. MHN medical centers are discussing the use of telemanagement services for patients with other chronic diseases, such as high-risk pregnancy, gestational diabetes, diabetes mellitus, asthma, chronic obstructive pulmonary disease, and depression. In September 2002, MHN presented results of its heart failure case management program to a national CHI leadership audience.

Figure 4.2

Indicator	Goal	MHN
Referrals	210*	182
Decrease in readmissions	50%	86.2%
Start-up costs	$74,830	$57,413
Annual operating costs	**$28,484**	**$24,686**
Patient daily call-in compliance rate	80%	93%
Rate of patient variance from preset parameters	10–15%	10.9%
Patient satisfaction: (1=low, 5=high)	4.50	4.82

*15 percent of hospital admissions for DRG 182 and principal diagnosis of 428.0.

The heart failure infusion clinic at the Heart Hospital has had similar positive outcomes, with decreasing hospital readmissions and increasing patient satisfaction. For 2002, the infusion clinic treated a total of 43 patients (1,387 total infusions) with Class III or IV heart failure diagnoses; this number was nearly 8 percent of the hospital's heart failure population. During that year, there were an average of two readmissions to the hospital per patient with a principal diagnosis of heart failure, compared to eight preinfusion therapy hospitals' admissions per patient.

Exercise endurance is an indicator used to measure clinical outcomes in patients with heart failure. As patients are treated in the infusion clinic, remarkable improvements have been noted in their ability to ambulate without shortness of breath and in the distance of the walk. Exercise endurance improvements contribute to the quality of life for patients.

CHALLENGES

Mercy-Des Moines faces six major challenges it must overcome to sustain and build its case management program.

Professional Collaboration

Case management involves delivering care across traditional professional boundaries. This means that care teams must work together as doctors and nurses, nurses and nurse practitioners, specialist doctors and primary care doctors, and other combinations of clinical caregivers. Turf battles and power struggles between and within professional groups must be broken down to enable collaboration for the patient's best interest.

Reimbursement and Misaligned Incentives

Third-party reimbursement for case management services is minimal. An organization must finance the overhead costs for case management from sources other than direct reimbursement. Health policies that reward organizations for case management programs that decrease costs and keep patients out of expensive institutional care would make more sense.

Accountability for Clinical Outcomes

Each patient is unique, so medical care cannot be completely standardized. However, clinical and financial outliers must be examined closely, and physicians' outcomes must be compared blindly to those of their peers. Although much progress has been made with approval of protocols and clinical pathways, the individual physician is still the person responsible for approving a patient's plan of care, which recognizes not only the medical problems but the patient's functional needs and responses to the diseases. It is a challenge to educate physicians about economic aspects of care and to change practice behaviors.

Access to Case Management

As in all medical services, a physician is responsible for referring patients for case management services. Access is unequal for all patients for several reasons. First, because Iowa is a rural state, many patients live in geographic isolation; therefore, patients may find it difficult to learn about case management services or may live too far from the nearest case manager. Second, the patient's physician may not understand the benefits of case management or may not have the time to facilitate setting up a patient referral. Third, the caseload may be too much. There could be such a high demand for case management services in some areas that some patients would not be served.

Motivation for Health-Seeking Behaviors

Some people do not follow treatment regimens. An important consideration of the clinical caregiver is the patient's definition of health. Is function more important than health? What is the person willing to give up to live a healthier lifestyle? At what point will a person be willing to adhere to treatment regimens and recommendations for improved quality of life?

Dual System Membership

Given the joint operating agreement between Trinity Health and CHI and the fact that MHN is itself a regional system, a challenge (and an opportunity) is presented by the overlaying organizational infrastructures. Not only are there two national systems with different management structures, policies, practices, and cultures, the Mercy hospitals in Iowa have their own unique cultures and practices. The advantage for MHN is having resources and know-how available for starting new programs and services and having benchmarks and systems to emulate for operating existing services.

KEY LESSONS

There are multiple reasons that case management may be successful in decreasing costs and improving quality of life. Several of the success factors experienced across MHN are described below.

1. *The successful case management program has physician, nurse, and executive champions.* Champions, described earlier in the chapter, formulated a vision that was articulated and shared across organizational and professional boundaries. Nurses, physicians, and healthcare executives are not only developing and implementing programs for their patients, they are helping others across the system learn about and implement best practices.

    The system has committed resources to coordinate and integrate best practices by sponsoring educational seminars, promoting regular meetings with key leaders, distributing reports, and comparing organizational performance and patient outcomes. Hickman, MHN's director of clinical integration, is a nurse with extensive management experience. He serves as an internal consultant to clinicians in the various Mercy organizations.

2. *Successful case management requires a systematic, organizational framework or plan that is agreed on by senior management and clinical leadership.* Based on best practices outside and within MHN, resources were dedicated to developing a framework for designing, implementing, and replicating case management programs. A system-based director of clinical integration was given the charge of overseeing implementation of case management across the network hospitals. It is essential that the organizational framework

be approved and supported by senior management and the medical staff.

The "Case Management Guidebook" (prepared by Mercy Health Network Medical Centers and Trinity Health) provides an organizational framework that includes guidelines for a steering committee, design team, project manager for development and implementation, and process for performance improvement. The steering committee oversees the design, implementation, evaluation, and continual improvement of case management. The committee comprises members of senior management and clinical leadership, those with broad organizational accountabilities, informal leaders, and people who understand and are committed to the case management organizational plan. The design team recommends the targeted population; coordinates the design and implementation; organizes the work for building the case management system; creates the formats, procedures, and role descriptions for the case management system; and reports progress to the steering committee. The project director manages the process, chairs the design team, and designs an ongoing structure to facilitate the evolution of the case management system. A management plan outlines the process for continual improvement.

3. *Based on standardized definitions and processes of case management systemwide, each organization should design case management to its own particular needs.* As discussed throughout the chapter, there are different ways to organize case management. There are also differing interpretations of case management, from coordination of home health visits for the patient with an episodic condition to providing telemanagement and infusion clinic services for the person with a chronic disease such as heart failure (disease management). The MHN lessons are based on similar processes and elements of both inpatient and outpatient models. Although the earliest case management programs in the mid-1980s were inpatient programs, there is inconclusive evidence about the effectiveness and efficiency of pure inpatient models (Cook 1998; Roggenkamp and White 2001). For some diagnoses, the cost of providing care exceeds the reimbursement amount; therefore, an admission is an automatic financial loss. Inpatient case management programs, then, may be efforts to reduce the magnitude

of financial losses. The cost of case management personnel and administrative overhead should be factored into a cost-benefit analysis to measure the exact amount of savings or loss to an organization.

Significant reductions in costs of emergency and inpatient care are possible through outpatient, community-based case management programs. Most programs like this are small and have evolved due to physician, nurse, or nurse practitioner champions. Reimbursement is minimal, so an organization must be committed to providing the service at a loss, but the loss would be larger if the service is not provided. With limited resources, the continuing lesson is how to design a case management program to have the biggest impact on improving patient care and decreasing costs.

4. *Nurses manage teams and clinics for improvements in patient outcomes.* Nurses are central to all the MHN case management models. They assume ongoing clinical management, under the direct guidance of the patient's physician and using protocols developed by the appropriate service. Case management can reduce the total demand for nurses and thus assist in a critical shortage, if sufficient inpatient admissions can be avoided and nonprofessional nurse extenders are appropriately used. MHN has begun to use social workers and nurse practitioners to supplement its nurses and primary care physicians (especially in rural areas), and nurse-managed teams and clinics are proving to be successful.

Given the use of evidence-based protocols and the availability of physician consultation when needed, nurses and nurse practitioners can provide superior care to persons with chronic illnesses. Nurses interact with patients and get to know their daily struggles. Nurses often uncover problems and barriers that undermine success, and they are able to help patients develop an individualized plan of action. Nurses play an essential role in empowering patients with chronic conditions to identify treatment options, develop self-care skills, and adhere to treatment regimens.

5. *Processes are streamlined and automated for ease of communication.* Nurse-managed programs for chronic conditions are facilitated by the use of software-facilitated communication systems. In a state that is mainly rural (like Iowa), geographic isolation may

contribute to patients' inability to access certain services. Software-facilitated programs that are used via telephone lines by nurses and patients are a way to stay in touch and to monitor disease outcome indicators. When problems arise, early interventions that follow physician-approved protocols may prevent more serious disease exacerbations.

6. *New methods of care are promoted by demonstrations and champions who can answer questions, reassure patients and physicians, and document their successes.* Telling the story of how an organization created cost savings and improved clinical outcomes is important for others to hear. Bringing clinicians and managers together locally, regionally, and nationally to discuss best practices and to offer advice and samples of policies, reports, and outcome monitors is beneficial. In this way, the opportunity cost by learning from others' successes is drastically reduced.

7. *Information systems aid work processes and workflows for managing care.* E-mail and shared electronic records are critical in getting the necessary physician backup. Although MHN has not developed a full telemedicine system, it has many of the components and will add the rest.

   Technology is important not only between nurse, physician, and patient. An information system must be designed to give information and knowledge resources quickly to case managers. The case manager must access reference databases for drug interactions, community or business resources, and references on evidence-based practice to provide health system guidance. A case manager must also know when a patient called for assistance after hours or when a patient is presented to the emergency department. Data must be collected on emergency visits and hospital readmissions and integrated with financial data to determine the ongoing effectiveness of the case management program.

8. *Evidence-based protocols are coordinated with performance-improvement processes.* Physicians must decide on clinical pathways and medical protocols for multiple diseases, and nurses must utilize research-based practice and follow nursing theory to intervene

with patient responses to their diseases. When deviations from physician-approved protocols occur or when other opportunities to improve patient care surface, case managers have a mechanism with which to work with performance-improvement staff to enhance outcomes. Trends are monitored and alternatives are explored for intervention.

BIBLIOGRAPHY

American Heart Association. 2003. "Heart and Stroke Statistical Update." [Online information; retrieved 4/2/03.] *www.americanheart.org.*

Cardiovascular Roundtable. 1998. *Congestive Heart Failure Prevention.* Washington, DC: The Advisory Board Company.

Chen, A., R. Brown, N. Archibald, S. Aliotta, and P. D. Fox. 2000. "Best Practices in Coordinated Care." [Online article; retrieved 4/2/03.] *www.mathematica-mpr.com/3rdLevel/bestprac.htm.*

Cook, T. H. 1998. "The Effectiveness of Inpatient Care Management: Fact or Fiction?" *Journal of Nursing Administration* 28 (4): 36–46.

Cudney, A. E. 2002. "Case Management: A Serious Solution for Serious Issues." *Journal of Healthcare Management* 47 (3): 149–52.

Daniels, S. 1999. "Using Hospital-Based Case Management to Reduce Payer Denials." *Healthcare Financial Management* 53 (5): 37–39.

Hospital Case Management. 1999. "Case Managers, Social Workers Thrive Under Triad Model." *Hospital Case Management* 7 (1): 3–5.

————. 2000a. "From Worst to First: A Physician Success Story." *Hospital Case Management* 8 (6): 83–84

————. 2000b. "Following the Path to Improved Outcomes." *Hospital Case Management* 8 (10): 149–50.

Porter-O'Grady, T. 1992. *Implementing Shared Governance.* Baltimore, MD: Mosby.

Powell, S. K., and D. Ignatavicius. 2001. *Core Curriculum for Case Management,* p. 3. Philadelphia, PA: Lippincott.

Roggenkamp, S. D., and K. R. White. 2001. "Is Hospital Case Management a Rationalized Myth?" *Social Science and Medicine* 53 (8): 1057.

Roggenkamp, S. D., K. R. White, and G. J. Bazzoli. "Adoption of Case Management: Economic and Institutional Influences." [unpublished].

Vinson, J. M., M. W. Rich, J. C. Sperry, A. S. Shah, and T. McNamara. 1990. "Early Readmission of Elderly Patients with Congestive Heart Failure." *Journal of American Geriatric Society* 38 (12): 1290–95.

Walters, J., C. F. Schwartz, H. Monaghan, J. Watts, G. J. Shlafer, G. M. Deeb, and S. F. Bolling. 1998. "Long-term Outcome Following Case Management After Coronary Artery Bypass Surgery." *Journal of Cardiovascular Surgery* 13 (2): 123–28.

Zander, K. 1988. "Nursing Case Management: Strategic Management of Cost and Quality Outcomes." *Journal of Nursing Administration* 18: 23–30.

Chapter 5

Prevention: Creating Healthy Communities at Good Samaritan Health System

BACKGROUND

Good Samaritan Health Systems (GSHS) is the local acute care provider for 100,000 people in five counties of central Nebraska. It serves a secondary service area of an additional 70,000 people in nine rural counties and attracts referrals from an additional 180,000 people living in a tertiary service area the size of the state of Indiana. Almost 18 percent of the population is over 65, and 9 percent is over 75. Cardiology and cardiovascular surgery, neurosurgery, and behavioral health are the principal referral services at GSHS, but it also has orthopedics, trauma, neurosciences, urology, and oncology service lines. GSHS has 287 acute beds, has a neonatal ICU, and is the hub of the Mid-Nebraska Telemedicine Network and a network of 12 Critical Access Hospitals. Approximately 27 percent of its outpatient visits and one-third of its inpatient admissions are from outside the five-county local area.

GSHS emphasizes family practice and internal medicine in its primary service area. It has a freestanding behavioral health center, and it has 22 skilled nursing beds, hospice, and a full array of home services. It recently opened a unit for Alzheimer's and assisted living and a fitness center that provides both rehabilitation and preventive exercise and wellness services.

Maintenance of market share is critical to GSHS's success. It faces three kinds of competition: integrated networks seeking to serve large rural areas, local hospitals in adjacent counties, and independent specialty centers. Its strategy is to compete on quality, cost, and customer service while collaborating—that is, serving as a resource to and referral center for those same entities. As Table 5.1 shows, GSHS has been suc-

Table 5.1 Major Performance Measures for Good Samaritan Health Systems

	1999	2000	2001	2002
People				
Employee satisfaction		3.40	3.84	
Physician satisfaction				
Turnover: organization	20.1%	21.0%	22.80%	18.58%
Turnover: RN only	15.7%	11.6%	10.1%	10.1%
Organization vacancy rate			4.1%	4.2%
Growth				
Patient overall satisfaction[1]	4.26	4.26	4.24	4.24
Market share	51.4%	50.4%	49.1%	48%
Performance				
Net patient revenue (thousands)	$101,111	$117,879	$126,566	$135,564
Operating margin	6.9%	6.0%	7.3%	9.6%
Total margin	10.0%	9.7%	8.7%	9.8%
Days of total cash	258	259	263	267
Debt to capital ratio	25.4%	24.9%	24.6%	21.8%
Cost per adjusted discharge[2]	$5,371	$5,831	$5,603	$5,914
Community benefit[3] (thousands)	$16,451	$20,008	$24,522	$25,465

Quality

Patient perceived quality[4]	4.49	4.47	4.46	4.36
Patients rating care as "excellent"[5]	44%	44%	42%	36%

Process and outcomes measures in use[6]	• Complete Y2K plans and training • CABG cost reduction by at least 2 percent • CABG average intubation time less than seven hours • ALOS for CABG patients within 0.5 days of national standard • Plant operations cost savings were $387,534.72	• Reduce initial patient-assessment time by 40 percent • 91 percent breast cancer and prostatectomy patients electronic pathway compliant • 90 percent of charts document pain as the fifth vital sign • Reduce mammography result notification time to 4.42 days	• New nursing patient care standards • 30 percent improvement scoring in safe medication practices • Six pathways online • Fractured hip pathway reduced ICU stays 66 percent, ALOS one day, and mortality 75 percent • 94 percent compliance, ASA on admission protocol • Implemented standardized orders and standardized patient education for CHF

continued

Table 5.1 *continued*

	1999	2000	2001	2002
		• Reduce home health cost to $68.00 per visit • Maintain or improve customer satisfaction of home health patients	• 90 percent of breast cancer surgeries on mastectomy/lumpectomy pathway • Use of improved breast biopsy requisition form • Home health productivity and patient satisfaction goals • Pain management protocol for indicated patients	• Antibiotic for pneumonia patients administered within two hours of arrival
Quality improvement focus areas[7]		• Y2K contingency team • CABG clinical pathway team • Plant operations process-improvement team	• Interdisciplinary documentation team • Oncology clinical-effectiveness team	• Medication safety • Infection control • Care of the CHF patient • Patient care standards

- Home health
  performance-
  improvement
  team

- Home health
  operational
  productivity
  planning team
- Pain-management
  team

Notes: Measures were entered as they became available.

1. Inpatient survey results. These values were estimated from a regression equation using all original values and dummy variables for each quarter except from July to September 2002. The equation has excellent fit and significance. The parameters for the quarters prior to the current vendor are similar and highly significant. The adjustment model incorporates any time trend so that none can appear in the data above. However, inspection of the adjustment coefficients and original data suggest that there was no trend, either up or down, in these measures.

2. Cost per case adjusted for severity using CMS's DRG index.

3. Community benefit is defined by Catholic Health Association and includes charity care, Medicare and Medicaid losses, education and research costs, and services or funds donated to community activities.

4. Inpatient, survey results; see note 1.

5. Percentage of inpatients surveyed rating quality as excellent.

6. Measures reported to the MBO board. In 2003, CHI will standardize many of these measures for comparative reporting.

7. Areas selected for intensive study by the MBO.

cessful with that strategy. For the residents of Buffalo County, GSHS has been able to move beyond that goal to a broader one of promoting a healthier community. It has systematically identified health needs beyond acute care and met them, providing its local citizens with patient-centered care.

Kearney, Nebraska, the city of 30,000 where Good Samaritan is located, is an unusual place, both in its fortunate economic circumstances and in the civic engagement of its people. Allen Johnson, Kearney's city manager and chair of the GSHS board, describes Kearney:

> Kearney is an agricultural trade center, but it's diversified enough to protect it from the cycles of the agricultural business. It has good employment but also clean industries. The income level is relatively high. It's an expensive place to live. The work ethic in this part of the country is unlike anything I've ever seen. There's a spirit of partnership involving governmental and nonprofit entities. The Chamber of Commerce has a "Kearney Tomorrow" program to establish priorities. It's an effort that draws from all sectors of the community. Leadership seems to emerge from the collaborative process. It's not a fad. In the minds of the taxpayer, it's become an expectation. One of the best examples is an interactive system of law enforcement. The city and county are in the same building, and they share all the operational aspects. If that were to go sour, the taxpayers would be irate.
>
> There's just an incredible amount of strong leadership in this city. Somebody sees something worth doing, and they are willing to invest themselves in it; they can get support. It amazes me what this city will invest in. We had a wellness facility and program fund drive. CHI got behind that, and we ended up with a million and a half dollars.
>
> You could do what we've done anyplace you could get the leadership. It's a lot harder where there's conflict. Some cities can't agree on the time of day. When you have people trying to work on common goals, willing to participate, you can do it.

THE ROLE OF PREVENTION AND OUTREACH SERVICES

Patient-centered care is the Institute of Medicine's third criterion for the American health system, after safety and effectiveness. The central goal of patient-centered care is not just to treat but to collaborate with patients to keep them well; "continuous healing relationships" should replace "patient visits." Patient-centered care envisions a system that helps patients identify and reduce disease risks, deal effectively with those that become reality, and maintain maximum quality of life thereafter. This vision will require massive shifts in attitudes, lifestyles, and the healthcare system.

This country has always emphasized treatment over prevention; in fact, it now spends only about 3.5 percent of its healthcare budget on public health. Lifestyles have created epidemics of smoking- and obesity-related diseases with documented loss of life years and quality. Payment systems reward care over prevention, intervention over counseling, acute care over continuing care, and institutions over homes. The physician supply reflects the payment system. Hundreds of billions of dollars are consumed in the care of preventable disease and disability. Our aging population, shrinking birthrate, and financial needs outside of health mean that we cannot sustain the present model. We must move to one that reduces disease incidence and its consequences. Ken Tomlon, CHE, CEO of GSHS, elaborates on this point:

> Kearney's larger employers posed the question, "How can we reduce the overall costs?" I said, "Two things. Work with us to increase the value of the services by improving the outcomes. Second, none of us are focusing yet on why people are coming into the healthcare system. Many of the reasons are things we do to ourselves. Until we focus on that, we won't improve our condition. We're a nation that wants it all. There's no limit when you deal with the disease side. We need broad-based support to deal with the prevention side—the lifestyle side." The message was well received. Our meeting with major employees was scheduled as a half-hour presentation. It ran for two hours as a dialog.

One way to understand what patient-centered care means is to explore the limitations of the services that hospitals and doctors currently offer. These limitations are what GSHS strives to overcome:

1. *Reaching out beyond patients.* Hospitals and doctors respond to "patients" who seek them. They don't reach out to "people" who

might prevent disease or disease consequences but who are not yet "patients."

2. *Serving patients with chronic disease.* Patients with manageable but incurable problems—heart disease, arthritis, pulmonary disease, diabetes, stroke, depression, trauma, AIDS—often have serious obstacles to recovery that arise from social, financial, and physical issues beyond the usual expertise of doctors and hospitals. The problems become more complicated when patients have two or more of these diseases, a situation that is now common among the aged.

3. *Supporting the infirm.* Many people require support to maintain their current functioning. The level of support ranges from relatively simple services like transportation to full nursing home care. A variety of home and community services, as well as several levels of institutional support, are required.

4. *Assisting the end of life.* About 1 percent of the American population will die each year; these people and their families face incalculable stress. They will consume about 10 percent of the total hospital and physician resources in the months before they go. (The exact fraction is difficult to estimate, but several studies place it at more than one-quarter of all Medicare expenses.) The role of the health-care system is to help these people fulfill as many of their needs as possible, while avoiding futile efforts. The hospice movement is an important part of the solution.

The typical hospital governing board is surrounded by signals that reinforce the traditional model of acute intervention. Unless it has some exceptional leaders, it is not likely to think how and why its patients arrived at the door nor what their needs are when they leave. "Acute care is our mission," its board members will say. "We are no more responsible for prevention and continuing care than we are for education or police protection. Besides," they will note, "no one will pay our hospital to do primary prevention, and the rates of payment for continuing care make it difficult to do even a minimally adequate job." In 1996, CHI explicitly rejected this perspective. CHI's vision espouses "creating new ministries that promote healthy communities." When CHI evaluates its MBOs, it looks for specific achievement in creating healthy communities. Almost all MBOs have some long-term care, home care, or hospice units. All MBOs have explicit healthy community initiatives that focus on coalition building and partnerships.

In addition to validating the concept, CHI created a central Mission and Ministry Fund, one component of which makes grants to MBOs and congregations of women religious to "break the boundaries of institutional care and build healthy communities." The Fund seeks programs that are "innovative in the way that they address long-term or emerging community needs, invite collaboration with community partners, and are replicable in other communities." By 2002, the Fund had distributed $11.7 million to 73 communities. CHI also offers loan resources through its Direct Community Investment Program "for organizations and projects that promote human dignity, social justice, and healthy communities." Since its inception in 1998, CHI has made loans at below-market rates to 34 communities, providing them with access to $20.5 million. So far, the program has had no defaults.

Vision alone is not enough. A practical program to improve community health must recognize some unpleasant realities:

1. *Programs must reach people who are most in need, and these people are often in lower socioeconomic groups.* "Social justice" is not an empty or idle phrase. Poverty is part of the problem.
2. *Programs must be designed around limited financial support.* Payment for primary prevention of disease (immunizations and disease-preventing lifestyle changes) is often unavailable, and payment for continuing care is substantially less generous than payment for acute care.
3. *Promotion and marketing are critical.* The people who need care are not immediately receptive to it. Popular habits, attitudes, and beliefs sometimes run counter to prevention and continuing care needs.

GSHS is CHI's model for dealing with these realities while achieving the criterion of patient-centered care.

COMMITMENT TO COMMUNITY HEALTH

GSHS's efforts to improve patient-centered care began in the early 1990s. Its 1991 report to the Sisters of Charity Health Care Systems, a CHI predecessor, indicated substantial interest and commitment, not only in Good Samaritan but also in the larger community, which had completed a variety of needs assessment surveys. A 1994 report to the GSHS's board, "A New Civilization—A Healthy Community," led to an expanded vision statement:

> Good Samaritan Health Systems will broaden its focus over time from acute, illness-based care to prevention/wellness-based whole person care that is patient, family, and community focused, collaborating with traditional and nontraditional partners who promote healthy living to provide a continuum of life long health care that ranges from prevention and health maintenance to acute care to chronic/long-term care.

Joan Lindenstein, FACHE, administrative director for community health development at GSHS, explains:

> When CHI established its mission, it was very definitive, the emphasis on new ministries and new ways to serve the broader community. At Good Samaritan, we set community health goals through our strategic plan. We had a community benefit accounting process and a community benefit task force that led to Healthy Communities. The early Healthy Community discussions were about providing access to healthcare. That evolved into a broader sense of what healthy communities mean.

Johnson remembers:

> When we started talking about the development of this healthy living center and the focus on health, my question was, "Is central Nebraska ready for this?" It was pretty radical stuff. The hospital's leader, the previous administrator, had shared that vision with the board. The fact that they had the margin to go with it didn't hurt; if the margin hadn't been there, it wouldn't have happened. Some of the leadership and vision came from the physician community. One doctor in particular, Bob Rosenlof, was a strong advocate; he sold the board on health. He was . . . tenacious but soft spoken. Some of the medical staff thought he was a bit eccentric.

GSHS implemented its vision with a three-pronged strategy.

1. *It catalyzed the formation of the Buffalo County Community Health Partners (BCCHP) to create a basis for collaboration on all kinds of health needs.* The Partners stimulated a cascade of health promotion and disease prevention programs that involve county government, private employers, social agencies, and citizens.
2. *It began developing wellness, prevention, and health education services, and it acquired a behavioral program with inpatient and outpatient services.* GSHS now offers a full spectrum of service for the well community, including acute needs, rehabilitation, chronic needs, and end-of-life care.
3. *It developed a program collaborating with Critical Access Hospitals and other rural healthcare to provide telemedicine, online consulting, visiting consultants, rapid transport, and management assistance.* The result is an integrated program of service to distant rural communities.

THE BUFFALO COUNTY COMMUNITY HEALTH PARTNERS

The partnership approach, essentially building teamwork among interested parties, led to an extraordinary array of services. As Table 5.2 shows, more than 30 different programs, ranging from pet therapy to winning a "Well City USA" award for Kearney, have emerged from these partnerships.

More than 20 organizations participated in the BCCHP community health improvement initiative. BCCHP's vision is

> to improve the quality of life of those who live in, work in, or visit our community. In so doing, our community focuses its time and resources on the things we value as a community, including:
>
> 1. strong sense of community
> 2. holistic health
> 3. education
> 4. environment
> 5. economy

Structure

BCCHP organized its stakeholders into seven constituencies—education; business and industry; government; healthcare providers; health-

Table 5.2 Outreach and Prevention Services in Buffalo County

GSHS *Programs*

- Community conference center
- GSHS Health Development Center, a facility and program for rehabilitation and wellness exercise and promotion
- Depression screenings, available year-round and free of charge
- Crisis intervention, initial assessments, and referral information to persons seeking mental or emotional health services
- Outreach clinics, consultations, and mobile diagnostic and screening services for rural areas, in collaboration with the medical staff. Eighty-eight clinics were held in 25 different communities in 2001
- Volunteer activity by GSHS associates on more than 180 boards, councils, community organizations, and coalitions.
- Recruitment strategy for primary care physicians in rural communities. GSHS operates a residency program with the University of Nebraska, assists physicians starting rural practices, and subsidizes a *locum tenens* program
- Mid-Nebraska Telemedicine Network, funded in part by federal grants, serving 12 rural communities. It has provided more than 9,000 patient encounters, 400 educational programs, and 100 administrative conferences
- Primary care clinics in three rural communities
- Healthy lifestyles educational programs emphasizing exercise, diet, stress management, and smoking cessation
- "Critical Incident Stress Management Team" of certified "debriefers" who can assist individuals dealing with stressful incidents
- "Corner Closet" that supplies clothing for needy patients

- Community Health Access Team, whose goal is to provide primary care access for every citizen "with zero racial and ethnic disparity"
- Pediatric trauma program to train emergency medical technicians and rural emergency staffs in pediatric needs, with the Nebraska Office of Highway Safety
- Wellness Works, a program to promote workplace wellness that has given awards to 24 businesses or government units and that earned Kearney "Well-City USA" designation in 2001

BCCHP- and GSHS-Sponsored Programs
(in collaboration with other community partners)

- "Health Ministry Network" to educate the faith community of Buffalo County regarding the establishment of health ministry programs
- Safe Kids, instruction in child safety emphasizing car safety
- "Safe Community Team" developing and implementing safety strategies with emphasis on traffic accidents
- Family Centered Services, with volunteers and state funds to assist families with nonmedical needs
- A parent assistance network providing a variety of services to parents of behaviorally disabled

- Transportation program that integrates several low-cost transportation services and served 50,000 riders in 2001
- Healthy family worker program to provide an array of nonmedical in-home services
- Volunteer program to mentor grammar school students
- An exhibition of hands-on learning activities attended by 8,300 people
- "School to Career" initiative to educate junior high and high school students in health careers
- Medical Explorer Scout post
- Day camp for families grieving the death of a loved one

continued

Table 5.2 *continued*

- Case management program for children from birth to three years with verified disabilities; the program included 134 families from nine counties in 2001.
- New blood collection center, with the American Red Cross
- Telephone interpreter service with AT&T
- "Positive Pressure," a grass roots coalition that addresses issues of alcohol and drug use among young people

children. Community volunteers and local organizations assist in making the program available in five counties.
- Education and support network for pregnant and parenting teens, with the State, Union Pacific, and Kearney Public Schools
- Pet therapy program for hospital and nursing home patients, with volunteers and the local university

- Domestic violence task force coordinating healthcare, law enforcement, and community resources to assist in "breaking the cycle of violence." The task force led to the Family Advocacy Network, a collaboration of 19 agencies serving 34 counties to break the cycle of violence and provide support for victims

care organizations; human services; and civic, church, and consumers. Representatives from these groups form BCCHP's governing board. Five "Vision Element Committees" provide organizational oversight of 15 priority health goals. A work group representing all seven constituencies mobilizes progress toward each goal. The work group is charged with developing an asset map and an action plan and working with BCCHP to measure results. BCCHP supports the work groups with technical consultation, recruitment of volunteers, and measurement. Denise Zwiener, director of BCCHP, explains:

> The concept of BCCHP was to impact several entities—the schools, agencies, spiritual leaders, healthcare providers—by getting us together to talk about our goals, what we wanted to do to create a healthier community. The board members come together with the belief that we can make a difference. We have support from our whole community because of the visibility we've achieved. We've done some "asset mapping" to identify what's valuable to our constituencies. We create "positions" to make sure everyone is in agreement. Even groups who doubt the value of BCCHP can join the board, dialog with it, and create more followership. The work touches many people in many ways. It's an entity in the community where people think of their needs and identify who cares about them.

Reverend Russell Sommerfeld, pastor of Holy Cross Lutheran Church and member of the BCCHP board, describes the collaborative process:

> The thing that attracted me was the overall philosophy that the Health Partners would become a conduit, rather than a managing agency. In the first summit, I saw people pair off and sit down who perhaps had never sat down together before. At first we had board members facilitating the groups, but we wanted leaders to emerge from within the collaborating organizations. We were not there to control or direct. It wasn't smooth as silk. It took a while.
>
> We had put Alzheimer's care, suicide prevention, and immunization into a group called "holistic health." As we worked together, we realized suicide had three risk groups—youth, mentally ill, and elderly. We assigned people to work on each of those areas.

Then something amazing happened. The representatives from Vocational Rehabilitation, the Goodwill Industries, Region III Behavioral Health Services, and the Nebraska Association for the Mentally Ill started to talk about the mentally ill. The need for employment surfaced quickly. These folks collaborated to develop a center where people could get support, mentoring, and accountability training. I sat there, the alleged leader, and I watched it take place. I didn't do anything but convene the group. Vocational Rehabilitation Services and Region III now fund the center.

You can be sure that all the groups weren't able to collaborate immediately. The immunization group wasn't sure how to connect. There were clinic providers, private providers, and schools, with no idea how to collaborate and no common database. They didn't click until several years later. Because of that initial BCCHP meeting, they got together and did a great job.

Dr. Clint Jones, a GSHS medical staff member and BCCHP board member:

The Partners required Good Samaritan to modify the traditional patriarchal approach that preceded CHI. It required collaboration and participation. We weren't doing enough for prevention or education, but the larger picture is a sense of belonging and an ability to engage the healthcare system. You have to see the Partnership in action to understand what it means to say to a group, "We'll only help you if you partner with another group." If you work together, you'll get the money.

Programs

BCCHP's sensitivity to constituency need drives its programs well beyond traditional concepts. Jami Anderson, chair of the BCCHP resource committee and deputy director of Mid-Nebraska Community Action; Sommerfeld; and Lindenstein describe some of the programs. According to Anderson:

Our Community Health Access Team (CHAT) is charged with increasing access for the underserved. One of the reasons CHAT was formed is the high rate of untreated chronic diseases among the

50-year olds. There's a phenomenon called "prairie pride." People who are hardworking poor don't want the stigma of Medicaid or free care. We want to develop a white paper on the problem, with data and proposals. It is moving tentatively. We've been to a national conference. We've been working on educating the physicians. We're trying to bring a speaker from that conference here.

Preventing teen pregnancy was a BCCHP goal. The work group brought a large group together to start educational workshops targeted at building self esteem for third to sixth grade boys and girls and provided some funding to help them continue their work.

Sommerfeld explains BCCHP's strong and successful connection to the faith community:

Today there's a better connectedness between the main line denominations and the evangelicals. In 1997, I suggested to the Ministerial Association that we bring together pastors and counselors for troubled youths. I hit a brick wall. There was fear that the therapists would bring ideas that were doctrinally uncomfortable. Now, there's a little more trust. The churches are beginning to use the services of the various family care agencies.

The most recent development was a dream for quite a long time. It was to see the churches saying "We have a role to play in improving health." At the Buffalo County Health Ministry Network, churches get together every month to network about what we are doing to improve the spiritual, physical, and emotional health of our community. Some pretty creative things have begun to happen, [such as] blood pressure clinics and car seat seminars, . . . regular care for elderly people, and personal contact with the elderly. Some of the churches have begun to provide healthier foods at their carry-in dinners. It might not seem like much, but we've had people coming to our dinners who couldn't come before.

Good Samaritan offered a workshop for nurses who wanted to do parish nursing. We are in the early stages of developing parish nursing. Four of the congregations have them, and they come to the network meetings; the nurses want to see [the program] extended to the smaller rural churches. There is a champion for

Stephen Ministries who is working on developing personal care and grief care.

These are things that have happened, and the Network is not even a year old. Health Partners helped this process. In January, it helped the Ministry Network fund "Health Ministry 101," a seminar by Interfaith Ministries of Nebraska. Now we see people who are interested in having these things in their churches dragging their pastors to the network meeting.

Measures

Measured achievement is a critical part of BCCHP. Each goal has measures, and each task force and work group understands that measures are essential. Carol Renner, assistant superintendent of Kearney Public Schools and chair of the BCCHP planning and measurement committee, explains:

> We say how frequently we'll measure the goal, what's the source of measurement, and we hold ourselves to that. We make sure we monitor what we do. We try to measure annually where we can. We publish our progress, so the whole community can participate and celebrate success.
>
> We've been through one cycle of learning how to set goals and measure. Our measurement has become a lot more realistic, and that lets us set goals that are a lot more realistic. We can say how much some things have improved , but we can't attach financial values to our achievements. The reader has to decide what the value is.

Measurement is not cheap. As Lindenstein explains, BCCHP completes regular surveys of Buffalo County citizens, conducted with the same rigor as national and state health surveys:

> When we had to rely on the state public health department for data about health needs, we got data that was two or three years old, and the samplings for Buffalo County were never large enough to be statistically valid. So BCCHP had to carry out the same type of studies, looking at the outcome indicators and risk factor surveys with an appropriate sample for the county. We wanted statistically

valid data that we could compare to the state and the nation, so we could set objectives for the county.

The measurement systems and the programs must be integrated. Zwiener describes how this happens in domestic violence:

> When we set our goal on domestic violence, we thought we could reduce violence, but we learned that we had to improve the reporting before we could reduce the violence itself. We had to change the goal to improved reporting. When we started in 1994, law enforcement and other agencies believed "what happens in the home stays in the home." Now we have more openness, and communication between the police, parole officers, the Safe Center, and the hospital. Now the community offers coordinated support to the victims, and they are more willing to step forward. The law enforcement officers have training and policies to keep victims safe, or detain their husbands. The Batterer Intervention Prevention Program can reduce abuse by counseling the abuser. We've extended the program outside the county, through the Family Advocacy Network. It uses the telemedicine capability to interview and counsel people in remote sites.

Finance

BCCHP is a grant- and gift-supported organization. Total grant support to BCCHP over the years has been approximately $300,000, including two planning grants from CHI of $75,000 each. Members of the BCCHP board contribute both cash and in-kind contributions as a part of an annual pledge process to the Partners. In addition, businesses and physician clinics assist with cash sponsorships of special events. BCCHP provides project grants and mini-grants to community groups that collaborate to attain the priority health goals. Grant funds come from GSHS, which donates approximately $100,000 per year to BCCHP through cash and in-kind donations.

Most BCCHP participants are volunteers or are supported by existing agencies. The annual budget for paid workers and office operations—$100,000 per year—is financed by contributions from sponsors. To reduce costs, the staff is employed by United Way and contracted to BCCHP, and the Kearney Area Community Foundation is the fiscal agent.

Anderson describes BCCHP's effort to expand the financial support:

> The resource committee's charge was to develop a plan for the sustainability of BCCHP. That involved collaborating on grants and developing a strategic resource plan. The funding from Good Samaritan will continue to be a major part of our support. We've also received funding from CHI and from the Robert Wood Johnson Foundation and W. K. Kellogg Foundation. We have a process for soliciting individual and corporate support, and we accept in-kind donations. BCCHP is not supported by the state or the county except through grants we are awarded, and the grants go mainly to the participating agencies.

Results

In 1996, BCCHP established 15 goals it wished to attain by 2001. BC-CHP's emphasis on measurement allows it to evaluate its progress (see the results in Table 5.3). The Partnership achieved four goals and made substantial progress on seven others. It did not achieve four behavioral health goals—alcohol use, domestic violence, obesity, and tobacco use. Those areas are problems for all communities, and the people in Kearney feel they have important and positive steps on each. BCCHP also carefully documented its specific and often extensive actions for each goal.

In addition to the BCCHP record on specific goals, the concept of wellness has certainly spread. The Partnership became the forum for Buffalo County health issues and has stimulated several programs that reach beyond its borders. In 1997, BCCHP was awarded a three-year, $60,000 grant by the Robert Wood Johnson Foundation (RWJF) and the W. K. Kellogg Foundation (WKKF) to support assessments, annual healthy community summits, and technical assistance to its work groups. The grant was part of the foundations' "Turning Point" program to transform and strengthen public health infrastructure. Annual national forums for grant recipients provided BCCHP members with valuable insights into leveraging their achievements.

The RWJF and WKKF Turning Point program also supported a similar healthy community effort in a nine-county region in northern Nebraska and the Nebraska State Health Department. The state's funds were to work with communities to carry out the core functions of public health in new ways. Since Turning Point, Nebraska has promoted the

Table 5.3 BCCHP's 1996 Goals and 2001 Achievement

Goal	Measure	Target	Baseline (1996)*	2001	Status
Assisted living	Available units	93	58	300	Achieved
Independence of older adults	Percentage of awareness of services from survey	74%	66%	72%	Progress
Alcohol use	Alcohol-related motor vehicle accidents	46/year	64/year	61/year	Not achieved
	• Driving under the influence	4%	8%	5% Not achieved	Progress
	• Binge drinking (from survey)	10%	24%	24%	
Domestic violence	Safe center clients/1,000 adult females	12.8	22.8	40.7	Not achieved
	Implementation of countywide measurement system	Increase public awareness	1 reporting source	7 reporting sources	Achieved
Child abuse	Substantiated cases/1,000 children	7.33	12.39	11	Progress
Suicide prevention	Suicides/100,000 population	11	18	10	Achieved
Alzheimer's disease	Available beds	50	0	34	Progress, met in 2002

continued

Table 5.3 *continued*

Goal	Measure	Target	Baseline (1996)*	2001	Status
Infant, flu, and pneumonia immunizations	Percentage of target population, by local surveys	Infant: 90% Flu: 75% Pneumonia: 50%	Infant: 81% Flu: 65% Pneumonia: 39%	Infant: 89% Flu: 55% Pneumonia: 51%	Progress Not achieved Achieved
Teenage tobacco use	Tobacco use, 11th grade survey	12%	30% (boys 38% girls 22%)	26% (boys 29% girls 24%)	Progress
Obesity	Percentage of population overweight	37%	38%	48%	Not achieved
Teenage pregnancy	Births per 1,000 females, 15 to 17	21/1,000	24/1,000	12/1,000	Achieved
Multiple prescription management	Percentage of hospital discharges admitted with prescribed drug reaction	"Reduce"	1.1%	0.5%	Achieved
Drinking water quality	Percentage , failing state standard	Unable to measure	Unable to measure	Unable to measure	Unknown
Transportation	Number of boardings of public transportation	34,000/year	26,000/year	87,000/year	Exceeded
Affordable housing	Units for low/moderate income population	1,025 additional units	1,465 additional units	Unable to measure	Unknown

* Baseline data were for 1996 or the most recent year available.

formation of district health departments that serve 30,000 people or more in contiguous counties, with support from a portion of Nebraska's tobacco settlement funds. BCCHP has been a model for communities embarking on healthier communities initiatives. The Partnership has a policy of "sharing our learning" with others. In 2002, Buffalo County joined with six contiguous counties to form a district health department that contracts with BCCHP for specific public health services for the county.

BCCHP has selected ten new goal areas for 2006. Environmental air quality, housing, and substance abuse goals were expanded. Access to care, safety, lead levels, spirituality, stress on the family unit, and infant mortality were added. The new goals are as follows (listed here as published):

- To reduce lead levels in children
- Environmental tobacco smoke—increase smoke free restaurants and workplaces
- Access to Health Care—100 percent coverage for children, using Kids Connection and Child Health Improvement Program
- Safety—youth seat belt use
- Stress on the Family Unit— youth and adult alcohol, tobacco, and other illegal drug use, depression and youth thoughts of suicide
- Reduce Obesity—exercise and nutrition for adolescents and an obesity goal for adults 45–65 years
- Health and Spirituality—"increased awareness of spirituality's effect on health and healing"
- Infant Mortality— perinatal and postnatal mortality
- Affordable Housing—"an adequate number of affordable housing units"
- Transportation—expand the successful program

In addition, BCCHP elected to monitor a variety of other measures of community health, including drinking water quality, recycling, toxic chemical releases, child abuse, domestic violence, voter registration, school attendance, injuries and deaths, teen sexual activity, number of homeless people served by agencies, unemployment, and three indicators of income or wealth.

The Workplace Wellness Program

As the BCCHP reaches out to fill specific needs, local employers have moved enthusiastically to support workplace wellness programs. A national nonprofit wellness organization awards gold, silver, and bronze status according to criteria they have established. Twenty-four businesses in Kearney have achieved this award. The national organization also gives awards to cities that excel in employee wellness participation. Kearney became the sixth city in the nation to win the award.

Karen Crocker, director of education at GSHS, tells how the workplace wellness program began and grew:

> We wanted to make sure that we improved health status, and not just focus on an award that would sit on the shelf. The Well Workplace taskforce went to the businesses and employers. The response in the community was overwhelming. Thirty businesses joined the effort. Good Samaritan sponsored a Well Workplace University to educate them on how to start worksite programs.
>
> There were two important components. One, you need to get the businesses to support the effort. Our businesses began to say that it made a difference in the lives of their employees. Many of them provided information that it made an overall difference in the business. Second, competition had a profound impact. "We're doing silver; you are only bronze" friendly competition. The pride in the city award developed into a true camaraderie and brought people together. The smaller businesses used the hospital's education programs. We had luncheons and celebrations. The entire business community was represented. We had 600 people at the award luncheon.

Johnson:

> The award became a point of intense pride for . . . employers. . . . The school district got the Bronze Award, and the city employees got the Silver, and it became a prideful thing. We tried to give it some prominence—an awards luncheon, with the leaders there. Eaton Corporation [a prominent local employer] had a lot of emphasis on safety and health to start with, so when a program like this comes along, . . . they see it as . . . contributing to their goals.

Zwiener notes that Workplace Wellness and BCCHP collaborate:

> The national organization provided a lot of the initial support. To sustain it, we needed to make it more local. We set up a membership organization called "Wellness Works." It's a membership organization with fees. We will keep the support local, make it more portable so more businesses come on board. We'll have a single point of contact.
>
> We have linked domestic violence to the well workplace. We have a violence prevention program we've offered in 20 sites. We stress the importance of having policies in the workplace to address domestic violence. We want to get the small town Mom & Pop retailers so they can help employees break the cycle of violence. We are making business aware that violence impacts their bottom line.

GSHS SERVICES BEYOND ACUTE CARE

GSHS provided much of the initial leadership for BCCHP. It continues to stay actively involved in the Partnership through representation on the board and the goal work groups. GSHS has several programs of its own that emphasize outreach, wellness, and prevention:

- A behavioral health program with both inpatient and outpatient capability
- A coordinated program for families
- Numerous free clinics and health fairs emphasizing early diagnosis screening
- A comprehensive array of continuing care services
- Healthy lifestyles programs, including integrative health modalities such as massage therapy and biofeedback

GSHS uses an outreach network to provide substantial assistance to families with difficulties, including programs for the safety, wellness, and parenting of infants and preschool children; safety and risk prevention for elementary school children; disease prevention, parenting, safety, and substance abuse for teens; and family support services for adults. Many of the services meet needs of challenged families, but many are aimed at awareness and education for well populations. Although lo-

cal service is often given through BCCHP, GSHS works with agencies
in other counties.

Screening

GSHS had an aggressive program of diagnostic screening clinics, including oncology, cardiology, podiatry, depression, and osteoporosis.
A "Women and Heart Disease" program of screening and health promotion attracted 5,500 people. GSHS offers screenings in the smaller
communities at health fairs, schools, and their affiliated hospitals. At
the peak, 40 sessions were offered in one year.

The medical staff forced a reexamination that reduced the scope
of screening. They were concerned that screening be limited to documented effectiveness, that preventive education be included with the
screening, and that individuals with indication of disease receive appropriate follow-up. The staff's medical education committee now reviews
and approves the kinds of screening, following the Guidelines of the
U.S. Preventive Services Task Force. A hospital committee reviews specific requests from the communities. Crocker explains:

> We accept only about 10 percent of our invitations. A committee
> of the services that normally participate decides how much time
> they will commit. They review each request in terms of their ser-
> vice's needs. If enough services are available, we participate. We do
> cholesterol and blood pressure screening upon request. The hos-
> pital has sponsored oral cancer screening conducted by the county
> dental society. In addition, some physician clinics do oral cancer
> exams and skin cancer screening.

Screening is a complex question. Identifying people who do not have
the disease and people whose condition cannot be helped is inevitable.
These cases can be frightening and frustrating for the patient and expensive for the healthcare system. There are no easy answers, as Dr. Jones
and Dr. Bill Vosik, chair of the staff's education committee, note.

Dr. Vosik:

> We felt we needed to treat people properly. The medical staff is
> supportive of screening that has proven medical benefit. A lot of
> what the hospital was doing seemed more like promotion than

prevention. The medical staff had a session with consumers participating and with every specialty involved agreed that we would only do screening when we understood why we were doing it and how we would do it.

Dr. Jones:

The medical staff, the administration, and the board have never gotten together on screening to the point where they know each other. That's been one of the big issues.

Dr. Vosik:

We still don't have a good answer. The hospital cut back on carotid screening. Now there's an outfit that comes into town and does vascular screening for profit.

Dr. Jones:

I think we'd have to say not all the doctors are comfortable with the solution. I had a patient where we found a micro cancer in the prostate. He elected surgery, and he thinks the surgery saved his life. I think it debilitated him.

Post-Acute Care

GSHS's program for long-term care includes the following:

- An extensive rehabilitation program that offers cardiac and pulmonary rehabilitation, arthritis therapy, and aquatics rehabilitation. This program is housed in the Health Development Center, which is also used for wellness/fitness programs. The combined visits of the programs total 120,000 per year.
- A home care program that provides nursing, social work, therapy, and aide services in four counties. In 2002, the program made 14,000 visits.
- A home infusion program that serves the central part of Nebraska. In 2002, the program served 90 patients
- A hospice program that serves ten counties
- A 22-bed continuing care unit
- An Alzheimer's and assisted living facility with 58 beds

Rehabilitation Program

The Health Development Center is an attractive 29,000-square-foot medical fitness facility. It features a large, dual-temperature exercise pool as well as large exercise areas, strength training and cardiovascular equipment, classrooms, and treatment areas. In addition to the usual post-acute rehabilitation and support, the center encourages self-referral for arthritis, minor injuries, and continuing exercise programs for chronic heart disease and diabetes. The center is open to self-referred people seeking an exercise program, either through individual or work-related group enrollment. Unlike a commercial exercise program, each applicant receives a health-risk appraisal and an activity-readiness questionnaire and is screened by a healthcare professional. Self-referred applicants at moderate or higher risk must obtain a release from a physician. Once screened, the applicant can seek guidance on exercise, nutrition, and stress management.

In fiscal year 2002, 110,000 of the 120,000 visits to the center were self-referred wellness/fitness customers, aquatics therapy pool walkers, and cardiac rehabilitation phase IV members. Self-referred users are expected to pay fees and are generally not covered by health insurance. Private-pay fees were 53 percent of the center's revenue. GSHS subsidizes a portion of its employees' fees and provides a 10 percent discount to employees of organizations that participate in the workplace wellness program.

Hospice Program

Last year, the hospice program served 120 patients, about half the adult cancer deaths reported for the counties and 13 percent of all adult deaths. These ratios are less than many hospices achieve. GSHS formed a task force on supportive care of the dying that conducted focus groups with patients, bereaved families, healthcare workers, and community members. Denise Waibel-Rycek, director of home care services at GSHS, discusses these focus groups:

> The themes that emerged from the groups were improved communication with physicians and other caregivers; greater family involvement in the communications; a more family-friendly environment at Good Samaritan, especially in the emergency room; more support groups; and earlier referrals. GSHS is working on all of these, and we expect to see an increase in hospice activity as well as improved care for all patients needing palliative care.

INTEGRATIVE HEALTH STRATEGY

CHI has made a substantial investment in integrative healthcare—a patient-centered strategy for delivering a whole person (body, mind, and spirit) care. Alternative, complementary, or nontraditional medicine has received increasing attention and respect in recent years. CHI established a council for integrative medicine in 1998. The council concluded that a vision was needed that embraced but went beyond alternative medicine:

> To provide a more holistic (mind/body/spirit) approach to health care that would include the clinical and philosophical rationale for combining different therapeutic modalities into a seamless unified approach.

CHI defined integrative care as:

> A personalized, comprehensive, and collaborative approach to assessing and responding to a person's body, mind, and spirit needs for healing. Compassionate and attentive listening to the whole person as a way of delivering clinical care, as a way of engaging staff loyalty, and as a way of assuring organizational alignment of inter-disciplinary resources, initiatives, competencies and infrastructure.

Depending on the needs of the patient, integrative care may or may not include the use of complementary therapies. The approach is patient centered rather than therapy centered.

GSHS has moved aggressively to actualize the CHI concept, and it has moved beyond it. Through a healthy lifestyles department and patient-centered holistic health teams, GSHS has implemented an integrative health strategy that combines rehabilitation, chronic disease management, and wellness. The mission of GSHS's healthy lifestyles department is "to create healthier communities through the provision of value-based, holistic (mind, body, spirit) programs designed around lifestyle models of prevention, disease management, and disease reversal."

The healthy lifestyles department offers more than 30 programs, ranging from yoga, massage, biofeedback, and meditation to family programs to "Learning Journeys," which are multiweek lifestyle change programs designed to affect such high-risk areas as tobacco usage, heart disease, and weight management. Some programs are designed specifically to complement workplace wellness programs and gain corporate support. Some are stand-alone programs and others are integrated within the GSHS clinical service lines. The offerings are based on discussions with the medical staff and the community to identify unmet needs. Measures of behavioral change are included in every program.

Each program includes a health-risk screening and limited physical screening on intake. Enrollees who need medical attention are referred to their personal physician. If they do not have a personal physician they are referred to a physician on the medical staff. A collaborative relationship is developed with each participant's/patient's personal physician during the screening process. Medical oversight of the programs is provided by the medical director in liaison with appropriate medical staff committees at GSHS.

In fiscal year 2002, the healthy lifestyles department served 800 people. It is projected to grow to 4,000 users by fiscal year 2006. All of the courses are offered for fees that are similar to competing sources of care. Most of the fees are not covered by health insurance. The healthy lifestyles department began in 1999, and the projected budget calls for continuing losses through fiscal year 2006, totaling about $1 million and continuing at the rate of $150,000 per year. GSHS considers the losses a part of its commitment to creating a healthier community.

Cindy Shultz, RN specialist at GSHS, discusses the healthy lifestyles department:

> This department is an outgrowth of the [BCCHP] survey five years ago. The survey indicated that 50 percent of priority health issues [were] related to lifestyle. Establishing the department was a real commitment on the part of CHI and GSHS . . . . We give people the power to make changes in their lives that either help keep them well or live better with their disease.
>
> The department has a diverse staff. We have a group support facilitator who is a licensed mental health provider, a massage therapist, a nurse, two stress management specialists, an exercise physiologist, a dietitian, and a medical director. The participant's physician also plays a key part. It's a partnership that includes the participants, their physicians, and the staff.
>
> "Learning Journeys" bring four components—nutrition, exercise, stress management, and group support—to change the

patient's lifestyle. Our heart disease reversal program has a documented success rate. Our smoking cessation program uses a 12-step model; it has a 70 percent success rate, which is very high.

We always contact physicians about their patients. Even if a patient enrolls on their own, we automatically bring their physician in as a partner. The "Learning Journey" programs require physician clearance. . . . For all the programs, we ask if they have any objection. We try to make the physicians aware of the plan, keep them involved in the decision making, give them feedback on progress, and involve them as an integrated partner.

We've created a database on progress and outcomes for every program. The data are fed back to the patients and their physicians.

Dr. Jeff Brown, the medical director of the healthy lifestyles department, discusses the approach:

Some of the programs focus on the care of people who already have some illness or have had a central event. Healthy Lifestyles is providing education, helping to put the tools where we need them, and putting the focus and the mindset of the care providers that they are providing care not just for the patient but for all the people around them. One of our goals is to increase physician awareness of our programs . . . . The medical community right now doesn't understand the role of the yoga and stress management activities. It's easy for a physician to manage the medical component; it's a little more difficult to encourage a holistic program. In my office, I don't have the time to go into that. Very few patients come in saying, "I need help to stay healthy."

It's a paradigm shift to move from treating the disease to promoting health. Our physicians are grappling with it, but it's difficult to get them to encourage concepts that they don't follow themselves. That's probably our biggest hurdle. We are a profession based on hard evidence, and we are just now starting to get the statistics and research to back up wellness.

In addition to the mind, body, spirit offerings of the healthy lifestyles department, GSHS has established ten different holistic health teams of employees, physicians, patients, and families reviewing all of its care delivery system. As of 2002, the teams were examining all facets of the patient and staff experience to develop plans for a healing environment.

SUPPORTING THE RURAL AREAS

The rural area to the north and west of Kearney contains 170,000 people, a small city scattered over a vast land area. Service to these people is part of GSHS's mission and is an essential element of GSHS's strategy. Dave Glover, CHE, senior vice president at GSHS, describes this multifaceted strategy:

> Our strategy now is to assist communities any way we can to establish a primary care presence, either with a local physician or with a group from another location. We'll put together a recruitment package with a community to help them get a doctor. Good Samaritan once owned seven rural physician clinics. We've supported transferring those practices back to their local communities. We continue to support three communities where the transfer hasn't happened. We agreed with our staff physicians not to buy primary care practices in Kearney. Good Samaritan concentrated on the rural areas.
>
> Our 12 hospital Critical Access Network is one of the largest in the country. Good Samaritan's medical staff has grown from 50 physicians to 120. The specialists at Good Samaritan do outreach to the rural areas.

Critical Access Hospitals (CAH) were given special Medicare financial treatment in 1997, provided that a state agency was supervising the program, the hospitals were 15 beds or less and met other federal criteria, and the hospitals participated in a network for referrals and support. The state established the necessary program, and it offers grant support to CAH networks. The GSHS network won grant support in 2000 and established goals relating to quality of care, transfer procedures, and improvement of individual CAHs. Progress was made in almost all areas. Glover describes the services GSHS provides on request and without charge:

> Good Samaritan shares a strategic planning model that includes data collection, analysis, and board education. We share it with all the Nebraska networks. We provide assistance in training the

workers in the hospitals. We help them develop measures of performance. We collect patient transfer surveys from all the hospitals and feed them back comparatively. We assist the boards in making credentialing decisions. We will advise on whether or not a specific procedure is appropriate for a specific doctor.

GSHS offers a family medicine residency in collaboration with the University of Nebraska. About three-quarters of the graduates of the program now practice in the area. GSHS and its medical community have expanded physician availability from 50 physicians to 120 in the past ten years. It operates a *locum tenens* service for these doctors that is partly supported by a state grant and partly by local fees. It also recruits mid-level practitioners.

With its medical staff, GSHS operates mobile ultrasound and telemedicine EKG sites. It provides outreach specialty consultations in most medical specialties. The furthest reaching and most extensive are cardiology and orthopedics, which offer 25 clinics a month each. Other specialties combined provide 50 clinics a month. GSHS provides helicopter and long-distance ambulance transportation and cooperates in a state program of ambulance support.

GSHS has had a telemedicine program for eight years, and it is now operating in 12 sites in Nebraska and Kansas. The program, supported by three grants totaling $3.5 million, is evolving as the technology improves. It has already proven its worth for education and for online consultations. By July 2001, almost 9,000 consultations, more than 400 educational programs, and 100 administrative meetings had occurred using telemedicine. Mental health consultations are the most common; speech pathology, orthopedics, and oncology consultations are also successful. Direct patient education in diabetes and arthritis and remote reading of images are the latest developments. Permanent funding has been a challenge for the program, but as Wanda Weekley, program manager, says:

Our focus is more timely specialist access. We had some champions in orthopedics and cardiology. We quickly reached 100 patients a month. Patient satisfaction is very high. Even elderly patients accept it very well. Counseling visits have been particularly acceptable.

There are cameras and microphones on both ends. Document cameras can show handwriting and data; we can view the x-rays. The lab data are usually faxed to us. A nurse at the remote site can do heart sounds and use otoscopes, and an advanced practitioner or physician can do physicals on camera. We don't routinely use physicians at the remote sites. Our physicians prefer to make the initial visits in person. Follow-up works really well. We've had patients tell us that they keep their appointments better because they only have to go to the local hospital. They don't have to take off work as long. They don't have to arrange a long car ride.

With the newer equipment, the cost has fallen. The whole unit sits on top of a TV, and is big as a VCR. The equipment is much more reliable. Troubleshooting is down 90 percent. Some networks do homecare on several hundred patients. We have the equipment and we have some patients, but we have not pursued it as aggressively.

Third-party payers are finally paying for most visits. Medicare pays for most services. The grants subsidize a portion of the physician fees and cover charity patients. We do a lot of education. Any CME offered to the Good Samaritan staff is available to the remote sites. Our EMT program is available monthly; we usually have 80 to 100 people attending education sessions.

Building on its success with BCCHP and its family support program, GSHS has won a three-year federal grant to develop a Family Advocacy Network to provide a coordinated response to all forms of family abuse, including neglected or vulnerable adults. The program involves 19 collaborating agencies and will serve 34 counties. The telemedicine network will be incorporated in the program to allow consultation and recording of conference information.

THE BENEFITS OF PREVENTION AND OUTREACH

The ultimate worth of outreach is a question that defies simple evaluation. Gains can come from improvement in length of life and quality of life, from increased productivity, and from cost reduction, but a longer life may be more expensive. Why then should a community health organization invest in it? There are three reasons:

1. *It improves achievement of a health mission,* when the criteria of health are the patient's. Kearney is a healthier place.
2. *It improves productivity.* The healthcare establishment can handle a larger patient load through the various outreach programs. The Kearney economy is stronger because of the collaborative efforts at wellness.
3. *Continuing a program limited to acute intervention will not be acceptable to society.* Kearney will be more attractive than other communities that have not pursued these programs.

Scientifically, these are speculative propositions. None of them can be proven in Kearney, and rigorous proof is lacking in general. The BCCHP has been able to show improvement in some health measures, and it has reached an impressive fraction of the Kearney population. But as the BCCHP concedes, it cannot attach a dollar value to its efforts. The Workplace Wellness programs may pay off as much in motivation as in health. Far larger populations than Kearney are necessary to make definitive statements, but the employers in Kearney, like many others, feel that the investment is justified. The screening, as revised by the medical staff, is justifiable in terms of lives saved, but it probably increases costs. Post-acute care meets a market test; people pay out of pocket for a substantial amount of it. But the people who most need it are least able to pay for it. The telemedicine is valued by its patients; it extends the reach of the GSHS specialists, and it is winning market support. But it does not appear to have reduced demand at GSHS. It is an add-on rather than a replacement at this time.

Strategically, however, the question is not of proof but of risk versus reward. Outreach and prevention are scientifically speculative, but most new business ventures are speculative. The questions governing boards must weigh are both the risks of pursuing the investment and the risks of not pursuing it. In this context, Kearney offers a lot of useful information.

1. *The investment in prevention and outreach is manageable.* GSHS's total outlay is less than 2 percent of its operating budget. A well-managed acute care organization in an economically prosperous area should have a cash flow (earnings plus depreciation) on the order of 7 to 10 percent of net revenues. At this level, outreach is clearly affordable. Organizations that fail to meet this standard

will be forced to use their cash for pressing acute care needs, rather than for prevention and outreach. The tragedy of this is that the areas of greatest need for prevention and outreach are those in disadvantaged settings. It is not an accident that the test case is in a wealthy, balanced economy with an enthusiastic community of volunteers and collaborators. Kearney is an ideal setting. It will be difficult to transfer Kearney's success to cities with impacted poverty and diverse populations, where, as Johnson says, they "can't agree on the time of day." But CHI is making the healthy community concept work in many communities. The concept is clearly viable for many American cities and can be a vision for all.

2. *The program is amplified and made cost effective by deliberately stimulating the contribution of many others, including government agencies, employers, and civic and religious groups representing customer stakeholders.* GSHS acts as a facilitator and stimulus, and it is highly selective in its own investments. It has drawn in as much outside money as it has spent. Its human resources investment is outweighed many times by the efforts of others on the BCCHP. The collaborative model is the only known way to address the outreach and prevention problem effectively. It arguably does three things—spreads the real costs over very large populations, promotes the concepts among those populations, and gives the populations served a voice in the direction of programs. The problem of broad participation is one of control—how to keep focus, settle arguments, and maintain efficiency. Kearney's solution relies heavily on the work groups that represent all the constituencies and that set measurable goals and its staff, which devotes much of its effort to measurement and celebration of achievement. As Sommerfeld says, "It doesn't always work, even in Kearney, but the point is that it sometimes works extremely well."

3. *The benefits of the program are diverse and accrue to stakeholders beyond the healthcare organization as well as to the organization itself.* Child health, for example, includes prenatal care, immunizations, screening, nutrition, safety, and domestic violence elements. These elements benefit children, parents, police, school systems, and employers in different ways and with different time lags. They probably cost the healthcare establishment more than the estab-

lishment earns in compensation. But no community healthcare organization is likely to deny the importance of child health.

The rewards of prevention and outreach are best assessed in the broadest terms of customer satisfaction, market share, and financial return for the organization as a whole. At this level, GSHS has clearly followed a winning strategy. For example, the Health Development Center is now breaking even on direct costs, but it makes no contribution to indirect expense. Revenue for the healthy lifestyles department is about $150,000 a year below direct costs. Randy DeFreece, president of the Good Samaritan Hospital Foundation, and Lesley Bollwitt, director of grants and special projects, note the offsetting fundraising opportunities.

Bollwitt:

> We have a foundation grants committee that meets on a regular basis to evaluate funding opportunities in terms of our strategic plan. One issue discussed with each grant is sustainability—what happens after the initial funding runs out.

DeFreece:

> The healthy lifestyles program and the healing environment program open opportunities for giving. People are interested in prevention; they want to be involved. Healthy lifestyles has an endowment. Our thought is that it will be used to assist people who have financial needs that prevent them from changing their lifestyle. We've raised $600,000 to date. There are also a lot of grant opportunities.

Bill Luke, chief financial officer at GSHS, recognizes the underlying issue:

> If you look over the years, we've gone from 6 percent to almost 9 percent margin. That's about $4 million more cash flow. The costs of the community programs haven't been terribly important in that context.

KEY LESSONS

GSHS, Kearney, and the Sisters of Charity committed to prevention and outreach before most of the nation. Their efforts preceded the IOM's criteria by almost a decade. They were one of the first "Healthy Communities." Here are the steps they took and that a community seeking to emulate Kearney should take.

1. *Local champions, the former CEO and a member of the medical staff, led an exploration of the strategic opportunity.* The effort was directly related to the GSHS mission and the concept of community bene-fit. A "continuum of care" committee was formed. The committee worked for two years, conducting several surveys and stimulating discussion. Its final report to the board and the medical staff called for a revised vision, emphasizing

   • transformation from illness-based care to prevention/wellness-based whole person care that is patient, family, and community focused and
   • collaboration with traditional and nontraditional partners that promote healthy living.

   Although "transformation" is one word used in the commit-tee's report, "filling the gaps" is another. GSHS has not directly modified acute care. Its programs supplement and complement the traditional services, and as a result it can coexist with multiple styles of acute practice. Similarly, "collaboration" expands the set of partners but does not bring them deeply into acute care.

2. *Efforts were begun to establish collaboration with local employers and other community agencies.* Collaborative programs were identified that led to Wellness Works and the BCCHP. GSHS provided important support, however, including the following:

   • Encouraging GSHS employees to contribute their time to various collaborative efforts.
   • Committing its employees to workplace wellness. As one of the largest employers in town, this commitment was essential.
   • Providing critical financial support and management time to establish BCCHP and Wellness Works.

3. *Despite the need to reinforce the autonomy of BCCHP and the wellness program, two critical ground rules were established.* Both programs are loose alliances that are difficult to sustain. Both have now succeeded in Kearney long enough to be reasonably permanent parts of the community. The first ground rule emphasizes formal collaboration. By giving the grant funds to the Partnership to disburse, GSHS demonstrated its intent to collaborate, not dominate. That allowed the programs to become independent activities, driven by their own constituencies. The concepts arose from the coalition rather than being imposed on it. All constituencies of BCCHP are represented in each of the work groups. No activity can come under BCCHP auspices unless it involves collaboration between two or more agencies.

The second ground rule emphasizes measurement. All the BCCHP goals must be measurable, and much of the effort of its small staff goes to measuring. The measures drive the work groups, the goal setting, and the celebrations. Wellness Works is a collaborative vehicle that also emphasizes measurement. Although the bronze and silver awards for wellness emphasize structure and process, the gold award requires "capturing concrete outcomes related to behavior change, cost effectiveness, and return on investment."

4. *The preventive and outreach programs emphasize celebration.* All the programs deliberately and consistently attach wellness to positive images and rewards. Fairs, parties, prizes, and hugs are the images and the reality. Encouragement is the motivator, not criticism or force. Even the workplace competition emphasizes the victories, not the defeats. Conflict is muted by politeness and patience. As Sommerfeld says, "it doesn't always work." The opposite approach is less likely to succeed.

5. *GSHS continues to be an active participant.* The stability of these programs depends on GSHS. Were it to withdraw, the programs would be jeopardized. GSHS is committed to an ongoing share of discretionary funds and human resources. To continue this commitment, it must value prevention and improving health status through outreach higher than competing opportunities. Some of these opportunities will have much larger income possibilities for

GSHS and its medical staff. Saying no to them will test the skills and leadership of GSHS and CHI.

Although many organizations are committed and some are powerful, a "prime mover" is usually required. GSHS deliberately plays that role, continuing to provide financial support, to volunteer assistance, and to contribute time of its managers. It has effectively moved itself and its physicians from providers of care to providers of health.

6. *GSHS's own programs are developed in close coordination with its medical staff.* Dr. Brown says that the paradigm shift from treating the disease to promoting health is GSHS's biggest hurdle. Dr. Jones says not all the doctors are comfortable with the screening solution, even after cutting back. These two members of the medical staff are reflecting something much bigger than the specifics they are addressing. Collaboration with the medical staff involves a workable structure, good rules, and substantial tolerance. GSHS reflects all three: (1) it has medical staff review structures to guide its integrative health strategy; (2) it uses the Prevention Guidelines, a national consensus on the evidence for screening, as its rule for evaluating local activity; and (3) it promotes its integrative health with an agreement that it is for those who choose to use it.

BIBLIOGRAPHY

Buffalo County Community Health Partners, PO Box 1466, Kearney, NE 68848–1466 (308) 865–2284

Callahan, D. (ed.). 2002. *The Role of Complementary and Alternative Medicine: Accommodating Pluralism.* Washington, DC: Georgetown University Press.

Emanuel, E. J. 1996. "Cost Savings at the End of Life. What Do the Data Show?" *JAMA* 275 (24): 1907–14.

Eisenberg, D. M., R. B. Davis, S. L. Ettner, S. Appel, S. Wilkey, M. Van Rompay, and R. C. Kessler. 1998. "Trends in Alternative Medicine Use in the United States, 1990–1997: Results of a National Follow-up Survey." *JAMA* 280 (18): 1569–75.

U.S. Preventive Services Task Force. 2003. [Online information; retrieved 1/03.] *http://www.ahcpr.gov/clinic/uspstfix.htm.*

Chapter 6

Support Services: Surpassing Benchmarks at St. Elizabeth Health System

BACKGROUND

St. Elizabeth Health System is the smaller of two acute care systems in Lincoln, Nebraska, a rapidly growing city of 250,000. It historically emphasized primary care, but in recent years it has added referral service lines in cardiology, orthopedics, neurology, burns, wound care, pediatrics, obstetrics, and neonatology. It maintains extensive ambulatory services, an employed physician network, occupational health, home care, and hospice care. It has a number of joint ventures, reflecting physician interest in new models of care delivery, and these compete with independent providers as well as the other healthcare system.

St. Elizabeth's core business strategy is to support the clinical service lines. It must make itself the source of choice for their needs, both to help attract solid patient demand and to keep the lines themselves from migrating to the competition. St. Elizabeth's competitive advantage is in supplying accurate, timely, efficient support to the service lines. Most patients will need diagnostic and treatment services—lab, imaging, operating rooms, emergency care, rehab—that the service lines themselves cannot conveniently supply. Similarly, logistic services—human resources management, plant and supply services, information, accounting, finance, planning, and marketing—underpin both the clinical lines and the diagnostic and treatment services. A breakdown in either diagnostic and treatment or logistic support mechanisms will make St. Elizabeth less attractive to its patients, attending physicians, and referring physicians and will threaten its future success.

St. Elizabeth has developed a comprehensive program to ensure excellence in these support mechanisms. That program has allowed the

159

service lines to succeed, and through them, St. Elizabeth succeeds. By 2002, St. Elizabeth had rising trends in most balanced scorecard measures, and it had risen to top quartile and better where comparisons were available. This was not always the case. As Table 6.1 shows, 1999 was "a wake-up call" to Robert Lanik, president and CEO of St. Elizabeth. A combination of factors pushed St. Elizabeth to the first operating deficit in many years. Its two competitors had merged, and the merged organization was competing more aggressively. Managed care led to the loss of some insured groups. The early efforts to build the physician network "made all the mistakes" and lost $10 million. The Balanced Budget Act of 1997 took its toll, and "Y2K" was a serious problem. Lanik says:

> In 1999, I saw our earnings and cash erode. I saw reasonable performance in our hospital, but not good enough by my standards. The physician network was where we had to take the most aggressive action. We had to support that by creating a sense of urgency and "turning up a notch" on the hospital side. I've never lost money before. I hated it. For me it was an opportunity to create a sense of urgency and a team, and we did.

St. Elizabeth's Response

The answer for St. Elizabeth is a management system that helps each support service identify its most promising opportunities for improvement. St. Elizabeth built its system around a solid tradition of financial budgeting, a successful continuous improvement program, a cooperative culture, and a dedicated senior management that was in place before the 1999 problems arose. St. Elizabeth recognized that healthcare is a team game, like football, where every player must succeed for the team to succeed and any individual failure can cause the team to fail. Behind excellence are whole processes of support that Lanik calls "blocking and tackling":

> Clear, concise, repeated messages. You have to do it every play. It's fundamental. If it doesn't happen, the whole thing breaks down.

In "A Work in Progress," a presentation Lanik made to his CHI colleagues in 2002, he identified four major steps to "turn it up a notch":

continued

Table 6.1 Major Performance Measures for St. Elizabeth Regional Medical Center

	1999	2000	2001	2002
People				
Employee satisfaction	4.20	3.91		3.85
Physician satisfaction		7.01		
Turnover: organization		27.5%	21.52%	17.18%
Turnover: RN only			14.2%	10.3%
Organization vacancy rate			8.3%	6.2%
Growth				
Patient overall satisfaction[1]	4.20	4.24	4.23	4.09
ER patient satisfaction[2]	4.63	4.50	4.62	4.17
Market share	31.1%	32.9%	32.0%	
Performance				
Net patient revenue (thousands)	$111,114	$125,283	$144,862	$180,583
Operating margin	(3.9)%	5.7%	10.2%	13.8%
Total margin	(1.1)%	7.8%	10.9%	13.9%
Days of total cash	81	135	165	148
Debt to capital ratio	11.6%	10.2%	8.0%	7.6%
Cost per adjusted discharge[3]	$5,712	$5,517	$5,648	$5,276
Community benefit[4] (thousands)	$8,380	$9,079	$9,772	$13,434

Table 6.1 *continued*

	1999	2000	2001	2002
Quality				
Patient perceived quality[5]	4.41	4.42	4.43	4.22
Patients rating care as "excellent"[6]	40%	42%	43%	30%
Process and outcomes measures in use[7]	• Mortality • Readmissions • VBAC rate; falls with injury; aspirin in 24 hours of MI diagnosis; surgical site infection for abd. hyster.	• Mortality • Readmissions • VBAC rate • Falls with injury • Aspirin in 24 hours of MI diagnosis • Surgical site infection for abd. hyster.	• Mortality • Readmissions • VBAC rate • Timing of prophylactic antibiotic for hip pros. patients • Falls with injury • Total patient falls • Surgical site infection—CABG • Pressure sores • Aspirin in 24 hours of MI diagnosis	• Mortality • Readmissions • VBAC rate • Timing of prophylactic antibiotic for hip pros. patients • Falls with injury • Total patient falls, • Surgical site infection—CABG • Pressure sores • Aspirin in 24 hours of MI diagnosis

Quality improvement focus areas[8]	• Asthma pathway; C-section pathway • Hysterectomy pathway; migraine HA pathway • CABG pathway; pneumonia pathway • Total knee replacement pathway	• DRG 89—simple pneumonia • DRG 98—bronchitis and asthma • DRG 107—coronary bypass with cardiac catheterization; DRG 109—coronary bypass without cardiac catheterization; DRG 370—C-section with CC • DRG 371—C-section without CC; DRG 209—total joint replacement; DRG 507—full thickness burn with skin graph or inhalation without CC or significant trauma	• DRG 14—stroke • DRG 89—simple pneumonia and pleurisy, age greater than 17 with CC • DRG 107—coronary bypass with cardiac catheterization • DRG 109—coronary bypass without cardiac catheterization • DRG 127—heart failure and shock • DRG—143 chest pain • DRG 209—total joint replacement	• DRG 14—stroke • DRG 89—simple pneumonia and pleurisy, age greater than 17 with CC • DRG 107—coronary bypass with cardiac catheterization • DRG 109—coronary bypass without cardiac catheterization • DRG 127—heart failure and shock • DRG 143—chest pain; DRG 209—total joint replacement

continued

Table 6.1 *continued*

Notes: Measures were entered as they became available.

1. Inpatient survey results. These values were estimated from a regression equation using all original values and dummy variables for each quarter except from July to September 2002. The equation has excellent fit and significance. The parameters for the quarters prior to the current vendor are similar and highly significant. The adjustment model incorporates any time trend so that none can appear in the data above. However, inspection of the adjustment coefficients and original data suggest that there was no trend, either up or down, in these measures.

2. ER survey results; see note 1.

3. Cost per case adjusted for severity using CMS's DRG index.

4. Community benefit is defined by Catholic Health Association and includes charity care, Medicare and Medicaid losses, education and research costs, and services or funds donated to community activities.

5. Inpatient survey results; see note 1.

6. Percentage of inpatients surveyed rating quality as excellent.

7. Measures reported to the MBO board. In 2003, CHI will standardize many of these measures for comparative reporting.

8. Areas selected for intensive study by the MBO.

1. Start with individual talent
2. Work on team dynamics and conflicts
3. Prioritize the strategic initiative
4. Adopt a results culture

Consistency is the key to these four steps. Implementing them steadily and uniformly allows St. Elizabeth to move forward without gimmicks or fancy technology. Although St. Elizabeth invents tools as it goes along, the "tried and true" is what makes St. Elizabeth work, not the "latest and greatest."

STARTING WITH INDIVIDUAL TALENT

St. Elizabeth places great stress on finding the right people and keeping them. It has a low avoidable turnover rate of 14.8 percent per year in a workforce of 2,000 employees (with 1,450 full-time equivalents). Its senior management team measures its longevity in decades. Despite that, its workforce is relatively young; the new recruits who arrive stay with the organization. A rich employment-benefit package—more than 30 percent of wages—helps keep them.

St. Elizabeth makes a deliberate effort to evaluate new hires carefully. Being in a university city that is one of the fastest growing in Nebraska, it has the luxury of an excess of applicants (4,690 applicants for 530 positions in 2002). It uses both screening and interviewing to identify candidates who are likely to succeed in its environment, and it has had remarkable success.

John G. Dumonceaux, Ph.D., vice president for mission and human resources; Greg Gillespie, coordinator of human resources; and Kim S. Moore, vice president of nursing, describe the activities St. Elizabeth undertakes to recruit people.

Dumonceaux:

> We work on recruitment relationships. We put people on the road to nursing schools, for example.

Gillespie:

> We ask our recruits what brought our job to their attention. The recurring themes are our faith-based mission and how they were treated here as a patient. Our own people are the key to the recruitment—how they treat people, what the image is. You can't put a

price on that. We've offered a bonus to staff who bring in recruits in pharmacy, and it has made a huge difference. We are looking at taking it housewide.

Moore:

> We are the preferred hospital for new graduates, but by 2010 we will need some fundamental changes in how we deliver healthcare. We have strategies for long term. We are looking at partnerships between colleges and St. Elizabeth so we can actually increase enrollment.

Recruiting is only a part of the program. Retention may actually be more important.

Dumonceaux:

> We have a performance improvement team (PIT) on recruitment and retention. We started pretty much at the national average, and now we are much better than that.

Gillespie:

> Three years ago we focused on turnover; turnover has declined continually since. This year we've reduced our turnover by 20 percent. Nursing turnover is only 10 percent. We're hiring new people, and keeping the people we have. Our average age in nursing is decreasing because we are keeping young new hires. We have a preceptor/mentor program for our new nurses.

Part of retention is training. According to Dumonceaux:

> We understand the value of training much more now than we did. CHI has contributed to that. They've helped us learn that an investment in training and retention is better than investment in recruitment. We offered 26,000 hours this year and reached 2000 associates. We provided 2400 hours for management.

The other part is supervision. Here's how St. Elizabeth selects and prepares its directors or first line supervisors.

Gillespie:

Part of our success is in selecting people for promotion. We use specific criteria, a group interview process, and a personality assessment instrument. We want to promote from within, but we never want to set someone up to fail.

Dumonceaux:

Any director-level position or higher must include a search for outside candidates. Insiders are encouraged to apply. We will hold a position open for a long time to find the right person. We have superiors, peers from other areas, and even subordinates interview candidates. We seek people who can break down barriers, build relationships.

All new associates get a two-day orientation. Managers get an additional orientation using a program developed by CHI. The program is two hours a week for nine weeks on the basics of supervision taught by members of human resources and educational services, and it covers goal setting, time management, effective authority, delegation, motivation of staff, decision-making processes, handling difficult people and situations, and staff development. The classes are case studies and real-life situations that individuals are experiencing along with weekly exercises and readings. New managers also get a mentor from another department.

Moore:

I think I've had the opportunity to hire more directors than anybody else. A year or two ago, I recognized that I had a lot of directors who were great at nursing, but not so great at some of the management skills. I couldn't risk people leaving in two years because we didn't have the right management performance. We have an orientation program for new directors that John was really helpful in designing. We've identified three-, six-, and 12-month behavior goals the new directors are accountable for. We give them a preceptor and a mentor.

I completely restructured my monthly meeting with the nursing directors. We spend half an hour on leadership. I needed my directors to understand their role in keeping talented people. Turnover is in our accountability standards for directors. They must reduce turnover by 10 percent from the prior year.

Nurse directors get some additional outcomes standards at various stages in their careers. They work with a preceptor/mentor for years. That person helps them with how to get things done. We've found that nurses develop a special friendship with their mentors.

Finally, part of retention is ongoing monitoring of satisfaction. At St. Elizabeth, worker satisfaction is surveyed regularly by an outside firm and is included in individual goals for all managers. In the most recent survey, St. Elizabeth scored in the 74th percentile among all clients. In counts of workers giving St. Elizabeth the top rating, it exceeded the 75th percentile on 8 of 12 questions and exceeded the 50th percentile on the remaining 4.

BUILDING TEAMS

The senior management at St. Elizabeth encourages team formation, beginning with the individual work groups. It designates councils to manage activities like cross-functional performance improvement and service excellence activities, and it encourages the councils to set up ad hoc teams as indicated. Senior management even uses teams to manage operations. The operations council, a subset of the senior management team, meets weekly to monitor all activities.

The teams support the culture of the organization. At St. Elizabeth, it is expected that you will put the patient first and be honest at all times, that you will stay and be a permanent member, and that you will help your colleagues and that your colleagues will help you. Lanik says:

> We start with an environment and a culture that's supportive. It allows people to make changes and do things. We work hard to break down barriers. When we have an issue—either a problem or an opportunity—we get people together at the table, work through our processes, and come up with a solution. We train our director and management-level people to do this.

Creating the Culture

St. Elizabeth uses its faith-based tradition to support these elements of the culture, but it also uses a number of nonreligious devices that continually reinforce the culture and values of the organization.

- Posters, newsletters, and other visual devices prominently display the organization's values (Reverence, Integrity, Compassion, Excellence).
- Recruitment information describes the work environment to attract like-minded applicants.
- Formal orientation and training programs carefully explain the culture and values.
- A day-and-a-half offsite orientation provided by CHI for all new appointments to director rank or higher.
- A special, mandatory training initiative in 2002, "Embrace the Spirit," reviewed elements of customer service and collaboration with coworkers.
- Mentoring provides one-on-one guidance to new workers and new managers.
- Worker satisfaction surveys measure loyalty to the organization and indicators of retention.
- Both recognition and tangible rewards reinforce the value program.
- Incentive payment and personal development programs reward longevity.
- Efforts are made to reduce use of temporary or agency workers.

Promoting Service Excellence

St. Elizabeth decided in 2001 that the traditional methods of promoting the culture were not enough. It began an ambitious initiative of worker training it calls "Embrace the Spirit" (see Figure 6.1). Moore and Libby Raetz, director of the emergency department, explain the program.

Raetz:

Bob Lanik suggested we could do a better job relative to customer service. The conversation at our management team meeting was about why we shouldn't do it, but then we concluded we couldn't afford not to do it. We developed the "guiding coalition," of formal and informal leaders—two senior management, four directors, and 17 hand-picked staff. Donell Martinez, director of marketing, and I were cochairs. We used some outside consultants, but we built what we thought would work here, with our culture and our people.

Figure 6.1 Embrace the Spirit Model

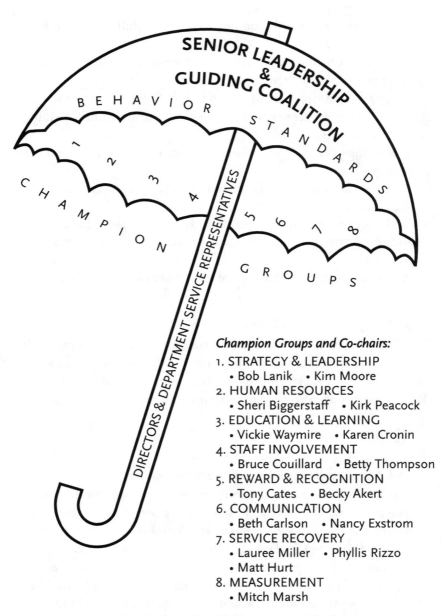

Saint Elizabeth Health Systems
EMBRACE THE SPIRIT MODEL

SENIOR LEADERSHIP
&
GUIDING COALITION

BEHAVIOR STANDARDS

CHAMPION GROUPS

DIRECTORS & DEPARTMENT SERVICE REPRESENTATIVES

Champion Groups and Co-chairs:

1. STRATEGY & LEADERSHIP
   • Bob Lanik   • Kim Moore
2. HUMAN RESOURCES
   • Sheri Biggerstaff   • Kirk Peacock
3. EDUCATION & LEARNING
   • Vickie Waymire   • Karen Cronin
4. STAFF INVOLVEMENT
   • Bruce Couillard   • Betty Thompson
5. REWARD & RECOGNITION
   • Tony Cates   • Becky Akert
6. COMMUNICATION
   • Beth Carlson   • Nancy Exstrom
7. SERVICE RECOVERY
   • Lauree Miller   • Phyllis Rizzo
   • Matt Hurt
8. MEASUREMENT
   • Mitch Marsh

Reprinted with permission from St. Elizabeth Health System, Lincoln, Nebraska.

The coalition defined what we wanted to do, what kind of behavior we wanted. One of the pivotal points was the strong need to somehow reflect our spirituality. We did an organizational assessment, talking to different staff and physicians, individuals, groups, and patients. The common thread that came out of our assessment was, "How do we keep the spirit of St. Elizabeth in our place of care or employment?" We decided on "Embrace the Spirit." Spirit can have more than one meaning. The coalition came up with the umbrella design, and senior management approved it. The coalition wrote out 12 behavior standards.

Last summer, all the staff were invited to an auditorium off campus. The guiding coalition did a skit on a patient's experience. The patient had a heart attack, and she relates her experience to a friend in a movie theater; the movie theater's audience was "overhearing" her comments. It was a lot of fun, but it showed how we needed to turn things around and what we needed to pay attention to. It was really well received. We served popcorn, candy bars. Over 1,000 people came. The skit served as our associate's recommitment to service. In January, and every month after that, we work on a service standard. We do games, a lot of story telling. We build it into staff meetings. Over a three month period, every employee attended training on the standards, "Fire in the Hole"— how to support someone who is being fired on by a customer; service recovery, "The Four A's"—anticipate, acknowledge, apologize, and amend. We use "Onstage/Offstage"—how to keep conversations appropriate. People now will say "onstage," and everyone will know that our customers can overhear the conversation.

The senior leaders and the guiding coalition collaborated to develop the plan for champion groups. [The champion groups are listed in Figure 6.1.] The champion groups are cochaired by two members of the coalition. Each group formulates activities for all the standards, for each month. The department service representatives (DSRs) are the group that carries the message to our workers. They meet every month. They have a choice of one of two sessions for convenience sake. It's a group of about 70 people representing every department. We prepare them for the coming month. We also get the word out on the street, any barriers to implementation. We always do story-telling. That's been the funnest part. The DSR representatives are the conduit to the guiding coalition and the senior leadership. They had to apply for the position. They went through a department interview process. They could not be on any work improvement plan, which is our disciplinary action process; they had to show that they exemplified good customer service skills; and they get training and special name badges and recognition. They are spokespeople at staff meetings. They hear back from the staff—what's working well, what are opportunities for improvement, what stories, what barriers. They become the eyes and ears of the organization.

Moore:

The representatives tailor the message to their unit. They are the key. They make it fit their unit. When we started we were ranked 24th in CHI for overall patient-perceived quality. Now we are 8th. We also built customer satisfaction into our merit raise incentive for associates. I think it helps reduce turnover. It's helping create the kind of work environment that people want to stay in.

Raetz:

We had a mandatory six-hour training program for all associates. If they did not go, they were not eligible for a merit increase. We trained 18 associates to teach the six hour programs. A member of senior management introduces the session, telling every associate that "Embrace the Spirit" is expected behavior and a condition of employment. The HR champion group changed our application procedure. Every applicant sees the 12 standards and signs an agreement to live with them.

We are including our physician providers. We recognize their key role to our success. The doctors have noticed that we are doing something that makes a difference. A couple practices have requested that we involve their office staffs.

Raetz and Moore discuss the service recovery part of the initiative.

Raetz:

"Make It Right" is our standard for this month. It's about service recovery. We created a "care kit" for each unit, including coupons for free coffee, gifts, meals, and a specific policy. We are document-ing with a log. If a coupon is used, the date, time, incident, and what was done will be recorded. We have another form for bigger issues, like writing off a portion of the bill. That goes through our performance improvement council for departmental action plan development.

Moore:

It's a record we can pass along, too. I don't have to listen to a ver-bal report that might get confused. I can refer to the log. In many situations, giving somebody a gift certificate is not the right an-swer; it might even make them mad. What they really want is just somebody to listen to them and solve their problem.

In the training program, we talk about "Complaints as a Gift." We try to tell everybody in the organization that a complaint is an opportunity to make things better. If we just give out coupons and don't do anything to anticipate the next problem, we'd drown in coupons and nothing would ever improve. Our focus is to take a step back when we get a complaint and say, "Why did this happen? What can we do to prevent it from happening again?" If you are just handing out coupons, buying dentures and glasses, you aren't getting at the root cause. "Complaint as a Gift" tries to make it clear that nobody will be punished or criticized for turning in a report. We tried to make it fun, with cartoons and things. It's in-cluded in the six-hour orientation, and it's reemphasized in the service recovery month.

Raetz:

In the emergency department, I'm not sure we've handed out a coupon yet, but people are empowered to solve the problem. I had a nurse this weekend give me a whole written document. Eighty year old female, such and such complaint. She did her four A's. She put down what she did under each "A." She called me today and said, "Have you called this lady? I think we should consider writing off part of her bill; will you support that?" This nurse had never done anything like this before. I thought, "This is the whole thing we are trying to accomplish, right here." Getting people to feel that they are empowered, they can go ahead, and make things happen and make it right.

Making Teams Productive

Taken in total, St. Elizabeth has the cultural elements of a "service excellence" program, deliberately building customer satisfaction through worker morale (see Chapter 7). These programs are more complex than they appear on the surface. In addition to the several elements of selection, satisfaction, training, and reinforcement, two common causes of dissatisfaction—inept supervision and inadequate support—must be addressed. St. Elizabeth's culture and values will not hold up if supervisors cannot answer questions effectively, and the most serious questions are often "Why are we short-handed again?" and "Why don't I have the resources I need to do the job right?" St. Elizabeth and other institutions that are successful at service excellence use a foundation of measured performance, goal setting, and continuous improvement to prevent these questions from arising.

Operations at St. Elizabeth are managed by the operations council. The members of the council are Moore; Jeanette Wojtalewicz, vice president of finance and CFO; Dumonceaux; and Pat Gilles, vice president for clinical and support services. They discuss the Council. Lanik and Charlotte Liggett, vice president for strategic planning and business development, who do not regularly attend, chime in.

Moore:

> The operations council meets every Thursday to resolve all issues; the senior vice presidents, except the VP of planning and the CEO, are included. It's helped break down the silos. There is also a strategic council that includes some directors, the planning vice president, CFO and CEO, and an executive council that includes both, plus some additional directors.
>
> Four or five years ago, we were having a bad year. Bob held a meeting with the management team. He helped us to focus on our "three Cs"—cost, customers, and capacity. For the last four years, we've tried to focus everything we do around the three Cs. Our role is to support our people. We create an environment that includes meeting expectations, helping people to learn, being ac-

countable. We've done a lot better job with that in the last couple years, creating an environment where people want to work.

Wojtalewicz:

Other organizations operate in silos. We are very different here. We are very integrated. When we have a problem, we pick all the people who need to be there to analyze and solve the problem. We are not trying to build our own empires, and we support each other. We recently had a project that was not going well. You would not believe the binding together that there was to get back on track.

Dumonceaux:

It starts with leadership and culture, then teamwork and process, then the expectations and confidence of the people you work for. Your problem is our problem, and we are going to do something about it. The council members are aware that they act on multiple levels, helping people solve problems while constantly reinforcing the culture.

Lanik:

You can't build culture quickly. You have to live it, to reinforce it. We've been able to do that because we've been here a long time. We worked hard on norms of behavior. We all attended a CHI course on teamwork. We celebrate as a team.

Gilles:

The culture is open, trusting, and empowered. The thing we have tried to change is adding accountability to our culture. The CHI regional conferences in the clinical and logistics support areas brought the right people together to solve some issues. The surveys of patient and worker satisfaction have been a help. The outside benchmarking has helped. People have the sense that they can do an awful lot of things, and they can.

Dumonceaux:

> Anybody who thinks "me first" won't last here.

Liggett:

> There was a time when two vice presidents had built some silos. It was the people at the director level that brought this to our attention. That was the beginning of really trying to break down the barriers across division lines and department lines. It started with CQI in 1993 or 1994.

Moore:

> Our values and our integrity help our directors be fair and open with physicians. It's the way we work.

Setting Improvement Goals

The operations council uses two major devices to keep the culture focused on service and improvement. First, they have rigorous accountability standards, as many measures as they can, and a procedure to set annual goals on important measures. That process creates balanced scorecard goals not only for every work group but also for every new program or capital investment. Second, they use performance improvement teams extensively to develop ways the measures can be improved.

Every director has written accountability standards that cover mission effectiveness (with emphasis on community service), cost management, quality of service, human resources management, medical staff relations (if applicable), strategic plan implementation, and situational leadership ("responds to changing circumstances . . . cooperates harmoniously . . . completes staff assignments . . . ."). All of these standards have weights used in the incentive pay calculations. Sixty percent is assigned to cost and quality, and many other elements can have negotiated weights. The standards, including the subjective ones, are judged on a scale of zero to four, where two is expected and four represents exceptional behavior. Goals are negotiated annually. (See Appendix A for a specimen accountability standard.)

The accountability standards are the foundation for negotiating the annual budget and other annual goals. Steve Bray, director of finance;

Wojtalewicz; Jean Dowling, director of financial services; Barbara George, director of critical care; and Moore describe St. Elizabeth's considerable effort to make the budget process participative.

Bray:

> The senior management team tries to identify and project the global activity. Finance tries to project that to each work group and proposes targets for labor, productivity, and supplies costs. We developed a spreadsheet that allows the manager to try many different solutions. It is linked to demand forecasts and labor ratios. The manager and the director can work together on this solution, and the "roll up" to higher levels is automated through linked spreadsheets.

Wojtalewicz:

> We recognize that some people are really frightened of these spreadsheets. We make them user friendly. We have one-on-one training in our computer training lab.

George:

> Each director has a management council which is made up of associates from the floor that help develop it, look at it, and track it.

Moore:

> The budget process is a lot easier for the nursing directors because it's more integrated. All the different spreadsheets talk to each other. The directors have the opportunity to play around with FTEs, skill mix, and cost per unit and very quickly see what the outcome is. Before, we had to do a lot of that work ourselves. We disciplined ourselves to identify how we will measure success as we start new projects. With our quality improvement plan, we've gone to 70 or 80 percent of the quality elements measured compared to about 20 when we started. The directors have the strategic plan in hand and the core strategies. Targets for growth, people, and quality and performance come from that.

Dowling:

> A lot of the quality issues are developed in the operations council
> and the CQI teams. They are not something new the day the bud-
> get comes up. They are already in place; you've started on them;
> you are working on them. They just roll into the budget and the
> accountability standards. The extra costs associated with that are
> built in too. If a quality improvement will cost us $50,000, that
> cost is built into the budget assumptions. Each service has a busi-
> ness plan that contains longer range targets.

Guiding Performance Improvement Teams

New goals require new processes to make them realistic. St. Elizabeth
relies on PITs to analyze and improve processes. PITs also change the organizational culture, promoting an atmosphere of mutual support. Improvement teams were rarities a decade ago, even within a single activity.
At St. Elizabeth, they are commonplace. Most operating units have one
or more teams analyzing processes that are important to their targets.
The managers have learned that most improvements to real hospital
services require collaboration with other services and caregivers. Cross-
functional teams attack problems of integration and coordination. The
performance improvement council manages the cross-functional teams.
Lori Burkett, director of performance improvement/outcomes management, and Moore describe how the performance council operates.

Burkett:

> Our performance improvement council is made up of 19 members:
> nine are physicians, two are from the senior management team,
> five are directors, and three are staff. The council has oversight
> of all clinical outcomes. We set goals, and review organization-
> wide quality outcomes. The council focuses on interdisciplinary
> groups. The departments are responsible for handling their unit-
> based outcomes.

Moore:

> When we did our CQI initiative, we looked at teams and groups
> and how we can drive the CQI process through the organization.

We wanted to avoid having a lot of teams doing different things without a central focus. In 1996–97 we were spreading ourselves too thin. People were spinning their wheels. We changed the whole performance-improvement initiative; we made it more interdisciplinary. The teams could work on service performance, not just departmental performance.

We put a step in place that encourages departments to work on any initiative within their department. They can go ahead with anything within their own team. They share their plan with us, but it does not require council approval. We approve and prioritize all the teams that are interdepartmental, that involve a lot of different disciplines. We built a grid of "Outcomes, Tactics, Responsibility, Resources, and Timeline" that helped us focus on the most important projects. The departments complete a request by filling out the grid. The council makes sure the team has all the bases covered. The council reviewed one last week where we added a physician to the team.

Burkett:

We also look at all our outcomes, compared to benchmarks and goals. If the council finds a concern, they can request a team.

Moore:

The council chooses the most noteworthy measures for quarterly reporting. [The quarterly report is shown in Figure 6.2.] We monitor the measures throughout the year, and any measure that identifies a need for improvement, then the council starts a team. The council also looks at any other measures that are not as expected. For example, last month we looked at ventilator-related pneumonias, from the infection control committee, even though it is not on the quarterly report. So some things come from the council, some things come from the departments, and some from groups of departments; the fourth place is administration. The senior management team has directly started several initiatives.

FOCUSING THE STRATEGY

Given two foundations in measured performance and team-oriented culture, how could St. Elizabeth go wrong? Where are the weak links

Figure 6.2 St. Elizabeth's Spider Diagram: Dashboard Compared to Target/Benchmark

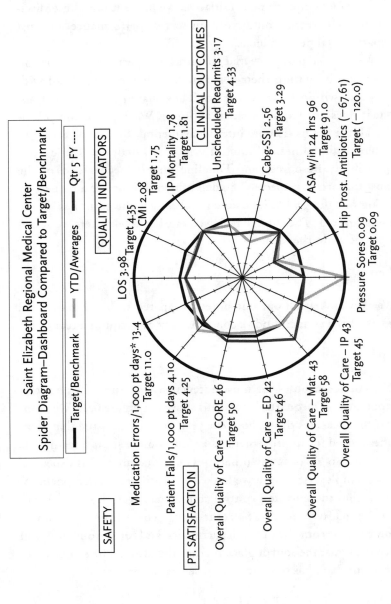

Reprinted with permission from St. Elizabeth Health System, Lincoln, Nebraska. Modified to protect peer-review confidentiality.

that might cause it to fail? The answer is in strategy—the management of matters that transcend all the components of the organization. If St. Elizabeth's strategy is not carefully managed, its associates will lose enthusiasm, its physicians will migrate to its competition, and its patients will follow. The third foundation of St. Elizabeth's effort is a program of strategic decision making that continues to direct its improvement efforts and its capital toward the best long-term opportunities. Lanik explains why focus and priorities are important:

> In 1999, we had a lot of strategic initiatives—a hospitalist program, maternal fetal medicine, Level 3 neonatal capability, rebuilding the physician network, a lot of healthy community initiatives, critical pathways, and Y2K. That's what we accomplished. There was other stuff we didn't do—a Medicare risk product, a rural care strategy, an independent physician organization, and an expanded managed care program. We had even more in the plan.
>
> We agreed that the strategies had to be prioritized. Leigh Hantho, CHI's vice president of strategy and business development, and I worked with our board. We worked on our decision process. We made sure that each project had a business plan, supported by data, strategic assessment, and political assessment. Before, the business plans had been just pro forma; now, we report progress quarterly to the board. When we submit our capital budget, it will include a one-page outline tracking achievement against the original plan for every approved initiative.

St. Elizabeth builds its strategy around CHI's balanced scorecard—people, quality, operating and financial excellence, and growth. Its strategic plan specifies four or five goals under each of these topics but does not describe specific initiatives. Instead, a set of initiatives are selected, developed, prioritized, and presented to the board and CHI for approval. These vary widely, from the "Embrace the Spirit" campaign to service line development and ventures with specialist and primary physicians to an extensive facility replacement and expansion. Lanik says:

> We really worked hard to have and execute a strong strategic plan. It included the physician network, cardiovascular care, hospital-

ists, and our orthopedics care. We worked on strong medical staff relationships.

Assessing the Environment

The critical part of St. Elizabeth's strategy is in the selection of the initiatives. The initiatives are generated and prioritized through a formal environmental assessment and a less-formal listening process. Initiatives come from any operating unit, and many of them appear in the capital budget process. The strategic council prioritizes the initiatives, but it is also responsible for making sure no important opportunity is left unexamined. Liggett and Curt Koesterer, director of strategic planning, are accountable for the planning process.

Liggett:

> We have a very sophisticated external assessment. Our supplier [a commercial company providing healthcare planning data] gives us quantitative demand and demographic information.

Koesterer:

> CHI has a national assessment. We add a state/county-level review.

Liggett:

> Then we do an internal assessment and a SWOT analysis. We take that to senior management for review.

Koesterer:

> We do SWOT analyses for each service line so that the clinicians who are taking care of the patients and know more about the clinical issues can give us input. We use a number of outside sources to identify trends.

Liggett:

> CHI has been helpful identifying trends from other markets. We listen to other markets and watch other trials. I just went to the

first meeting of the CHI planning vice presidents. Those meetings will be helpful.

Lincoln is a prime target for some for-profit competition. Do we sit back and wait for it to happen or are there some areas in the city that could be underserved—growing population, young families? We'll do a study of this in the next 60 days, including Lincoln and the surrounding counties, It will require capital from CHI. I don't want to send in something frivolous, but I don't want to get caught asleep at the switch.

Our focus has been about creating relationships. About 1991 we bought a computer system that tracks our customer database. That allows us to communicate with our consumers, with surveys or information, and also gives us statistical information; we added the physicians a little later on. Next we developed a marketing system with two components. One is nurse triage; the other is a system to measure consumer response to our advertising. All of these efforts are meant to raise awareness of St. Elizabeth in the marketplace and to build long-term relationships. It costs more to gain a new customer, so it pays to develop loyalty. We do community attitude surveys every two years. We feel that information helps us understand our market and design our messages. It tells us what the consumer attributes to St. Elizabeth. We use that information a lot. It also gives us market share.

I see marketing as a three-legged stool. One piece is consumer and competitor intelligence. The second is advertising. The third is building customer (physician and patient) relationships. We have done a little "image" advertising, but a lot more selective, targeted advertising. The targets are the service lines in our strategic plan. We won two Tully Awards for our ads on perinatal and cardiology services. We are selective in the campaigns, because they become expensive. The nurse triage component is a very good connection for physicians. Physicians are a big piece of marketing. It does a nice job for family practice physicians and pediatricians. They contract with us for their patients who can call in to the triage nurse. It helps them handle patient relations. The physician doesn't get called if the nurse determines the patient can do self-care according to protocols. We also place telephone orders for prescriptions for the physician.

CHI has given us a huge advantage with our website. Their communications group selected a web site development company that is effective and inexpensive. We are just moving to make it more interactive. We want to offer online registration and add health risk surveys. Generation X is interested in doing those things on the web.

Internal Listening

The formal assessment is only part of the issue. St. Elizabeth also does a lot of informal listening. It supplements the formal goals and accountabilities and generates ideas that lead to opportunities. Bray; Mike Hopkins, director of radiology services; Jan Wadell, director of hotel services; Jeff Weissert, director of physical and occupational therapy, Dumonceaux; Liggett; and Lanik list the methods of internal listening used at St. Elizabeth.

Bray:

Finance uses open-ended surveys of its internal customers.

Wadell:

The cafeteria uses surveys too. But frankly, this organization is open enough that if I had a problem with an area, I could go to the person involved and work things out before it became an issue.

Liggett:

We survey the directors about whether they are comfortable approaching other units. We survey our physicians to track their satisfaction.

Dumonceaux:

CHI is working on standardized human resources surveys, and we already have an employee attitude survey.

Hopkins:

We know we are doing excellent work because we ask our physicians, patients, and coworkers. We ask about quality, timeliness, and their perceptions.

Weissert:

> We survey our rehab employees, and we encourage them to stay. Our PTs have an average of ten-year longevity. We measure length of stay and recovery and use national data for benchmarking. It's harder on the outpatient side; we hope to get better numbers.

Bray:

> CHAN has focus areas that are established nationally. The reviews help identify process changes and improvements. They also follow-up after a period of time to see what improvement has been made.

The focus on listening is deliberately extended to the medical staff, as Liggett explains:

> Our strategic plan for a long time has been developing relationships with physicians. We've done it through our clinical centers, on an informal basis—how we work with them; we keep working at that. You have to be careful; physicians cannot believe you are taking them over. You have to figure out how to be good partners and help them to work things out.
>
> We hold physician forums on an annual basis. The forums are set up to allow all active physicians to come and talk with Bob about various issues or concerns. Last year we had just gotten back the results of our physician attitude survey so we fed back the results and asked physicians for their input on issues. This was a way to combine qualitative and quantitative information related to physician satisfaction. The forums seem to be well attended when there is a major issue affecting the medical staff.

Dr. Cary Ward, chief medical officer and director of inpatient medicine services, notes:

> The doctors in our Physician Network participate actively in quality issues and monitor patient satisfaction. We meet quarterly to discuss issues that affect our practices and to participate in continuing medical education. We are developing a dress code; it came

out of the hospital policy. The hospital's "Embrace the Spirit" program promotes professional behavior and dress. The doctors are required to participate in the campaign.

When I started here, I went to a four-hour session. I thought it would be a waste of time, but we learned St. Elizabeth's four core values and that's the attitude you are going to have at this hospital. We will set ourselves apart and live by those core values. The administration truly believes in those values, and you can tell that throughout the entire hospital. I've had experience at several other hospitals, particularly the other system in town. There truly is a different sort of ethic and value here. Patients are treated in a different way, and doctors are treated in a different way. That's one of the reasons I chose to work at this hospital.

Most of the relationships between the specialists and primary care doctors are out of the hospital's hand. Because of the competition, the doctors have to provide good service, and they do. There's a very good relationship; I don't see problems with this relationship. St. Elizabeth's Physician Network allows them more say in what physicians will do. The ER doctors, some obstetricians, internists, occupational medicine, are all employed. That group has a stronger desire to work with the hospital and have a common goal: much more teamwork.

The Capital and New Programs Budget

Part of a successful investment strategy is sound management of capital expenditures. Projects at St. Elizabeth now are better thought out and more carefully prepared, reducing the risk of unexpected costs or late completion. The capital budget is managed to the quarter, rather than the year, to protect the cash position. Lanik, Wojtalewicz, and Moore explain how capital is managed at St. Elizabeth.

Lanik:

> We are much more disciplined about capital. It is rare for a physician to approach me directly. I refer them back to their directors. We're respectful; we listen; we hear their issues and their needs. Physicians tell me they expect a different behavior from St. Elizabeth, and they get it.

Wojtalewicz:

> We receive our capital spending caps from CHI. Vice presidents review specific requests quarterly, and we allocate capital spending based on presentations from the directors. The needs are prioritized within the units. In the OR, for example, the team coordinators work with specific surgeons to identify needs. The surgeons have input, but the team coordinators decide the final priorities. In cardiology, though, the physicians are submitting a prioritized list of needs.

Moore:

> Over the last four years, the surgeons have developed a better appreciation of the capital constraints. We kept communicating back to them that we had limited resources, involving them, asking if a piece of equipment could work for another year, another quarter. Lots of dialog. They appreciate that we've been honest with them.

GETTING RESULTS

Good people, good culture, and good strategy are the foundation, but they do not automatically make real improvements and make them last. St. Elizabeth managers have measures and rewards to encourage them. They can document some impressive improvements.

Progress Reports

The system of setting goals on measured performance is a powerful incentive in itself. As of 2002, a St. Elizabeth manager received the following measures for his or her unit:

- An accounting report, similar to those generated by most commercial accounting systems, that shows full detail of costs and revenues and counts of service and case-mix adjustment and that is available within ten days after the end of the month. St. Elizabeth constructs the report to show each item for the accounting period and year to date and compared to budget. Productivity measures, such as cost per adjusted discharge, are calculated. The manager can specify measures of particular interest to be displayed at the start of the report.

- A spider chart in color, showing safety, clinical outcomes, and patient satisfaction measures versus target is available quarterly two months after the quarter closes.
- Employee satisfaction surveys are conducted every two years, available through the CHI surveyor.
- Market share and demand information is given at an annual budget briefing to assist in devising new targets.
- Access to specific information is available as needed, through support services in planning, marketing, and finance.

A two-page monthly report for associates is widely distributed. It contains the major balanced scorecard dimensions, with emphasis on financial budget achievement. It allows associates to track their incentive compensation possibilities.

Incentives
St. Elizabeth's culture is reinforced by an extensive program of recognition and tangible rewards and help for managers who do not achieve them. St. Elizabeth has a unique incentive plan that ties annual wage and salary adjustments to goal achievement. The intent of the pay program is that each person in the organization will be recognized for personal achievement as well as organizational achievement. Each year, a base-pay adjustment is budgeted. In 2002, the full adjustment amounted to 3 percent. Associates who meet individual goals earn half of this amount. If corporate goals for operating margin and patient satisfaction are also met, the associate earns the other half. Additionally, a lump sum bonus, usually 1 to 3 percent of base pay, is awarded if the associate qualifies for his or her individual increase and the organization exceeds its goals.

Managers and vice presidents can earn base salary increases between 0 and 7 percent based on how well they perform against their accountability standards. Managers also participate in the same lump sum bonus as do associates. Vice presidents are under the same incentive plan as the CEO and can earn a bonus of up to 20 percent.

Dumonceaux explains how the pay-at-risk concept keeps people focused on achieving goals:

> The first year of the program, everyone got their increase. But in 1999, the organization failed to meet its goals and associates

learned that the pay adjustment and bonus were not an entitlement, they had to be earned. Every year since then, we have succeeded. This year, the associates will get a 3 percent lump sum bonus. For a full-time kitchen worker, that's $480. That's an incentive to stay with us and to be part of a team effort that can help us meet our goals.

In September, our directors go on a two-day, offsite retreat to lay out the next year's goals. They come back and share those goals with the associates. On a monthly basis, we also share our financials and patient satisfaction scores. In this way, everyone knows throughout the year how we are doing and whether or not a bonus is in reach. It all fits together. Not everybody likes a system that puts part of their pay at risk based on goal achievement, but we are building a workforce that understands that their efforts affect how the organization does, and how the organization does affects how much they get paid. It is very powerful.

Position Control

In addition to goals and incentives, St. Elizabeth uses position control to promote careful expansion of the workforce and to keep all the vice presidents familiar with the full organization. Any new position, even part time and temporary and even if approved in the budget, is presented to the operations council by the director or manager involved. Units on a "productivity watch list" must present all new hires, including replacements, but most units can fill existing positions without review. A written proposal is circulated in advance. The review covers need for the position, skills sought, goals to be attained, implications for other units, and opportunities for collaboration.

Although this review can easily deteriorate to micromanagement, the council uses it to build understanding of what's going on in the various units and to impose rigor on the workforce management. Any manager who wishes to add a position must explain what the position will contribute to the annual targets and the overall strategic plan, how the person will fit into the organization, and why a new position is necessary. That explanation becomes a record to evaluate future achievement. Wojtalewicz and Gilles explain why they use position control.

Wojtalewicz:

> It's so easy to just throw people at a problem. The position control review helps our directors make sure they don't overreact.

Gilles:

> Labor is an important cost, but our position control meetings also open the door to get into operating issues. We've been able to look at premium pay and the use of temporary people and get a common understanding of how things are done in the organization. It's a way to keep informed and understand what's going on in a department.

Examples of St. Elizabeth Success

St. Elizabeth can document a number of specific campaigns that lie behind its overall success: the redesign of its employed physician network, the development of its hospitalist program, and its growing sophistication in outsourcing.

The Physician Network

Jim Weems, executive director of the St. Elizabeth Physician Network, discusses the past failures of the physician network:

> We made a lot of the same mistakes everybody else did. We paid too much for the physician practices, we had physician contracts that did not tie provider income effectively to productivity, and we tried to manage the network and the practices like hospital departments.

Lanik expands on this point:

> We had a major, high-profile national firm to help us establish that compensation model. We knew we needed expertise and, to be honest with you, we didn't get what we needed. We hired somebody to run the clinics who was good at strategy but not at operating. The information systems were not adequate. We were flying blind; we couldn't even find where our costs were. We weren't efficient in collections. We bought two clinics that were closed panel

HMOs. The production in those clinics was low. We bought them in July and spun them off by January. It took a quarter to realize our mistake and another quarter to divest of it. Those clinics generated 10 percent of our hospital admissions. It was a real challenge to divest them in a way that maintained hospital admissions. We succeeded because we had long-standing good relationships with the physicians. We had worked with them better than our competitor did. We'd worked them into some of the medical staff leadership positions. It was hard for them to adopt a private-practice model.

We got more selective about physicians. We made a whole strategic plan based on CHI's "Macbeth process," with production standards. We showed our doctors a profile that works in terms of what they want to accomplish, what patients they want to see and can see. That was the artery that was bleeding, and we stopped that.

The "Macbeth" process revises contracts to put physicians at-risk for their earnings, much as they would be in private practice. (The name is derived from "Management Assistance Clinic Break Even Team"). Following the process has not been painless, but it has resulted in major improvements in St. Elizabeth's and CHI's margins. Weems explains:

St. Elizabeth started the physician network to create a critical mass of primary care physicians. It now has 60 to 65 employed physicians, and it loses about $35,000 per provider per year. We're hoping to reduce that to $20,000 to $25,000. The Network focuses on areas where private physicians have not adequately responded to community needs. St. Elizabeth approaches this as a community partnership, rather than directly competing with our private physicians. Relationships with physicians is one of the things that has made St. Elizabeth successful.

Many hospitals looked at the losses and reversed their strategies. St. Elizabeth took a different approach—more introspective and strategic. We decided it was still a valid strategy. We started to fix the problems. Macbeth devised cost-finding standards and identified best practices in specific cost elements. We studied our three urgent care centers and reduced them to two. We actually increased revenue but eliminated many costs. We decided to sell the HMO panels. We vacated some contracts and rewrote others. We

encouraged some physicians to either leave or restructure themselves into private practices. We redesigned physician contracts to
tie income to productivity; that took several iterations.

The best model is the private-practice model, where the incentive is to make the business successful. We are trying to move all
our physicians to a similar model, where we can take the best of
private practice and add our skills in billing and practice management services. We can free the physician to what they really want to
do, what they do best, which is patient care. We can relieve them
of the day-to-day practice management responsibilities. Some of
our physicians—the hospitalists and the emergency doctors, for
example—are on an hourly rate. The physicians in primary care
practices and some of the specialty practices are on volume-related
compensation. The current contracts do not have either quality of
care or patient satisfaction components built in. We are consider-
ing that. The Network has a quality committee that is developing
measures. We just completed our first patient satisfaction survey.

The Hospitalist Program

Dr. Ward has led the hospitalist program since its inception. It was devised to provide 24-hour service for any hospitalized patients. Some of
St. Elizabeth's goals were

1. to improve quality of care by having a group of physicians who
   could respond quickly to problems and play a leadership role with
   quality initiatives,
2. to provide service to admitted patients who do not have physicians,
3. to have physicians whose interests are aligned with the hospital's,
4. to provide greater efficiency of care,
5. to increase referrals to the hospital due to the convenience of using
   the hospitalist physicians, and
6. to increase nursing and staff satisfaction.

Dr. Ward describes the success:

> Six doctors are employed full time as hospitalists and provide 24-
> hour in-house care. The hospitalist admits the patients, offers con-
> sultation, or accepts the patient on referral. We are now rounding
> on approximately 45 patients a day. Our most common diagnoses

include COPD, chest pain, pneumonias, and strokes. About 15 percent are ED referrals without any primary physician. About 50 percent are from primary care doctors here in town. About 30 percent are consults from specialists—orthopedic surgeons, general surgeons, cardiologists, for example—whose patients have medical issues they'd like us to manage. A small number are referrals from rural physicians.

Physicians cover the service in one week blocks to ensure continuity of care. We have great communication to the referring physicians. Our summaries are transcribed and in the doctor's office either the day of discharge or the next day. The main advantage is the experience. A primary care doctor might see two or three hospitalized pneumonias a year; the hospitalists see 20 or 30. They know where to turn, how to answer the patients questions as well as the treatment protocol.

About 70 percent of family practitioners and general internists have referred to the hospitalists. We survey physician and patient satisfaction. We've never had a physician stop referring patients, and the survey data are very positive. When we started this program, there were a hundred different models out there. CHI had four or five hospitalist programs underway. We communicated with them, and visited several. Yearly, all the medical directors meet to discuss best practices and management issues.

Outsourcing and Competitive Bids

The outsourcing concept thinks of services as elements that can be "made" internally or "bought" from an outside supplier. The more completely a service can be measured, the easier it is to specify a purchase contract. An outside vendor can use advantages from scale and experience to replace an internal service. Conversely, an excellent service can consider becoming a "vendor" and transferring its expertise to other sites. A system like CHI often has multiple options—"make" at each MBO site, "make" at regional sites and sell to others, "make" at one site for the entire system, or "buy" from one or more independent corporations.

Modern technology makes new outsourcing models possible in many clinical and logistic services. "Just-in-time" deliveries eliminate local inventories. Filmless x-ray makes remote reading and interpretation feasible. Many human resources and marketing tasks can be performed remotely. The existence of these alternatives profoundly changes the marketplace and the operating standards.

CHI and St. Elizabeth have used the outsourcing opportunity sparingly. CHI provides a number of specific services to its MBOs, and CHAN is a service purchased from an independent company. CHI has not pursued centralizing services such as human resources, however. St. Elizabeth outsources housekeeping and food services to commercial vendors. It outsources hemodialysis, lithotripsy, and radiation therapy to various joint ventures. It formerly outsourced most laboratory services and wound care service but has brought them in house. Gilles; Liggett; Wadell; Liz Bechtle, director of health information management; and Koesterer discuss outsourcing decisions for logistic services.

Gilles:

> Our outsourcing for hotel services gives us a guaranteed budget that's competitive against national cost data. The contract has several measures of quality and response, with goals that must be met.

Wadell:

> One of the other outsource opportunities we have looked at several times is our laundry service.

Gilles:

> So far, laundry has turned out more cheaply to do in-house, but we are hitting a point where we will have to make major equipment replacements and we face a significant space issue. So we will revisit it again.

Bechtle:

> We evaluated outsourcing for transcriptions. We had a hard time finding a supplier who could meet quality standards.

Liggett:

> CHI has done a really good job of developing advertising graphic standards. They are trying to show us the gains from common work. It's very helpful.

Koesterer:

> We don't hire a lot of outside consultants, but we use them to check our own work. I do a medical staff plan every year. Every four or five years we hire an outside firm, as a cross-check. We do a lot of planning ourselves, and we hire somebody to look it over.

Gilles and Liggett go on to discuss outsourcing of clinical support services. The opportunities are more complex, and the "make or buy" decision is not simply cost comparison.

Gilles:

> Lincoln once had a centralized laboratory serving all three hospitals and the region. Costs got out of line, and Lincoln was subsidizing the rural areas. So we insourced our laboratory. Outsourcing laboratory services was a great concept, but it lost its way over the years.

Liggett:

> You need to watch the dynamics in each particular area. You have to know the outside vendor is truly functioning more efficiently and delivering high quality. We looked at radiology several years ago. We didn't do it. The outside vendor would supply the equipment. They would have either hired our staff or supplied their own. They would have anticipated our needs, and we would have paid them per case. It's not clear they could have gotten the capital as inexpensively as CHI. It's not clear we could have translated our culture to the outside group.
>
> We outsourced our wound care center. We created a relationship; we learned their processes; and then the people wanted to work for us. We negotiated out of the non-compete clause and took the center in-house. I'm not sure they would ever have been able to get where we are today.

Outsourcing to the parent company or across several MBOs may be the most complicated of all. CHI might at some point become a vendor, providing services to its MBOs or on the open market. Ad hoc service organizations may serve several clients in a region. CHI has been deliberately conservative in offering centralized services. In information systems, for example, it offers a choice of two packages, and as Woj-talewicz notes, MBOs can terminate some CHI suppliers:

> We outsourced collections. CHI had ownership in a company that did not meet our St. Elizabeth expectations. We renegotiated the contract to include specific performance criteria; that's something you have to do in any outsourcing agreement. The company was unable to meet the performance criteria so we terminated the contract. We negotiated a new contract with a local company. We've had no quality problems, and collections are better.

A cautious policy toward outsourcing has considerable justification, but CHI and St. Elizabeth cannot fully honor their commitment to the Lincoln community unless outsourcing alternatives are carefully compared to in-house suppliers and selected when they have a clear competitive advantage. With balanced, multidimensional measurement, it is relatively easy to specify the terms of an outsourcing contract and write a request for proposal. The proposals returned offer a new kind of benchmark. The in-house provider can then see the competitive standards and can adapt to them as necessary.

Shared services can also be developed with competitors. St. Elizabeth has tried this in the past with a centralized laboratory that did not work. In the future, it might open discussion with its competitor on healthy communities concepts. These would benefit the community as a whole and would do better with both hospitals supporting them.

KEY LESSONS

A healthcare organization that wants to emulate the St. Elizabeth success would need to take the following steps. They are not difficult, and many hospitals have begun the journey. Competitive pressure—both for patients and for skilled personnel—is likely to make the rest follow suit. The environment that results provides a foundation for quality and cost control, improves strategic thinking, and creates an attractive work environment.

1. *Verify or acquire budgeting and cost-accounting systems that can deliver timely, accurate cost reports.* The focus is on direct costs controlled by the service, and the goal is to have all managers comfortable with using cost reports to identify areas for improvement. St.

Elizabeth already had this in 1999. Standard accounting information packages are satisfactory. Most hospitals have them, but their accuracy depends on the input data. Many hospitals must make extensive revisions to definitions and data collection to produce reports that are credible to managers.

2. *Develop an expectation-setting process that makes first-line managers accountable; gives them information on corporate needs, history, available competitor positions, comparative standings, and benchmarks; and requires them to establish goals for performance improvement.* St. Elizabeth had much of this in place in 1999, and it expanded its effort with the accountability standards. "Accountability" is one key element of the St. Elizabeth culture. Every associate understands that service is the goal, and good service is his or her best job security. Managers must become comfortable with setting and achieving realistic expectations. Setting overly ambitious targets is dangerous. Every time a unit fails to meet its expectations, it triggers a retrospective search for causes. These searches are rarely as productive as a performance-improvement program that is seeking future opportunities.

   In a unit that is performing well, the goal-setting process will not be difficult. The unit will have human, financial, and informational resources to evaluate the opportunity and respond appropriately. The poorly performing unit that starts this process will need substantial support. The manager must be trained to study process, not people, as a source of improvement. The associates must learn that job security comes from service to the customer, rather than from management or a union.

3. *Install nationally administered patient and worker satisfaction surveys and add them to the expectation process.* Satisfaction measurement is no longer a "do-it-yourself" area. National survey firms have expertise in question design and sampling strategies, and they can generate comparative data and benchmarks. Even the largest systems have difficulty matching these advantages.

4. *Begin a process of measuring quality that permits each service to compare itself to national benchmarks.* St. Elizabeth and CHI are building these as they go, but they draw heavily on associations and

programs that address specific services. National organizations like the National Quality Forum are working on standardized measures.

5. *Improve selection and training processes, both for associates and for managers.* Selection and training allow St. Elizabeth to build a workforce that shares the service value. The shared value allows quicker, more efficient communication, and that in turn makes performance-improvement and service-recovery programs more effective.

6. *Start or revitalize a program of continuous performance improvement, encouraging teams within services and creating several teams that address major cross-functional systems such as diagnostic test ordering and reporting, charge reporting, safety, or patient scheduling.* As at St. Elizabeth, the teams should be charged to return with documentation on improved processes, performance measures, investment requirements, and expected returns. They should be encouraged to study best practices from elsewhere and to review outsourcing opportunities.

7. *Review the strategy-setting process, basing it more soundly on measured performance and extensive listening, tying it to the needs revealed by the performance teams, describing specific initiatives in terms of their impact on future performance, and prioritizing initiatives.* Strategy is a governance, not a management, activity, but the quality of the strategy depends heavily on three management contributions—a far-reaching search for alternatives, a careful evaluation of costs and contributions of each alternative, and careful implementation. St. Elizabeth has steadily improved its capability in all three of these areas.

8. *Begin a program of recognition and rewards for achieving or exceeding expectations.* Reporting, assistance, encouragement, recognition, and celebrations are critical foundations of a reward system. Managers at all levels must be confident that at least most of the time they will achieve their goals. These elements are more important than financial incentives. Growing numbers of hospitals also use financial incentives. St. Elizabeth's strategy of tying the rewards

to institutional performance overcomes one major drawback of incentive systems. Keeping the rewards modest for directors and associates prevents occasional failures from being destructive. Distributing the reward through the annual increase is rare; cash bonuses are much more common. It seems to be effective at St. Elizabeth.

9. *Insist on results.* St. Elizabeth succeeded in large part because its senior management team thought they should and they thought they could. The message of CEO and senior management replacement elsewhere in CHI was clear enough. CHI's support helped them conclude that they could. The support came in the form of capital, training, encouragement, and the timely installation of important components. CHI selected the patient satisfaction survey and installed the CHAN audits. These two steps substantially improved the measurement capabilities.

The elements of service excellence begin at step five—recruiting selectively and expanding training. Two other elements—empowering workers and assisting them to satisfy customers—actually run in parallel to the steps above. They can be started as soon as management can solve recurring difficulties by improving processes, and they should start as early as step two—the initial goal setting.

It is not likely that service excellence programs can be sustained without the first six steps. Workers who cannot solve recurring problems are likely to be frustrated and lose motivation. Conversely, when performance improvement programs address and remove these problems, a substantial synergy develops. St. Elizabeth's experience suggests that much of its success comes from selection, training, and culture, but much also comes from the organization's rigorous emphasis on numbers and processes. The whole appears to be substantially greater than the sum of the parts.

St. Elizabeth had a head start on the nine steps. It had the structure that St. John's found necessary to build (see Chapter 2). That foundation of commitment to honesty, accountability, objectivity, and improvement is essential. St. Elizabeth's long-tenured senior management and the vast majority of its associates take that for granted. Also, Lanik had been building the budget system for 25 years. In 1999, the senior management team began to emphasize selection, culture, and train-ing. Those advantages allowed St. Elizabeth to show improved results each year. A hospital in a similar position should be able to get similar results.

BIBLIOGRAPHY

Wachter, R. M., and L. Goldman. 2002. "The Hospitalist Movement, 5 Years Later." *JAMA* 287 (4): 487–94.

APPENDIX A: ST. ELIZABETH HEALTH SYSTEMS

FY 2002 ACCOUNTABILITY STANDARDS

POSITION TITLE:	Nursing Director	JOB CODE:	1103
RESPONSIBLE TO:	Vice President	DATE:	11/01
DEPARTMENT:	Nursing	PAGE:	1

ITEM #	RELATIVE WEIGHT	PERFORMANCE IS VERY GOOD WHEN
1.0	**5% FIX**	**MISSION EFFECTIVENESS**
1.1	5%	The total value of SEHS Community-Focused Initiatives of charity care and "in-kind services" will be between $12,190,000 (8.2% of net patient service revenue) and $12,799,500. (CORE)
2.0	**40% FIX**	**COST MANAGEMENT**
2.1	20% FIX	Consolidated operating margin before investment income for SEHS will be between $10,948,000 (FY02 Budget) and $11,495,400 (FY01 Budget plus $547,400, a 5% increase in operating margin % to 7.5%) with a minimum of 7.1% margin before investment income (FY02 Budget). (CORE) Expense per Departmental Statistics. Variable departments labor cost/UOS from 98–102% of budget.
2.2	10% Dept #1	Labor cost / UOS will be $163.66 and $173.34 (98–102% of 167)
2.3	5% Dept #2	Labor cost will be b/t $632,593-$658,414 (98–102% of $645,504)
2.4	5% Dept #3	Total cost will be b/t $405,897-$422,464 (98–102%)
3.0	**20% FIX**	**QUALITY OF SERVICE**
3.1	10% **FIX**	SERMC mean score for Overall Quality of Care core composite will rank in the top 20 of CHI hospitals (top 10 to exceed). (CORE)
3.2	6% FIX	Overall Quality of Care for unit will be between 4.27 and 4.3. TJO survey results looking at overall quality, pain and staff responsiveness
3.3	2%	Increase reporting of incident reports by 10%, showing evidence of a non-punitive culture
3.4	2%	Implement a patient complaint tracking system and incorporate into the quarterly board report

continued

4.0	**7% VAR**	**HUMAN RESOURCE MANAGEMENT**
4.1	3%	Associate relations in the department are determined by the evaluator to be very good. Evaluation will be based upon associate attitude survey, peer review, problem resolution, policy compliance, turnover rates, informal observation, and exit interviews.
4.2	2%	Turnover rates will decrease by 10% from FY01. Turnover will be below 20.13%
4.3	2%	Contract labor for nursing division will be reduced by 25% from $1,023,248 to $766,713 by June 20, 2002
5.0	**5% VAR**	**MEDICAL STAFF RELATIONS**
5.1	5%	Maintains positive physician relationships as observed from physician comments, observation of physician problem solving capabilities, and feedback from Medical Staff leadership. Develops and implements a plan to continue to manage increased capacity—encouraging RNs to attend ACLS classes.

Chapter 7

Service Excellence: Building the Future at Franciscan Health System

BACKGROUND

Franciscan Health System (FHS) is a $500-million-a-year integrated delivery system serving Tacoma, Washington, and the southern Puget Sound area. It provides a comprehensive array of service lines through three hospitals, with a total of 536 beds, a hospice, and a long-term care facility. Its 1,400 affiliated physicians and extended role providers are in independent practices, a physician-hospital network, and an employed Franciscan Medical Group. More than 55 percent of FHS revenues are from outpatient services, one of the highest percentages in the nation. FHS has 475,000 emergency and outpatient visits a year from a service population of just over 1 million people. Its outpatient contacts are 15 times as frequent as its inpatient admissions.

FHS has compiled a steady record of growth, almost doubling its net revenue since 1999, and it has simultaneously won several national and regional recognitions for excellence. Most of its growth has been in market share. FHS earned small positive margins in 2000 and 2001 but a healthy 5.9 percent in 2002. It has maintained median to excellent scores in overall patient satisfaction and worker satisfaction throughout a period when patient contacts increased by 50 percent and full-time-equivalent employees increased by more than 40 percent (from 2,500 to 3,600) (see Table 7.1).

FHS achieved its growth in the face of a number of challenges. Puget Sound is a mature managed care market, one of the lowest-cost health-care locations in the nation. Almost half of FHS revenue is from managed care. St. Joseph, FHS's flagship hospital, is located in the poorest section of Tacoma and is a closed shop with 12 unions. The physical

Table 7.1 Major Performance Measures for Franciscan Health System

	1999	2000	2001	2002
People				
Employee satisfaction		3.69		3.67
Physician satisfaction				
Turnover: organization	20.2%	21.3%	20.77%	17.01%
Turnover: RN only	19.7%	18.5%	14.0%	13.4%
Growth				
Patient overall satisfaction[1]	4.15	4.17	4.19	4.15
ER patient satisfaction[2]	4.39	4.34	4.19	3.88
Market share[3]	28.8%	29.9%	30.7%	
Performance				
Net patient revenue (thousands)	$283,364	$328,847	$411,310	$467,479
Operating margin	(5.3%)	2.0%	2.9%	5.8%
Total margin	(3.7)%	3.5%	3.5%	5.9%
Days of total cash	106	66	81	93
Debt to capital ratio	71.2%	68.4%	63.3%	57.7%
Cost per adjusted discharge[4]	$4,649	$4,956	$4,722	$5,210
Community benefit[5] (thousands)	$14,500	$14,459	$17,979	$25,073

continued

Quality

Patient perceived quality[6]	4.40	4.42	4.48	4.25
Patients rating care as "excellent"[7]	39%	40%	41%	36%
Process and outcomes measures in use[8]	• Patient satisfaction • Inpatient mortality • Restraint use • Employee injuries • Blood-borne pathogen exposure • Nosocomial infections • Regulatory inquiries • Care management days • Readmissions • Bill denials • Pregnancy related indicators • Patient falls	Same measures as 1999	Same measures as 2000 with addition of cardiothoracic profiling	Same measures as 2001

Table 7.1 *continued*

	1999	2000	2001	2002
Quality improvement focus areas[9]	• Patient satisfaction • Nutrition support • Pregnancy related indicators • Patient falls • Medication incidents • Blood utilization • Returns to OR	Same focus areas as 1999	Same focus areas as 2000 with addition of: • ICU antibiotic for pneumonia patients • PICC line placements	Same focus areas as 2001 with addition of: • AMI • CHF • CAP With the deletion of: • PICC line placements

Notes: Measures were entered as they became available.

1. Inpatient survey results. These values were estimated from a regression equation using all original values and dummy variables for each quarter except from July to September 2002. The equation has excellent fit and significance. The parameters for the quarters prior to the current vendor are similar and highly significant. The adjustment model incorporates any time trend so that none can appear in the data above. However, inspection of the adjustment coefficients and original data suggest that there was no trend, either up or down, in these measures.

2. ER patient survey results; see note 1.

3. Market share is calculated for inpatient care in the primary service area using data from a commercial supplier.

4. Cost per case adjusted for severity using CMS's DRG index.

5. Community benefit is defined by Catholic Health Association and includes charity care, Medicare and Medicaid losses, education and research costs, and services or funds donated to community activities.

6. Inpatient survey results; see note 1.

7. Percentage of inpatients surveyed rating quality as excellent; see note 1.

8. Measures reported to the MBO board. In 2003, CHI will standardize many of these measures for comparative reporting.

9. Areas selected for intensive study by the MBO.

plant is a maze of buildings constructed at various times, including an architecturally distinctive inpatient tower that features 12-bed nursing stations. When Joseph Wilczek, CHE, president and CEO, arrived in 1998, he found an aging plant and even more serious deterioration in morale. The program of service excellence was started with two goals in mind—to improve FHS attractiveness to its customers and its workers. Wilczek explains:

> Our motto is to make Franciscan the best place to provide care and the best place to work. When I first came, I met an old gentleman at a high school football game. He asked me what I did, and I told him. He said, "You are lucky to work there. My wife died there, and she got the most compassionate care she could ever have had." That's the thing we were lacking after some financial cutbacks and layoffs. Morale was miserable, we lacked money for infrastructure improvements, and patient satisfaction was down. We had high turnover.

WHY SERVICE EXCELLENCE?

The "service value chain" arises from marketing studies that show the importance of customer retention and the role of direct contact workers in achieving customer loyalty. Its advocates note that only "delighted" or exceptionally satisfied customers will make an effort to return and that satisfied workers do a better job of delighting customers. Conversely, they note, replacing workers who leave because they are dissatisfied and attracting new customers are both extremely expensive. The service value concept invests in worker satisfaction and worker effectiveness to increase customer loyalty and market share. Several companies in service industries other than healthcare have applied the concept with notable success. Disney World, Southwest Airline, and Ritz Carlton hotels are often-cited examples. A growing number of hospitals have also tried the concept, although published reports of their achievements are limited.

Customer satisfaction and worker retention are clearly critical for hospitals in the coming decades. The importance of the personal contact between caregivers and patients is indisputable. If the relationships claimed for the service value chain are true, all successful hospitals will eventually adopt the concept.

But will service excellence work with a company with a more traditional business plan and more limited resources? What are conditions necessary to make service excellence work? When can it be started, and when should it be avoided? And will it work in hospitals, some of the most complex organizational environments man has ever created? The FHS story adds substantially to our knowledge of these questions. Wilczek says he is sure of one lesson—service excellence is a complex, permanent change in how business is done:

> When we started the senior management retreats, I got an earful: "This is flavor-of-the-month again. It's nothing but common sense, and we do it already." I told them, we are not the best organization we can be, and it's going to help us move ahead. It's going to make a difference between us and our competitors. My wake-up call was about eight months into the program. I took a tour, and the nurses asked me, "How do you expect to have service excellence when we've got brown stains in the bathrooms, and leaking sinks?" If you get into this type of program, when the employees tell you what needs to be fixed and you say "I'm sorry. I'm too worried about the bottom line," you'll never change the culture. They will not listen to you. They'll think you are just a bureaucrat, and rightfully so. You can't say you want them to be top-notch if you don't give them the tools.

June Bowman, chief nursing officer and CEO of St. Joseph Hospital, adds:

> I think quality improvement is the major umbrella; service excellence is one of the spokes. What we're doing is creating a culture of quality improvement. Changing the culture is very difficult to do. You have to do it for the whole organization, and be extremely focused all the time. It can't be the flavor of the month. It has to be a clear, strategic plan. If you can't maintain it over time, I think you are wasting your money to get into it. Getting this up and running the first year is the easy part. Maintaining it over time is the difficult part.

Components of Service Excellence

Service excellence programs systematically encourage workers to identify and meet customer needs. To do that, they must simultaneously address causes of worker frustration and dissatisfaction. The organization's commitment to the customer must be as strong as the workers' to keep the program effective. A comprehensive hospital program has

- measures of both worker and customer satisfaction in enough detail and frequency to report reliably to most treatment areas;
- explicit identification of values, attitudes, and behaviors that are known to contribute to customer satisfaction;
- a program to change the culture of the organization to accentuate those values, attitudes, and behaviors;
- selection mechanisms to attract applicants comfortable with the service concept;
- intensive orientation for new workers in desired values, attitudes, and behaviors;
- training for workers in specific job competencies;
- training for managers at all levels to equip them to support workers;
- resources to respond to identified service issues, such as equipment needs, process redesign, and expanded measures of performance;
- a service-recovery program that allows workers to make immediate and direct adjustments in cases of customer dissatisfaction; and
- celebrations and rewards for both workers and managers.

Although most of these elements can be implemented independently, the service value chain concept is that they are synergistic; the biggest gains come from having them all. This is the program Wilczek elected to introduce in a financially and emotionally stressed organization. It was a bold move.

BUILDING THE SERVICE EXCELLENCE PROGRAM

FHS became the pilot for a service excellence program developed by CHI for its MBOs. The pilot provided guidelines on measures, detailed instructions and materials for changing the culture, the design of service recovery, and suggestions for celebrations. Although this is not a complete package (because it does not directly address the training components or the resources to respond to service improvement issues), it provided FHS with substantial help.

Structure

The FHS organization structure has four levels of management and matrix assignments to centralize both service lines and support services while maintaining geographic accountability for each of the three inpatient sites. FHS uses task forces and committees extensively. It implements the service excellence program through the guiding coalition, a permanent committee composed of 21 members who are deliberately chosen to represent a cross-section of the organization. FHS relies on frequent direct contact between upper management, first line managers, and workers to supplement this structure.

The coalition's role is to give increased visibility to the service excellence program and to facilitate communication between units of the line organization. The coalition has heavy interaction with the senior management team. It serves the function of a performance improvement council. It has several teams and committees reporting to it and communicates frequently with performance improvement teams that address various projects.

The FHS program identifies service representatives from each department who work directly with management to develop departmental goals and improvement plans. It also used 12 cross-functional "champion groups," with physician, worker, and management membership. The champion groups contributed material for the service standards (described below), but they also pursued specific strategies such as reward and recognition, human resources systems, employee involvement, patient/family involvement, and marketing. As the program matured, the groups were disbanded and their activities were absorbed into departmental responsibilities.

The culture and the structure diminish the importance of rank and encourage open communication. Taken as a whole, FHS's management probably spends more time communicating with each other and its workers than many similar systems do, and it argues that the extra time is a virtue, not a liability. Wilczek notes:

> **People want to know how they are doing. If your department managers don't take the time to give people evaluations and talk about the principles you espouse, it's not going to work.**

Sara Brown, ambulatory care center staff nurse, and Michelle Pruitt, ambulatory care center charge nurse, discuss service excellence from their perspective.

Brown:

> My biggest role has been in the guiding coalition. They meet monthly. There's a real broad definition. They oversee the service reps; they make the disbursement for the Idea Mill. We're involved in the picnic, process improvement, and environmental improvement.

Pruitt:

> I've been here 12 years. I had a different manager and a different team when I started. I worked night shift then; I couldn't have told you who the CEO was. It got better when June [Bowman] got here. She's so much more on the floor and interactive. It's really awesome because I felt like she knows my name. She knows who I am, which really makes me feel like I'm an important part of the organization. That's one of the great morale things—that we know we are supported by our administration. That's huge.

Brown:

> Lois Erickson [ambulatory care center's manager] has an open-door policy. She listens. She doesn't always promise to do something because sometimes people just need a sounding board. She's always there for us. You always have a sense of fairness. The fair thing will happen; it will get worked out. You can rely on that.

Measures

Service excellence programs must make performance and satisfaction measures available to individual managers frequently enough to identify important opportunities for improvement. CHI assesses worker satisfaction at 18 month intervals, and customer satisfaction quarterly. It will be adding physician satisfaction measures. Large samples and high response rates are required to provide reliable, current data to relatively small units. FHS supplements the patient survey measures with informal contacts, subjective evaluations, and complaint data, and it supplements the worker surveys with turnover, absenteeism, grievance, and safety data.

Wilczek:

> The first time we did an employee survey, we got about 48 percent response. Last time, we got smarter. We gave them prizes, and worked on our internal process. We got 80 percent!

Service excellence tends to generate new measures beyond surveys as well. When improvement opportunities are analyzed, they identify processes that can be measured directly. For example, a concern with patient waiting times leads to a study of intake process that in turn is likely to generate several different measures of delays.

Bowman:

> The measures are changed as the teams' needs change. For example, one indicator we worked on in the emergency department was "door-to-doctor time"—the time from arrival until they see a doctor.

Changing the Culture

FHS capitalizes on the CHI values of Reverence, Integrity, Compassion, and Excellence. Like other MBOs, it attracts many associates who gain satisfaction from those values. The values are also reinforced through extensive display, repeated reference in orientation and other training, and as the foundation of the "Spirit at Work" program described below.

To achieve the goals of service excellence, values must be translated into behaviors that are explicitly encouraged and discouraged, a step that goes substantially beyond dissemination and display. Service excellence changes the culture of the organization to one that emphasizes cooperation to please the customer. The focus moves from inputs to outputs, loyalty shifts from the unit to the system, and managers become partners rather than adversaries. Extensive retraining is necessary to build the new culture.

FHS undertook the cultural change as "Spirit at Work," a 24-month campaign. The campaign began in mid-1999 and was a major focus of attention through mid-2001. Some of the key events included the following:

1999	
July	Organizational assessment by consultant
	One-day initial retreat for guiding coalition
November	One-day offsite kick-off for all managers

2000	
January	One-day offsite kick-off for all associates; 1,000 (about 25 percent) associates attended
March	One-and-a-half day offsite retreat for all managers to explain service standards, structure, and department improvement strategy
April–June 2001	75 one-day retreats for staff. Retreats were mandatory, and 88 percent attended. The retreats used 14 trained managers as facilitators and introduced the structure, standards, and process
April–March 2001	Each service standard is emphasized for one month through displays and departmental meetings
May	One-day retreat for departmental representatives, which included some leadership skill development
May	Implement "Idea Mill," a suggestion system that asks for ideas that "improve employee and customer satisfaction"
October	Service standards added to all job descriptions

2001	
March	New hire orientation expanded to two days
April	Idea Mill revised to use the departmental representatives to rank ideas submitted. A budget of $5,000 per month, managed by the guiding coalition, is established to implement ideas. Criterion changed to ideas "improving first impressions or internal quality"
April	Half-day management retreat to review Idea Mill changes, the process for ongoing service standard emphasis, and "Franciscan Greetings and Responses" scripts for various recurring situations
July	"Healing environment" standards (customer friendly design elements) for new construction
July	Performance evaluation tool for managers that links service standards to incentive compensation

The "Spirit at Work" campaign identified 12 service standards as the focus of a month-long promotional effort. Each standard is associated with a CHI value. Each champion group was assigned a standard and developed specific behaviors, skits, and promotional material for the monthly efforts. Much of the detail in the standards can be described as simply good manners, but some elements raise fundamental issues of work life, such as acknowledging mistakes; recommending changes to procedures and environment; behaving in a collaborative, supportive manner; appreciating coworkers; resolving conflicts; and being sensitive to individual privacy needs.

1. Pass a smile! (First impressions—Reverence)
2. Make it right! (Service recovery—Integrity)
3. Welcome to our home! (Safe/healing/calm environment—Compassion)
4. Thank somebody! (Recognition/appreciation—Excellence)
5. Celebrate differences! (Diversity—Reverence)
6. Let's talk! (Communication—Integrity)
7. Keep in touch! (Provide information and explanations—Compassion)
8. Show the way! (Giving directions—Excellence)
9. Look the part! (Professional image—Reverence)
10. Lean on me! (Teamwork—Integrity)
11. Privacy matters! (Privacy/confidentiality—Compassion)
12. Keep growing! (Technical competency—Excellence)

"Spirit at Work" creates some controversy. Not everyone likes to be told to smile, although others agree with Wilczek that FHS could do better. Brown and Pruitt discuss this issue.

Brown:

The first year, they did the standards every month—like "Pass a Smile"—and everybody would work on that; the next month "Show the Way." It was basic golden rules—how to behave in kindergarten stuff. But it was really important to build that awareness, and it really did change behaviors. You always have naysayers. But as you get that positive energy building, and the rule becomes the standard, you hear less and less of that.

Pruitt:

Instead of being a policy written on a piece of paper, it brought it to life. It made it real for everybody.

The controversy was not trivial. Wilczek and Bowman held a special meeting to help manage it.

Wilczek:

> You can't avoid some conflict. June and I sat through a tough meeting with about 100 nurses. We had some angry nurses. Some of [the anger] was [about] "Spirit at Work," and some of it was a recruitment bonus that they viewed as unfair. We stuck to our guns; we were honest. They had some great points, and we adjusted to them mid-stream. But we said, "We think it's important for you to reaffirm the things we want you to do."

Bowman:

> I would change the way we started the program. We put all the employees together. I'd separate clinical and nonclinical staff. The nursing staff said "We're professionals; we know how to behave." I think they were right about that. They took that back to the medical staff and made disparaging remarks. We could have avoided that.

Some of the more fundamental shifts in the culture were hard for some of the employees to learn. Some nurses may have left because of them, as Bowman says:

> Spirit at Work addresses the relationship between employees. They work in an atmosphere that can be very difficult if they don't feel that they trust and care for each other. We had nurses who had bad attitudes; they were not incorporating the values. Some of them have gotten on the bandwagon. Some of them are no longer here. We've made a major effort to help the managers identify who hasn't learned.

With time, the controversies get resolved, as Brown and Pruitt describe.

Brown:

> We didn't do the monthly focus after the first year. Spirit at Work has become the norm and faded into the background, but the standards haven't; the attitudes haven't. In every staff meeting, we are

talking about it. We are always doing "Caught in the Act" [a reporting system that recognizes employees "caught" making an exceptional effort to meet a customer's needs]. It becomes part of the life. You don't hear the naysaying because it's what we are; what we expect; the Franciscan way. Sometimes that's said in a joke, but it's awesome. We love that.

Pruitt:

Some of the service standards have really helped us, so that when you get a new person, we're very friendly and open. We have a traveler nurse today. The first day she worked with us, she said, "This team has a kind of energy that's palpable. You are the first unit that made it okay to be a traveler."

Brown:

It was the hugest compliment, because all we did was say, "Are you doing okay?" Give her a hug. Ask her "What can I do for you?" Gave her a tour when she came on.

Applicant Selection and Orientation

Service excellence organizations deliberately seek new employees who will be comfortable with the concept. Not every new hire is comfortable, particularly in the management ranks. Wilczek comments:

Some of our hires did not fit. We use a matrix-style management system compared to the silos you usually find; some people like silos. When we interviewed for St. Joseph's COO, people came in and said, "I can't accept responsibility for something I don't have direct control over." That's not the type of managers we want. We want people people. When I hire an executive, I look at how they work with people, how they focus on retention, what they want to do to make this a better place to work. We hire for attitude.

The senior management team has to want to work with each other. Just one or two people on the team who don't want to work with the rest can destroy teamwork. They have to get off the bus. They want to pull the bus in a different direction, and you can't have that. That's a key element.

FHS has developed a video emphasizing its desired values, attitudes, and behavior. All individuals seeking employment are asked to view the video, which explains that application signifies agreement. FHS has found the video valuable both for prescreening applicants and as a promotional tool with schools and colleges. Lisa Morten, director of employment, discusses hiring goals:

> We know that a major part of our success is hiring the right people. We have begun a behavioral interview format assessing behaviors and values.

The desired behaviors must be taught to each new employee. FHS doubled the length of its employee orientation to two days. The added time is devoted to the standards of behavior and to bringing the worker's new supervisor and senior management into the orientation. They increased the frequency to twice a month to reduce the delay for new employees.

Employee Training

Organizations that succeed with service excellence invest heavily in training of all kinds. The desired changes in behavior often depend on specific, learnable knowledge, skill, and attitudes. A very substantial effort is necessary to initiate the program; virtually every manager and worker must be retrained. To continue the program, specific skill education must also increase to match process changes generated by the expanded improvement activities. Managerial skills, knowledge, and attitudes are a particularly sensitive component. As Wilczek notes, the managers keep the program in place after the initial efforts.

John Mueller, director of education services, explains the efforts to reach current staff and the revision of the orientation program:

> Staff retreats started in April 2000. My staff helped 14 managers from across the system facilitate the programs. We scheduled as many as 50 employees in a day, purposely mixing staff from all hospitals and many departments. We used the Apollo XIII moon mission as an example of what committed staff can do against very long odds. Staff had the opportunity to see some of their managers in white jump suits with NASA insignia and baseball caps.

We anticipated that many veteran staff would voice bitterness over past FHS downsizing and "takeaways." We trained the facilitators how to allow venting and how to suggest convincingly that the past was past and the event was the start of a very different future. We presented 75 retreats, reaching 3,305 employees in 14 months. We covered evening and night shifts and did several retreats on Saturdays. Evaluations repeatedly mentioned reconnecting with Franciscan values and trying to regain a sense of community that many felt had been lost.

We started working on a redesign of our orientation program in the winter of 2000. The literature abundantly indicated that in addition to supplying key information to employees, the program should engage and integrate them into the culture of the organization. We reviewed studies that demonstrated remarkable decreases in new hire turnover, increased productivity, and greater organization effectiveness. We wanted to do the same. We drafted a design that would explicitly welcome new employees; create a distinctive theme to communicate FHS history, values, and culture; provide amenities like meals and contest prizes; and use a variety of formats.

We also wanted to minimize the time between hiring and orientation; cover an expanded list of mandated regulatory content; and directly address service excellence, service standards, and service recovery. We used a workshop to help our facilitators with presentations, slides, and handouts. We implemented the new program in March of 2001. So far, 1,086 employees have completed it. Ninety-two percent of course evaluations were "satisfied" or "very satisfied."

FHS also invests in management development. Mueller explains the evolution and content of that program:

Management development was restructured in 1997. The human resources people here at that time felt that management skills contributed to a large number of avoidable and unfortunate employee-relations issues. They purchased a curriculum that emphasized communicating, delegating, performance assessment, coaching, and conflict resolution and implemented it through a local consultant. To date, the consultant's two facilitators have completed ten iterations reaching 250 employees. The bulk of our managers and directors have gone through the program. The current classes include new managers and staff at the coordinator, shift lead, or charge-nurse level.

In 1999, we asked the consultant to develop a supplementary program. They designed a four-day program on leadership. The sessions address effectiveness under pressure, building trust, involving a team in a vision, managing divergent opinions, and negotiating. That program has been offered seven times to 92 managers, directors, and vice presidents. It has evolved to incorporate both the FHS mission and values and the "Spirit at Work" initiative.

Mueller and Morten discuss the other training that FHS uses to support its managers and clinical workers.

Morten:

Our approach is different from when I started. The HR department has become more responsive to our customers. We've moved to a partnering approach. We have developed tools for effective interviewing and we constantly refer to the behavior standards, but we also educate our staff on performance-improvement methods. We explain the Joint Commission program. We use our evaluation tools to identify training needs and opportunities.

Mueller:

There's a lot of focus on our clinical staff and our managerial staff. We have done focused programs on management in St. Joseph and St. Clare. In a clinical area, we identify the patients' needs and tailor the communication skills to their age. We have a tuition assistance plan, and 56 percent of those taking advantage of it are in nursing programs.

FHS plans to continue and even expand these programs, but Mueller cautions:

We can't prove that these programs have paid off. Course evaluations have been positive. Our turnover rate has been decreasing recently, although the decline did not begin until several years after these programs began and after the "Spirit at Work" campaign. We want to support the management group with mentoring and coaching as well; we'll move ahead with this in the coming year.

Resources to Implement Opportunities

Service excellence programs encourage workers to identify opportunities for improvement. The improvements are usually process changes that require testing and training and frequently require capital. FHS has modified its capital budgeting process to meet the sorts of needs that service excellence seems to generate. It has created a category of capital expenditures less than $75,000 and used this category to protect the amenities-oriented and "soft" benefit proposals that often lose out in competition with proposals that directly affect safety or income.

FHS created the "Idea Mill" program to encourage staff to identify ideas that would improve customer service and to keep focus on customer satisfaction. A committee of department representatives reviews suggestions and narrows the list to five each month. The guiding coalition selects the final items for funding, with a $50,000 annual budget. So far, over 600 ideas have been funded, and the budget has been increased to $75,000 in 2003. All submissions are sorted and returned to the relevant department. Many of the items not covered by the "Idea Mill" funds are later incorporated into departmental budgets.

Syd Bersante, chief operating officer of St. Francis, notes that FHS has also created small discretionary funds for its managers:

> To get more decision making at the staff level, we are giving each manager a dollar amount they control, $125 per FTE, to improve the workplace in their department. The managers collaborate with their employees to decide the best use of the funds.

Service Recovery

Service recovery trains and empowers workers to deal directly with incidents that cause customer dissatisfaction. It is taught using the "four As"—anticipate, acknowledge, apologize, and address. The training emphasizes preventing difficulties by continued study of processes and analysis of errors, but it also encourages workers to solicit comments and respond to nonverbal cues from customers. Workers are taught how to listen to complaints, acknowledge mistakes without attributing blame, and avoid becoming defensive. The program encourages workers to "take complaints as a gift," apologizing and expressing appreciation for the information conveyed. It empowers them to make modest adjustments, such as issuing gift certificates or meal certificates, and to report matters that might require more extensive response.

Pruitt and Brown discuss how service recovery works in the ambulatory care center.

Pruitt:

> I think the big thing is service recovery. "Spirit at Work," and us as managers teaching it and being role models for it, is making it front line. I've seen it happening in the frontline people, secretaries, nurses. In the ACC, sometimes we do one recovery a week, sometimes none.

Brown:

> Sometimes a CNA knows how to make it right. You have somebody who's getting uptight; the CNA says, "Oh, let me fix that for you. Let's take care of that." You go a little farther to take care of the problem, and it's done. You have a happy person because they feel like they were listened to.

Pruitt:

> I feel like I'm getting fewer complaints. They just don't get to me.

Celebration and Rewards

FHS quickly learned the power of celebration in motivating workers. As Pruitt and Brown said, the managers make personal contact a reward. Senior managers are expected to visit all their work units weekly, and lower level managers are taught to respond positively to most worker actions and requests. The initial assessment for service excellence uncovered a desire to reinstate an annual picnic that had been discontinued some years before. The first response was in 2000, when 2,500 attended. The picnic has been held annually since, with growing crowds. In 2002, 3,500 attended.

In fiscal year 2002, 271 employees received the "Caught in the Act" award recognizing an exceptional effort to meet a customer's needs.

Each department has a "Recognition Tool Kit" with gift certificates, movie passes, and a variety of rewards. Any employee or manager may nominate an awardee for further recognition. The manager and employees select winners who are recognized in the employee newsletter and are eligible for a monthly drawing for a $100 gift certificate. Bonnie Bush, education coordinator of organization development, explains the goals for celebration:

> We want to recognize teams as well. We plan to add a quarterly team award and an organizationwide year-end celebration. When we make organizational progress, we want every employee to share in the wealth.

FHS does not have incentive pay for workers. It started a bonus plan for managers two years ago and is improving the evaluation process. Its evaluation form has five sections addressing management skills, core responsibilities, values-based service standards, work habits, and goal setting. Several sections address supervisory and leadership issues. The service standards section assigns satisfactory/unsatisfactory scores for all 12 service standards. The sections are subjectively combined into a four-point rating, and an improvement plan is required for any area rated unsatisfactory. Morten explains:

> The goals for our managers are very clearly defined. Most of our managers are eligible for a bonus that's based on meeting FHS's strategic goals and work unit goals for satisfaction and quality. There are thresholds that determine the bonus, which has been as high as 12 percent.

Most managers have earned their bonus. Wilczek reinforces an important point: bonuses should be attainable:

> I want everybody to make their goals; that means they've all done a good job. We don't set goals that are so goofy that people say, "What's the sense of trying?" If you do that, they start looking for an organization that's reasonable. Out of 115 eligible, five or six people have missed three bonuses and seven or eight missed two. Everybody made the financial goals. Two other criteria are "the light switches" that turn on the bonus. One is the patient survey;

most people made that one. The other is timely employee evaluations; that's the only reason those people didn't make a bonus.

RESULTS

The global results speak for themselves. In terms of the CHI balanced scorecard—performance, growth, people, and quality—FHS has achievements in every category. Wilczek lists some of the more impressive achievements:

> Inpatient volume is up 5,000 days in the last year. We are the third busiest hospital in Washington. We increased 70,000 outpatient visits. Our emergency visits increased 20,000. We've added 28 beds. We earned $361 million revenue in 2000, we'll have $520 million in 2003. We provided $25 million in community benefit in 2002. Our capital campaign has exceeded its goal. Our avoidable turnover went from 7.4 percent to 3.4 percent. Our cost structure is low compared to other Washington hospitals. The other hospitals averaged 2.2 percent margin last year; we had 5.9 percent.
>
> Our competitor won the consumer choice award twice before we started this program. Since then, we've won the award or tied with our competitor. We've always been a prize-winning hospital, and we continue to be. St. Joseph has been a "Top 100" hospital for six years. Now St. Francis and St. Clare are as well. We won two awards for our hospice program. Without service excellence, we could never have accommodated the growth. We would not have had the people here to serve the volume.

These results put FHS in a leadership position in Washington. They occurred in spite of the capital shortages, the geographic location, and other history.

Costs

It is difficult to identify the marginal costs of service excellence. Bersante records out-of-pocket costs such as training-program amenities, gifts and prizes, and consultant fees; these total about $100,000 a year only. The "Idea Mill" requires $75,000 a year. The picnic costs $70,000. The discretionary funds to improve the workplace cost $500,000 per year. The balance of new capital requests generated from service excellence falls within the capital budgets. The emphasis on customer satisfaction may shift expenditures in a different direction, but it would be hard to argue that the shift is wrong.

The time spent on training is the largest cost element. According to the American Society for Training and Development, all companies that contributed usable data to their survey expended about $650 per employee on training in 2000, about 2 percent of their payroll. Leading companies expended $1,550, more than 3 percent of their payroll. Healthcare organizations that responded spent only $284 per employee, about 1 percent of their payroll. They were much less likely to be in the leadership category. FHS training costs are $507 per employee. This expenditure, over $2 million in 2002, probably puts FHS in a leadership position among healthcare organizations in the United States.

Mueller:

> Four years ago we had 8½ FTEs in training personnel, now we are budgeted for 13½. The growth was largely in clinical areas— med/surg and critical care. We used managers from other areas to do the "Spirit at Work" training. We identified managers we thought could be effective facilitators, provided them with training, and brought them to a point where they are very effective in delivering eight hours of content to a group of employees.
>
> There are any number of hidden costs. The facilitators' time is probably the biggest. When we started, we invited them to a meeting. A number of them were really surprised, and there was a lot of doubt. Our plan was to replace them after a year, but when the first year ended, to a person, they wanted to continue. They thought it was worthwhile.

Although the training budget goes up, Morten notes that the human resources total cost remains competitive:

> We monitor how we spend our dollars very closely. We are completing a comprehensive review of policies, and we hope to have all policies online shortly. We centralized our recruitment and application process. And with our growth, we could afford to add a nurse recruiter, a person in compensation, and a Family Medical Leave Act specialist.

Many elements of the service excellence program—the guiding coalition, the departmental representatives, time off the job for training, and various media expenses to communicate the concepts—may not be additional costs. FHS's managers spend a lot of time in personal contact with workers, in service excellence-related meetings and programs, and in resolving issues identified in satisfaction surveys and service recovery events. FHS has the same supervisory structure and overhead costs that it had before; it has not added employees or supervisors to make service excellence work. FHS's indirect costs were 33 percent of total costs in 2001.

Quality of Care

FHS's several prizes and awards support its quality of care, and available measures are both competitive and improving. They have used a board-level retreat to stimulate continued improvement. Laure Nichols, senior vice president for strategic planning and business development; Bowman; and Wilczek discuss the quality leadership program.

Nichols:

> We have a board leadership retreat each year, where we bring board members, physicians, managers, and community leaders together. We have a performance quality leadership group that includes board members, physicians, senior managers, some directors, and staff. It meets monthly and cycles through all aspects of the organization.

Bowman:

> Physicians and other caregivers work in teams in our service lines. Each team has its quality indicators and we monitor them over time. The measures are changed as the teams' needs change.

Wilczek:

> We are looking at medication errors, and we will have some people working full-time on reducing errors for the next couple of years. Our medication error rates as reported have gone up. We think

that's because we are getting better reporting. We are creating a culture where you can report without fear.

Service Improvement

The service excellence program encourages a variety of customer-listening devices to help work groups identify opportunities for improvement. Bush describes the ones used at FHS:

> We have several listening devices, including mystery shopping, patient shadowing, patient mapping, and "Walk in My Shoes." Departments can ask their internal or external customers or their own employees to mystery shop. All managers are expected to round in their departments and to touch base with both employees and patients. Volunteers run a patient advocate program; they go into patients' rooms and interview patients. In patient shadowing, we accompany patients. With their permission, we go through the care process step by step, recording not only what happens but how they feel about it. We do patient mapping, and take the flow chart to patient focus groups to verify their reactions. We do "Walk in my Shoes," where department will sit down with internal customers and get feedback. The departments have the option of applying the tools best suited to their needs.

It is also true that the results took a long time to happen at FHS. Evidence on the rate of improvement suggests that old cultures die hard. Areas that had the most problems at the start have improved, but they still tend to lag. Mueller observes:

> The people who have been here the longest are the toughest ones to change. They are used to their routine, and they are waiting for the program to go away.

Workforce Reduction

Managing layoffs is a special problem. FHS has been able to keep the number small and to take special steps to minimize adverse reaction. Morten explains:

> We've used retraining and planned workforce reduction to avoid layoffs. When they occur, we have a competitive severance package.

Wilczek:

> We've shut down programs, but if you shut down programs you must have a plan. When we closed our home care program, we made a concerted effort to keep the people, and we kept 70 percent. If top management eliminates a program and doesn't both give a good severance package and do everything we can to get people reemployed, it won't work. People understand that you have to close some programs. What they don't understand is if you treat people brutally, if people say, "After 22 years, they kicked me out with two weeks severance, without helping me get a job.," I have to tell you it won't work.

Emergency Department

Two exceptionally critical areas—emergency and nursing—suggest the sorts of opportunities and management activities that service excellence stimulates. FHS's emergency departments are victims of their own rapid growth. Visits to the three sites have increased 25 percent since 1999, to 124,000 per year. Patient satisfaction scores are among the lowest reported for FHS (see Table 7.2).

The CHI average suggests that emergency services may be a widespread source of customer dissatisfaction, but that theory does not change the goal. FHS must work to improve this area of service, which accounts for one-quarter of its patient contacts. As Bowman says, the problem is complex:

> The ED staff gets caught in a bind. If there are no open beds, patients have to wait. Many ED patients will need a critical care bed or a bed with cardiac monitoring, so we studied the use of critical care beds and created 2 units with telemetry. That allowed us to move more patients through.

The FHS management team has put a lot of effort into managing emergency patient care. The process improvements that are in place so far stretch from demand management to bed recovery:

- Expanded the Franciscan Medical Group clinic hours to divert demand from the emergency department to less-expensive clinics

Table 7.2 Patient Satisfaction, July 2001 to March 2002

FHS ER Site	Mean Score	Percent Excellent	CHI Rank
St. Clare Hospital	3.97	37%	38 of 59
St. Francis Hospital	3.91	31%	50 of 59
St. Joseph Hospital	3.62	24%	59 of 59
All CHI	4.02	39%	

- Established a performance improvement team (composed of nurses, doctors, departmental staff, and an outside consultant) for emergency departments across the three sites
- Established triage and an urgent care system staffed with a physician assistant and an RN using patient care protocols
- Created standing orders to allow triage nurses to order certain diagnostic tests so that the results are available when the doctor sees the patient
- Used a team-building exercise for doctors and nurses so that information flows easily between the two groups
- Assigned social workers to the emergency department to resolve complex patient problems
- Added 24-hour holding beds for observation
- Opened 22 telemetry beds and installed $2 million worth of monitors
- Used the hospitalist program to reduce delays in admissions. Hospitalists care for 75 percent of all inpatients, and they have reduced length of stay.
- Sent admission nurses to the emergency department to start the admitting process
- Flagged diagnostic tests for patients being discharged so that the results come back promptly
- Used a beeper system with housekeepers to reduce bed turnaround after discharges to 30 minutes

Service excellence may be a way to keep the emergency department situation from deteriorating further. Worker satisfaction scores and turnover suggest that the departments continue to be difficult places to work, but turnover improved from 34 percent in 2001 to 29 percent in 2002.

Nursing

Nursing is central to patient satisfaction, and nursing recruitment and retention are critical to success. Bowman must deal with full capacity, an aging plant, and an inner-city location at St. Joseph. The 2002 St. Joseph patient satisfaction scores were below CHI medians in inpatient, outpatient, and maternity care. Bowman says:

> We have a nursing practice council that meets on a monthly basis. It's composed of all nursing directors across the system. The council sets policy and practice for nursing. The council works a lot on retention and recruitment. We've done some major work with directors and managers, looking at their positions as retention officers. We are one of 40 charter members of a national best-practice group in nursing. The group's staff comes here and works with the council.
>
> The council checks its policies with the service standards. Also, each nursing unit has at least one service improvement project. We look at indicators across the three facilities. One we are looking at now is patient falls. Each director and manager works with their staff to reduce falls. The Council doesn't really get into unit staffing patterns; that's done in the budgetary process. About two years ago, when I first took this job, we did an extensive project reviewing our core staffing, including all three hospitals. My belief, having worked in nursing for many years and various settings, is that each unit must have an adequate core staffing plan—that is, the staff you need to hire for your unit to handle the average daily census. When the staff needs additional help, we have several sources. We pay "extra shift bonuses" to nurses who sign up for extra shifts; we have "travelers"; and we use local agency nurses. When we can't meet staffing requirements, we close beds. We don't do that frequently, but it happens. I'm not going to allow these nurses to work understaffed. I think that's the worst thing you can do to your staff.

FHS needs a steady stream of new nurses to handle the remaining turnover and growth. The hospital has experimented with various approaches to recruitment. "Warm bodies" are not enough; the nursing recruits must fit the emerging culture. Bowman continues:

We've helped our nurse managers understand that they are better off not hiring anyone than hiring someone whose attitude they are worried about. My whole career, I've known nurse managers who'd get in a panic and hire anybody that came along. The wrong kind of people get you even more problems. We could certainly hire more people here, but if they aren't the right kind of people we don't want them.

We paid a recruitment company $20,000 per nurse for recruits. We were in a real shortage, and if we didn't get them, we'd have had to cut out vacations. The nurses here did not like it. We showed them the numbers. If every one of the recruited nurses left after one year, we would still have been better off financially than if we'd hired agency nurses, and we would have delivered more co-ordinated care. We agreed we would not take any nurse from our nearest competitor who worked more than six tenths full-time. Most people were recruited from the Northwest.

Out of the recruitment company's engagement came a more deliberate, locally oriented program that has been successful. Morten describes the second initiative:

We held a "100 Day Campaign" to recruit experienced nurses. We hired 67 experienced nurses and 42 new graduates. Our vacancy rate has been decreasing for several years. We used recruiting fairs, advertising, and other devices. The managers spend time with the new nurses, beginning with the interview. It's made a huge difference. Their comfort level has improved. Evidence from our recruits suggests they perceive a difference between Franciscan and its competitors. We are still short of nurses, but we're not as short as some of our competitors.

The initial orientation and support are a key to retention. A program of "clinical residencies"—10- to 12-week educational opportunities for new graduate RNs—has become an important component of nursing recruitment and retention. The programs combine classroom instruction and individually preceptored clinical experience. FHS offers them in medical/surgical, critical care, perioperative, labor and delivery, emergency, renal dialysis, and nursery specialties. Mueller justifies the program:

Changes in nursing school curricula have virtually mandated that new graduate nurses begin professional employment with a residency. Three different pathways lead to entry at the RN level. Our experience indicates that few graduates from any pathway are prepared to assume independent clinical responsibilities without extensive support and supervision.

The programs cost about $10,000 per nurse, most of which is salary costs for the resident. The labor and delivery and perioperative programs will soon be offered by a consortium of local hospitals. Pruitt talks about what the programs mean to nurses who followed her:

> Orientation has made a lot of difference. I had a week of in-house orientation and two weeks on the floor; my first days I didn't know what to do. It's much better now. You learn how to order on the computer? Who can help you if you have a problem? How do you reach them? a lot of things you need to know as a nurse.

Physicians' Role

The service excellence program at FHS has concentrated on hospital workers and so far has not addressed either the physicians or their office employees. In a mature managed care market, primary care physicians tend to have limited contact with the hospital, although they remain the first point of patient contact. Wilczek observes:

> We still haven't done a good job integrating our "Spirit at Work" program with our medical staff. Our community physicians don't come to the hospital as much because of the hospitalist team. We solved one problem—improving quality of care—with our hospitalist program, but we've created another problem—how do you get the primary care doctor wanting to work with us and feeling that they are part of our institution? Their interaction with the hospital is a fax machine. You've got to monitor them more, make sure you talk to them. Freestanding centers are telling them they can do a better job and try to get their loyalty.

Bersante explains what she is doing about physician involvement:

> I've been at St. Francis for a year. Because of the administrative turnover, the level of trust is not as high as at the other two hos-

pitals, both with employees and physicians. Physicians have become very disconnected. They perceive FHS as centralizing decision making that reduces their autonomy.

Senior leadership has been focused on relationship building, going out to the physicians' offices to identify their issues. I have a whole spreadsheet identifying the area of practice, issues, suggestions for enhancing services. We think the way to reach them is to identify the dissatisfiers.

In Washington's very low cost market, physician income may be a hidden "dissatisfier." Resolving the division of outpatient revenues is a problem that will not go away under service excellence. Wilczek discusses the implications of financial relationships with physicians:

We joint venture with doctors. I'm not afraid to take a third of a business; it's better than nothing. We have a surgery center in Gig Harbor, with a solid contribution. Four orthopedic surgeons contribute 85 percent of the revenue. Now they want to go on their own. The first financial analysis said a freestanding center would reduce our margin substantially. If I say no, I will lose even more. I'll probably have to shut it down. Now I have an incentive to help them grow business.

WHAT IS NEXT FOR FHS?

As FHS progresses with service excellence, it is identifying specific activities that need improvement. The plan for 2002 included expanded orientation and mentoring for new managers and increased contact between managers and workers through rounding and participation in the representatives' meeting. The "Idea Mill" criteria were changed to emphasize "first impressions" and "internal quality," the programs that serve the direct caregivers. Wilczek told his managers:

If we want to be seen as the best place to work, we must provide excellent internal quality to our staff. For example, people become frustrated because they desire to provide excellent care but lack the equipment. If we want to be seen as the best place to receive care, we must excel in our service from the moment the patient and family walk through our doors. The first impression we create must be impeccable. The Idea Mill will be focused on access, scheduling, and first impressions. In the next quarter, we will emphasize the standards that impact first impressions—Pass a Smile, Look the Part, Welcome to Our Home, Show the Way, and Privacy Matters. We will also be implementing standard greetings.

The program for 2002 also expanded screening for "service-savvy people" and added the hiring video and a performance evaluation tool that includes behavior standards. "Spirit at Work" was offered to interested physicians' office staff, and FHS promised to meet at least three needs identified in the physician satisfaction survey.

FHS's service excellence strategy tested several known limits. Most prominently, FHS lacked the capital for improvements, did not have a uniform culture across their three sites, had some serious misalignments of service and demand that required closures and layoffs, and had closed-shop unions in its largest facility. But FHS still made the strategy work. The 12 unions in St. Joseph include both service workers and nurses, but they were not a problem. Bowman observes:

I thought when I came, I'd spend a lot of time in grievance resolution. In the two years I've worked here, I think I've had two grievances reach my level.

KEY LESSONS

When the service excellence pilot program was reported back to other CHI MBOs, many had misgivings. Yet St. Elizabeth, in a very different environment and with a different history, adopted several elements including a "Spirit" campaign (see Chapter 6). Service excellence is entirely consistent with the CHI values. It expresses the values as key drivers of performance and mission effectiveness. It articulates the heritage of CHI in everyday behaviors.

Deborah Lee-Eddie, CHE, senior vice president of CHI, observes:

Virtually all the markets I work with have incorporated service excellence into the fabric of how they do business. The leadership teams in many MBOs have modeled service excellence to their unique environment. While the approach and implementation differs from market to market, a common thread is the expressed desire to create and demonstrate a distinctive culture that is mission, vision, and values rooted. That may sound like a cliché, but these systems count service excellence as a key driver in documented improvements in patient satisfaction, employee engagement, and operational success.

The question of when and how service excellence fits a hospital's strategy has answers more complex than "yes" and "no." The service excellence concept has three premises:

1. Delighting customers—earning excellent ratings—is essential to market growth or even retaining market share if your competitor succeeds at it.
2. Worker satisfaction and worker empowerment help delight customers. They also make recruitment and retention easier.
3. A battery of specific activities improves worker satisfaction and empowerment. From the FHS experience and the literature on the service value chain, these activities include the following:

   - Applicant screening
   - Applicant orientation
   - Technical skills training
   - Values training
   - Behavior standards
   - Performance measurement
   - Process improvement
   - Managerial training
   - Service recovery
   - Programs to encourage process improvement, like the "Idea Mill"
   - Programs to reward customer-oriented behavior, like "Caught in the Act" and incentive payment plans

A substantial body of marketing studies documents the validity of the first premise, and it fits most people's personal experience. We do not make an effort to go back to a place that is only average, without any distinction. The second premise is similarly justified. Again, the surveyors have data that show strong, convincing associations between worker and customer satisfaction. We do go back when workers answer our questions correctly and with a smile, especially if the smile is genuine. The conclusion on attracting and retaining workers is unshakeable.

So everybody's strategy should include satisfying workers and attempting to delight customers. The question comes down to the best way to go about it. CHI has concluded that a value chain requires a systemic endeavor and a permanent commitment. It must be integrated with leadership selection, management development, and physician loyalty.

The key lessons CHI draws from the FHS pilot are as follows:

1. *Start with values.* Imbed them in the management structure and expect them of associates. Values need to be imbedded in business decisions like the capital budget priorities and the work of performance improvement teams as much as in greetings and standard behaviors. CHI policies, like the CHAN audits and compliance officers, suggest that Integrity may be the starting point, not because Reverence, Compassion, and Excellence are less important but because they are unattainable without Integrity.

2. *Develop rigorous balanced scorecard measures.* These include worker and customer satisfaction, but in a context of financial and operational performance. Measures, particularly when they can be compared to benchmarks, motivate managers and associates to improve. They also help prioritize needs. Priorities are critical when resources are short.

3. *Train associates in technical skills and train managers in managerial skills.* People who do not know how to do their jobs cannot be rescued with a "Spirit at Work" campaign. Standard behaviors are no substitute for professional competence.

4. *Emphasize process improvement, explicit goals, and a carefully managed capital budget.* A "performance improvement council" is a stronger symbol than a "guiding coalition."

5. *Provide powerful incentives for balanced scorecard performance.* Celebrations are certainly appropriate. Incentive pay based on quantitative goals and accountabilities, like St. Elizabeth, will probably yield more permanent gains.

6. *With these five strategies in place, use the balance of service excellence—standard behaviors, service recovery, spirit campaigns, idea mills, "Caught-in-the-Act"—to substantiate, authenticate, and energize them.*

That said, was Wilczek's bold move right? The record shows it paid off. He had several factors that made his case unique and justified a heavy emphasis on meeting worker and customer needs. His costs were already near benchmark; process improvement would not yield big gains, but market share would. He had evidence of a serious morale problem, and he did not have enough capital to correct his facility problems.

For CHI, Wilczek and the Seattle team served as path breakers. They pushed the envelope of service excellence and showed that it can make a major difference in a challenging environment. The concept of the service value chain is now understood across the system, and several MBOs, including St. Elizabeth, have begun incorporating it into their organizations. CHI will help them with a program of core value assessment and development using the value chain tools.

BIBLIOGRAPHY

American Society for Training and Development, 1640 King Street, Box 1443, Alexandria, Virginia, 22313–2043; web site: *www.astd.org.*

Freiberg, K., and J. Freiberg. 1998. *Nuts! Southwest Airlines' Crazy Recipes for Business and Personal Success.* New York: Bantam Doubleday Dell Publishing Group.

Heskett, J., W. E. Sasser, and L. Schlesinger. 1997. *The Service Profit Chain.* New York: The Free Press.

Chapter 8

Thinking Forward: Completing the Transformation

THE SCALABLE MODEL

We believe CHI has built a model that has the power to transform twenty-first-century healthcare and promote healthy communities. CHI's model is not unique, but we believe it is effective. The strength of the model is its ability to identify and build an environment that is attractive to both customer and provider stakeholders. Communities that adopt the model will find they have a vehicle to find solutions to the problems of healthcare that other approaches cannot.

Like Henry Ford's assembly line, the CHI model can be made bigger, copied, and improved. It is scalable. It works in 47 MBOs; it can work in 470 or 4,700. It can be copied. CHI has no secret components or unique advantages. The model will be improved; in fact, improvement is one of its components. To convey fully what is involved, this chapter discusses the systemwide components that CHI uses to stimulate its MBOs, the risks and threats that CHI and others must successfully avoid, and the ways the model can be used to strengthen healthcare in non-CHI communities.

HOW CHI STIMULATES IMPROVEMENT IN ITS MBOS

The CHI model is an empowerment model and a learning model. Its strength comes from its ability to support its caregivers and frontline personnel, both as they do their jobs and as they improve them. The CHI corporate office stimulates the MBOs by making the opportunities and rewards for improvement clear. It provides the incentives, the common language, and the supportive environment—"the way we do things here." The culture is maintained by five foundation elements:

1. commitment to the core values,
2. measurement and goal setting,
3. strategic and financial planning activities,
4. centralized services and resources, and
5. rewards management.

These elements are used repeatedly in ways that interconnect and complement so that managers and associates are steadily encouraged to improve.

Commitment to the Core Values

CHI's core values—Reverence, Integrity, Compassion, and Excellence—are exceptional in their relevance and universality. These are values that many will embrace and few will oppose. They begin the reward process for associates because they add meaning to the work. They attract patients because they commit explicitly to patient needs. CHI uses these values to clarify its commitment to health. It also uses them to change the way decisions are made and the way people relate to one another within the organization. CHI makes its values real to its associates, and these values become its source of practical strength.

The Reverence value emphasizes "profound respect for every person and for a diversity of people and perspectives." That concept establishes essential ground rules for workplace behavior. Race, gender, income, and professional status are no longer acceptable distinctions. As a result, patients and workers from disadvantaged groups feel more welcome and are more loyal. The Reverence value makes clear that disagreements will be resolved in an atmosphere of mutual respect, using fair processes. Associates whose views did not prevail will still feel fairly treated and remain loyal to the process and the organization.

Integrity is doubly important in healthcare. Patients and families seek providers they trust. CHI's "deep sense of vocation or spiritual calling" attracts caregivers who intend to honor that trust. The vocation also stands for a long-term commitment that is critical in attracting physicians. A medical practice cannot easily be moved; most physicians make a lifetime commitment to one location. CHI associates can use their common commitment to resist expediency and resolve conflicts. The "transparent honesty" built at St. John's carries the concept a step further by committing to conflict identification and prevention.

The Compassion and Excellence values create care that meets the safe, effective, patient-centered, timely, efficient, and equitable criteria of the Institute of Medicine. Similar phrases appear in hundreds of vision statements. CHI's efforts to integrate them into its balanced scorecard reporting, strategic planning, and rewards have made them a real part of each associate's daily life. CHI has begun a program to help each MBO align its activities with the values, integrating the elements more completely. It will use a criteria and scoring system similar to the Baldrige Award to encourage each MBO to identify ways it can improve the actualization of the core values.

Measurement and Goal Setting

Modern healthcare is evidence based. The ability to use quantitative information is a foundation for improvement in healthcare organizations. It is also an indicator of fairness in making decisions. Decisions that are based on carefully assessed evidence reduce tension and frustration in an organization, particularly when they are approached with reverence and integrity.

CHI ensures that decisions by its MBOs will be evidence based. It specifies much of the balanced scorecard, defines and standardizes measures to allow comparison, audits to ensure accurate reporting, demands explicit improvement goals, and uses benchmarking and networking to establish these goals. The result stimulates not only performance improvement but also scientific objectivity. Decisions that once were made on rank, authority, or simply shouting louder are now subject to a simple test: "The _____ MBO does it differently and reports better results."

Quantitative measurement is subject to two recognized groups of hazards. One is honesty in reporting. The more reward is attached to a measure, the greater the temptation to falsify that measure. CHI addresses this with its value and culture of integrity and with its audit activities. Each MBO CEO and CFO must attest quarterly to the honesty of the figures reported. The CHAN audit verifies their attestation. CHAN provides all the usual internal audit services and more. The audit extends to some performance measures. The auditor has direct access to the MBO CEO; the MBO board or finance committee; and, through his or her CHAN supervisors, to the corporate office.

The second problem of measurement is reliability and validity. In healthcare, reliability and validity are obtained by careful definition, rigorous sampling, and complex statistical adjustment. The clinical performance measures in particular are estimates that must be carefully evaluated before they are applied. CHI uses its scale to provide reliable and valid measures and to train its associates to interpret complex statistics correctly. A consequence of CHI's efforts with auditing and measuring is that any manager or team can say, "Yes, this measure has limitations, but we can be sure it's the best available. We cannot safely ignore what it is telling us."

Strategic and Financial Planning Activities

A solid business plan and a solid financial plan must complement values and measurement. Empowered performance teams can improve processes; it takes additional resources and a different team membership to evaluate strategic questions like "What constellation of processes best serves our community?" or "With whom should we partner?" CHI's strategic planning process has helped all levels of its organization understand and support its strategic vision. The CHI process includes the following:

- A standard data system that reports community needs and analyzes markets. Although the system itself is commercially available, CHI provides training and consultation on its use.
- A formal requirement for an annual planning retreat attended by national staff and MBO leadership that examines strategic issues and builds consensus on direction.
- A structured process that evaluates capital requests, mandating a business plan and check points for implementation in each request.
- Corporate approval of the capital and operating budgets.
- Enhanced borrowing capability through pooling of risk and strong overall financial management.
- Corporate review of affiliation and partnership opportunities beyond the level of individual MBOs.

This process may provide a critical advantage to CHI MBOs. These are substantial protections against the common dangers of strategic planning. MBOs are significantly less likely to ignore emerging opportunities, to reach hasty conclusions about investments, or to encounter capital shortages than their competitors. In addition to its process strengths, CHI's bond rating and its cost of capital are more favorable than most independent hospitals.

Centralized Services and CHI Burden

CHI's services have so far emphasized leadership development, networking, and auditing. It has deliberately avoided a model of central corporate services replacing functions like billing, laundry, or laboratory. This strategy reduces the risks of high central-office overhead costs, and it is consistent with empowering the local MBOs and reducing the cost burden of system membership. CHI's success has allowed it to acquire capital more cheaply than most.

CHI's networking and training take advantage of electronic communication. The system encourages direct networking between the MBOs as well as communication with the central office. Most managers have "affinity groups" of counterparts in other MBOs. They are encouraged to share and copy. Occasional central meetings review major new directions and allow face-to-face interaction. Recognized experts are identified throughout the system; many continue to work at MBO sites rather than the corporate office.

CHI now offers auditing, information systems, capital finance, cash management, health and other employee insurance, purchasing, training, and networking through its national structure. It holds these activities to competitive standards and, in general, allows MBOs to pick alternatives. It mandates only those programs where 100 percent participation is essential to the common success. It abandoned regional organizations, but it has task forces studying shared service opportunities. Given the power of electronic communication, the optimal structure for services like human resources, accounting, or imaging remains to be discovered. It is likely that additional sharing will emerge, but only when the gains are apparent to the MBOs.

CHI charges its MBOs a flat fee of 1.25 percent of their operating expenses; that fee covers most CHI services. Beyond it, MBOs are required to participate in certain purchasing agreements and in centralized insurance programs for all the usual business insurance, pensions, employee life insurance, and malpractice. Health benefits are limited to three options, and all MBOs are migrating to a shared health insurance program. The MBOs are also required to purchase internal audit services from CHAN and clinical engineering services. A few MBOs also participate in shared services for billing or information services. Each of these items is individually priced and carefully monitored for competitiveness. A concerned MBO board member can request full pricing information and often can also get comparative pricing for similar service purchased elsewhere.

Geraldine Hoyer, CSC, CHI chief financial officer:

> CHI is a mid-range system in terms of its cost to MBOs because CHI provides more services than other systems. I would never say CHI is a low-cost provider because there are systems that provide relatively few services. CHI just took over a hospital from another not-for-profit system; that resulted in a reduction in fees to the acquired facility. We have as "straight arrow" pricing as we can. We don't cross-subsidize anything. Cash is one example. We credit back the interest earned on cash. It's a transparent system.

Rewards

CHI is reward driven. It has deliberately stimulated a culture of celebration. "We laugh a lot," they said at St. Elizabeth and FHS. The "Spirit" programs at both institutions emphasize celebrations and rewards. Perhaps reflecting their acceptance of the values of reverence and compassion, most associates want people they meet to feel good. Despite the rigor of the last few years, most of the MBOs have records of improvement that give them reason to celebrate.

CHI recognizes the importance of the workplace environment as a reward. Its efforts to incorporate the service value chain, to develop leaders at all levels of the organization, and to be responsive to worker and physician needs pay off with reduced turnover and improved morale.

CHI offers financial rewards as well. These are in addition to base compensation that is carefully scaled to national and local competition. CHI provides substantial bonus incentive to its CEOs, tied to achieving goals in the four strategic platforms—people, quality, performance, and growth. Most of the CEOs have extended the same plan to their senior team. Many have programs for other management; St. Elizabeth is among the few that have programs for all workers. Practice opportunities for physicians accept the market realities of modern insured healthcare. Employed physicians are offered incentive opportunities. Joint ventures and contracts with physicians include financial incentives. The result is that a great many influential people have financial rewards in addition to intangible ones.

Incentive compensation is difficult to manage. The incentive must be clearly related to goals that improve the economic functioning of the firm. It must be perceived as fair. It must be realistically attainable, which means that the firm must provide the resources necessary to achieve the goals. It cannot overcome cultures that do not respect workers or that cannot answer the workers' questions. CHI's success with incentives reflects the strength of its integrated foundations.

The CHI Advantage

Taken together, these elements allow local MBO stakeholders to reach and implement a consensus on hospital operations that is more attractive in the marketplace than most competitors can achieve. This attractiveness is what has allowed CHI to thrive since 1999, growing and improving when many other hospitals and systems were struggling.

Stakeholders by definition have conflicting aims. The typical hospital is impaired by these conflicts, which often remain concealed or superficially papered over. CHI deliberately uses its central power to keep the stakeholders from exploiting one another. It minimizes the opportunities to deceive, divert, or defraud. Each group leaves the boardroom with less than its wildest hopes but with confidence that the disappointments were fairly shared and that the reality will match the agreement. The effectiveness of this consensus-building mechanism is as close to a "secret weapon" as CHI has. The mechanism allows associates to identify goals they can share and to use the sharing to improve the work environment. The result is a substantial reduction in tension, an improvement in morale, and forward motion on the shared goals. The silos and the turf disputes are replaced with recognition of the value of collaboration. When people see the advantage of the CHI approach, the rest, as Edison said about invention, is simply "perspiration"—the effort necessary to make the consensus a reality.

ADDRESSING RISKS AND THREATS

American healthcare faces several serious threats in the years ahead. CHI believes it has responded appropriately to them, deliberately pursuing strategies for the long term. Its operating model will keep it more effective than most in dealing with these threats.

Funding Adequate Healthcare

Funding difficulties threaten the entire national healthcare system. The three major financial engines—employment-based insurance, Medicare, and Medicaid—will continue to constrain growth even in the face of rising demand. Most Americans will struggle to pay for the kind of healthcare they desire. Financing for long-term care will be a growing problem as the population ages. Drugs for chronic disease, nursing home, home, and hospice care are among the least well-funded parts of healthcare, but demand is exploding. The inadequacies of Medicaid and the growing numbers of uninsured Americans impose an extra burden.

CHI's first response is an exceptionally broad and thorough effort to improve safety, effectiveness, and efficiency. The programs described in this book eliminate errors, improve outcomes, and lower costs. They succeed by restructuring the fundamentals of providing care. CHI's success in Franciscan Health System indicates that it can make its model work in one of the nation's lowest-cost communities, on terms that the caregivers and patients find acceptable. The healthy communities movement is a very long run opportunity that could have major consequences for the 2020s and beyond. All the MBOs are on learning curves, with opportunities to copy from path-breaking leaders. They will continue to improve.

CHI will not abandon its commitment "to emphasize human dignity and social justice." It will provide at least its share of care for the poor in its communities, and it will reach out to meet their special needs. But it must balance its portfolio of sites, selecting markets where it can be effective and avoiding an unrealistic commitment to sites with exceptional losses from Medicaid and the uninsured. Finally, CHI uses its success to promote appropriate directions in health and acceptable levels of payment. The respect and gratitude it generates in its communities help CHI make its case in public arenas. It uses its economic power to promote socially responsible action by other corporations. We believe CHI's response is at least as effective as any competing alternative.

Although its MBOs are not operating in some of the most financially threatened locations, CHI feels it has adequate funds. Sister Geraldine notes that everyone would always like more money but states:

> I think CHI has adequate capitalization. No MBO did not replace something that broke. CHI will continue to improve its capital position, but it's not something of such import that we won't move forward. When you are strapped for cash—and CHI is not—you have very little tolerance for risk. But when you have too much, you don't think as well. You tend to spend it on things you don't need.
>
> It doesn't take money, it takes work to improve an organization. When you have a problem, it is either a market problem, or a problem with payers, or systems within the organization that

don't work, or what I'll call a public relations issue—some conflict between your organization and its community. None of those are cured by money. You can't invest in an organization until you have those problems solved.

Recruiting Adequate Personnel

The national healthcare system may be more constrained by personnel shortages than funding shortages in the years ahead. Recurring shortages of nurses, primary care providers, and specialist physicians are inevitable. CHI's response is to create an attractive work environment. The evidence so far suggests that it will succeed at least as well as its competition. Its model provides both psychic and tangible reward, and it reduces the tensions and frustrations of caregiving. To some unknown extent, making the work more attractive helps relieve the shortages. It provides positive images for young people seeking careers. It keeps people in the workforce who might otherwise leave it.

CHI is also working directly with schools that supply healthcare workers, helping to recruit students, arrange affordable education, and keep educational programs aligned with current practice. Its internal educational programs help workers achieve their highest level of productivity. Its care systems promote use of lower skill levels. Community-based programs move caregiving out to nonprofessionals. Telemedicine extends the services of specialists. Team medicine extends the reach of the most-skilled professional members.

Supporting Specialist Physicians

Specialty physician shortages and relationships represent a unique challenge. A move toward separatism by specialty is creating freestanding services in cardiovascular intervention, imaging, orthopedics, eye disease, and cancer. These may generate great efficiency, safety, and timely care for those who can afford the service. They may reduce or destroy the patient-centered, effective, and equitable aspects of care. The freestanding centers are often models of attractiveness, quality, and efficiency, but they typically exclude the poor and uninsured and the high-risk patient with complex disease. They draw revenue and profits from the most needy, destabilizing the overall operation. Programs for prevention, emergency victims, patients with multiple diseases, the chronic sick, and the poor are at risk unless the system is designed to keep resources in balance.

CHI is working with its specialist physicians to provide the facilities and services that allow them rewarding practices and competitive incomes. Its ability to continue to do that depends on its ability to provide service and improve efficiency. It will position itself to give each specialist a rewarding practice but in a collaborative rather than a separatist context. The history of medicine suggests that there are always doctors who agree with CHI's vision and support collaborative efforts; those are the doctors CHI will seek. CHI's success will be improved by national programs that guide physician income to long-term health goals rather than excessive rewards to the dramatic episodes of care, and CHI will seek and promote those programs.

Making Strategic Choices

CHI and its MBOs make strategic commitments each year that determine the nature of care delivery. The risks inherent in these decisions are substantial. Any wrong investment impairs the future economic health. Too much capacity, or capacity in the wrong place, can be fatal. The wrong services mean higher cost and lower quality than might have been attained. The wrong partners mean that problems that might have been effectively addressed are not.

CHI's systems for making strategic decisions are robust. Proposals are subject to multiple reviews from differing perspectives. Expected outcomes are rigorously quantified. Ratios of costs and benefits are compared to alternative investments. Innovation is prized. Financing is kept at low cost and low risk. Implementation is audited. MBOs are expected to grow at an average rate of 6 percent per year, enough to keep facilities current and within conservative financial limits. CHI has a level of strategy beyond the MBO. It can and will collaborate with like-minded organizations, including for-profit providers. It expects to expand beyond its current sites by 4 percent per year, suggesting one or two acquisitions or partnerships in each year. It also can divest MBOs, and it is willing to do that in situations where all parties benefit. The acquisition and divestiture strategy is consistent with a limited risk to the existing MBOs. CHI will neither acquire nor divest in ways that appear to endanger its current affiliates.

Maintaining a Competitive Environment

CHI welcomes fair competition. Many of its MBOs compete aggressively and, like St. Elizabeth, regard competition as valuable for their community. Competition that delivers long-term value must balance customer and provider stakeholder needs. Unfair competition arises when the balance is disturbed. Unfair competitors can offer incentives to caregivers that drive up the cost of care or drive down the quality of care. They can dump nonpaying patients. They can divert resources to internal stakeholders at the expense of customer stakeholders. All of these are recognized dangers in the complex world of healthcare.

CHI is committed to delivering full measure to both customers and providers. Its strong compliance activity is designed to minimize the risk of false claims, fraud, or abuse of physician privileges. Its internal audit system protects against illegal gains both by CHI itself and by individuals in its organization. Its open stance with community boards is carefully designed to protect customer interests. Its pricing systems are designed to be just to all stakeholders, including CHI itself. It offers single hospital communities prices similar to more competitive situations.

The devices that protect fair competition—antitrust, fraud and abuse, antikickback, false claims control—are improvable in many ways. Despite their limitations, their continued uniform enforcement is essential to CHI's health and the health of other well-intentioned, not-for-profit healthcare providers.

Moving Beyond Benchmarks

One strategic risk is to fail to identify the disruptive innovation that undercuts the existing market leader and generates a new one. CHI protects against this by empowering its MBOs, freeing them to examine and develop new opportunities. It has explored several frontiers at the corporate level, with generally positive results. The business model itself is an advance over much current practice, and its record suggests greater customer satisfaction, efficiency, and effectiveness. Its healthy communities program promotes an underlying shift from cure to prevention. The national office is also currently pursuing programs for improved and increased palliative care, integrative or nontraditional medicine, and physician practice management.

CHI's argument is that it has a better model for dealing with the exigencies of the twenty-first century than its competition. It will achieve, in fact is achieving, greater efficiency than many other systems. It can identify the needs of caregivers and build environments that are attractive to them. Its strategic and financial planning models and its control of major capital expenditures will not guarantee that every strategic decision is correct, but they will improve the odds. It will provide community benefits that are more valuable than the taxes paid by for-profit systems. It will explore the frontiers that might hold the solutions to the future.

EXTENDING THE CHI MODEL TO OTHER COMMUNITIES

CHI's strategy is to continue to exploit its model, teaching its MBO leadership to set goals, helping them to achieve those goals, and rewarding them for doing so. CHI expects to document steady gains on the balanced scorecard in each MBO and move its watch-list organizations toward its leaders, reducing the variance among sites. It will use its partnering networks and educational activities to ensure that the path-breaking successes that has occurred at St. John's, Memorial, Mercy, St. Elizabeth, Good Samaritan, and Franciscan becomes routine in CHI's other 41 sites.

CHI will also remain alert for opportunities to advance its goals by collaboration in the communities it serves. CHI is open to joint efforts with its competitors and others. The healthy communities agenda is particularly suited to collaborative approaches. In many communities, competitors can expand offerings of low-volume services by cooperating. CHI intends to stay within both the letter and the spirit of antitrust law. It will continue to reduce its costs and to price for the margin needed to sustain growth and innovation so that its savings are passed on to its customers.

CHI is also open to the acquisition of additional MBOs, but only on its terms. Commitment to its values and its approach are essential. CHI does not offer temporary support or short-term affiliations. It will not enter an agreement that endangers or impairs its existing MBOs. If it acquires a healthcare organization, CHI requires community support and a viable long-term plan. This strategy has a promising record of transforming healthcare in the communities where CHI has a direct presence. It falls dramatically short of transforming the nation, a task that requires a hundredfold expansion.

CHI hopes that any healthcare organization, even the smallest, can use the stories from its six sites and can emulate their success. Most healthcare organizations in the United States already belong to systems; as the systems are made more effective, more organizations will join. Strengthening the systems, therefore, is the critical step for the transformation. A realistic plan to complete the transformation includes three elements:

1. strengthening existing systems,
2. forming new systems, and
3. maintaining fair competition between systems.

Strengthening Existing Systems

We believe that CHI's approach is a template against which other systems can be judged and that the balanced scorecard approach provides the necessary measures. Governing boards of systems can and should insist on balanced scorecard measures, benchmarking, and continuous improvement. They should insist on independent auditing. System governing boards provide the discipline to local boards. Employed accountable managers should link the two.

Transforming Holding Companies to Operating Companies

At its root, the transformation begins with a change in the consensus about direction, toward one that is explicitly focused on success by meeting customer needs rather than one that implements a set of compromises to distribute effort and benefit. Many existing systems are burdened with historic, sometimes unmentionable compromises among former owners, physicians, unions, and other organized stakeholders; these compromises must be swept aside. Joining CHI explicitly required permanently accepting a "lay and religious partnership" to implement an explicitly universal vision. The second step, driven by fiscal necessity, was the move to measured performance and realistic goal setting.

Fiscal crises are useful because they make clear that older models are no longer effective, and they stimulate previously competing stakeholders to collaborate. Many systems will use fiscal crises to make the transition. The best managed, or the luckiest, systems will avoid crises. They will sell the transition by comparison of performance, by documenting acceptable alternatives, and by negotiation.

The move to operating control must be justified to the stakeholders in terms of their own long-run success. The simplest expression of the argument is that working together is better than working apart. For that to be true, the operating company must demonstrate its ability. It must deliver on service, price, work environment, compensation, and rewards.

Improving the Services of Central Organizations

The services of a successful operating company must be subject to the same rigor and continuous improvement as its affiliates. The cost of central services should be public and benchmarked against similar structures in healthcare and other industries. Comparison to the hospitality industry, for example, would indicate limits on central service costs tested in highly competitive markets. It might also reveal best practices for support that go well beyond current CHI offerings.

The notion of changing systems affiliation is forbidding, so the board of any local subsidiary should have assurances of value from its system. System performance on scope of service, price, and acceptability should be quantified. The board should be able to document to community stakeholders the value added by the system and the system's performance compared to realistic alternatives.

Guarding Against Strategic Error

The record of large corporations of all types makes clear the danger of failure of centralized governance. Strategic decisions that are bad, self-serving, or even dishonest are an obvious risk. The ability to assemble a knowledgeable, ethical, and committed system governing board, and support it with effective senior management, may be the limiting factor in system progress. Several tools are available to improve strategic capability and minimize the danger of centralized governance failure:

- Implementing an objective information and financial system with independent auditing
- Using a strategic process that involves broad discussion, widespread checking of assumptions, and modeling of expectations
- Training subsidiary boards on strategic and community responsibility
- Maintaining the independence and diversity of selection and nominating committees
- Developing managerial talent including preparing senior managers
- Instituting planned rotation of key figures in management and governance

Providing Public Accountability

Not-for-profit organizations have been allowed a level of privacy that tolerates incompetence and encourages deceit. Systems should be accountable to the public. CHI publicly releases its financial information each quarter. (See *http://www.catholichealthinit.org/blank.cfm?id= 37582&action=search.*) All systems should routinely release reliable data that allow comparison and informed choice. The information should include the major elements of the balanced scorecard. As the systems grow larger, they should have the same level of public attention as do other large corporations.

The lack of reliable information contributes substantially to healthcare's current problems. A system of secrecy designed to be self-serving has become self-defeating. It is not possible to document either the problems or the opportunities because the data are concealed.

Forming New Systems

Systems provide about two-thirds of acute healthcare, but more than half the systems have revenues less than $1 billion per year. Many are smaller than the systems that were originally merged into CHI. Independent hospitals are generally even smaller. In terms of the national healthcare economy, both the smaller systems and the independents should thrive in all situations where they have real advantages. Competition from larger systems will challenge many existing small providers. The transformation of healthcare should lead to growth for some and closure for others.

To promote an optimal overall configuration, we believe that every community should have the opportunity to join healthcare systems that are willing and able to document their contribution. Ideally, every hospital's governing board should be able to consider offers from competing systems and compare its results under continued independent management with those offers. That action would place the systems under competitive pressure similar to those in other service sectors. We believe that level of competition would be a major step toward transformation.

New and larger systems will require capital. The present payment structure does not offer many incentives for improvement of performance. Programs that attach financial rewards to effective performance would be an important incentive toward consolidation. Effective joint ventures with organizations using equity capital may be a useful avenue. Existing equity providers have so far failed to demonstrate an advantage in either quality or cost performance, and many of their competitive gains involve selective marketing to the less sick and the better insured. Under expanded public information and scrutiny, they may have a renewed role. A program that attaches the not-for-profit tax advantage to documented community benefit and public release of information would stimulate constructive competition among not-for-profit providers. The Institute of Medicine's proposal for systematic demonstrations is certainly a start.

Maintaining Fair Competition Between Systems

Communities are the appropriate customers for the larger healthcare systems. They compete with one another, even when their healthcare systems do not. Given unfavorable comparative information about the cost and quality of healthcare, a community board would have strong motivation to insist on improvement. Restructuring its provider organization by consolidation or affiliation would be a promising avenue.

For the competition to be socially constructive, however, it must be fair. Today, communities are exposed to a number of forms of destructive competition; the most important are

- selective marketing by competitors that concentrates the expensive patients and the uninsured patients in a few organizations,
- programs that exploit high-paying procedures but do not provide a comprehensive system of care,
- flaws in the systems of physician contracting that make it difficult to support primary care and chronic care compared to specialty intervention, and
- monopolistic pricing supported by lack of comparative information.

Although many of these are addressed in current law and regulation, they remain hazards for systems like CHI. Improvements that clarified the intent and increased the specificity and integration of current regulations would help keep competition on a constructive path. We believe that improvement would lead to the restructuring of existing systems. As a result, more communities would be better served.

KEY LESSONS

Someone who was an influential citizen in a community, active on a healthcare board, and unsure of the performance of the community's healthcare system would be wise to gain support for the following steps.

1. *Review the values of existing healthcare organizations.* In most communities, acute care is provided by not-for-profit organizations that hold values similar to CHI's. Even the published values of for-profit organizations are not dramatically different from those of not-for-profits. Sound values emphasize respect for others, integrity, and excellence; these are concepts that form a solid platform for improvement of safety, effectiveness, timeliness, and efficiency of care.

   The issue is often not one of defining goals but of increasing commitment and achievement. Periodic review is valuable in itself. The process helps clarify the stakeholders' individual desires, identify the goals that can be shared, and build consensus. It leads to identification and prioritization of areas for improvement.

2. *Request balanced scorecard measures, benchmarks, and annual goals.* The scorecard is the best-known way to review the complex demands on a healthcare enterprise and to support a program of continuous improvement. The annual goal-setting process is now routine in most industries, and it should be in healthcare. The more the dimensions are quantified, the harder it becomes to evade or ignore important areas of disagreement or failure. Comparative data and benchmarks create their own dynamic and can be used to identify realistic goals.

3. *Restructure the finance committee, substantially strengthen the independence and resources of internal auditing and expand its scope, and strengthen the contract with the external auditor.* This is a critical step to achieve transparent honesty, and transparent honesty is a foundation for programs that motivate providers. Not-for-profit healthcare has escaped the worst scandals of auditing failures, but many institutions will be strengthened by greater independence of the auditor, the financial management staff, and the internal auditor. CHAN's system of complete independence will be a long-term competitive advantage. Similarly, the external auditor should have no other financial ties to the organization and should receive instructions from and report to an independent board member who chairs either the finance or audit committee. Periodic replacement of the external auditor is wise.

4. *Invest deliberately in an expansion of networking, education, and performance improvement.* Given a chance to set improvement goals, most people would like to accept the challenge of meeting them. To do so, they must learn new techniques, develop new methods, and install new equipment. All of these activities cost money. Although they will eventually be self-financing, they need initial funding change.

5. *Encourage celebrations and offer tangible rewards for success.* Caregiving is an emotionally demanding activity, especially when it goes badly. An environment of trust, mutual respect, and celebration supports staff in many different and subtle ways. Creating and keeping that environment is a major step in dealing with caregiver shortages. Those organizations that have a supporting environment are substantially more successful at recruitment and retention.

   CHI also uses tangible rewards extensively. CHI's successful experience is leading it to expand its monetary reward programs. Despite the complexities of bonuses and similar devices, they are well liked and no longer rare in the workplace.

6. *Identify customer needs and strengthen customer relationships.* Customers have choices and they exercise them. Hospitals that respond to customer needs will thrive at the expense of those that do not. The old silos of traditional hospitals are disappearing because customers are better served by service line structures. Focusing on customer needs explains the transition and clarifies the goals for the new organization. Job security and organizational longevity are earned from the customer.

7. *Strengthen physician and nurse support so that the organization is viewed as a preferred employer.* CHI has documented that the path created by these steps is one that can be rewarding to both physicians and nurses. An atmosphere of trust, an environment where questions get answered, and a culture of respect and reward attract the best caregivers. Recognition of their professional, personal, and financial needs and ongoing dialog on how to meet them helps keep these professionals.

   Competitive compensation is part of the package. CHI monitors patient care salaries for nurses and is prepared to make mid-year adjustments when necessary. It is open to contracts with physicians that incorporate competitive rewards for quality and customer performance.

8. *Publish the major balanced scorecard measures.* Published results on quality, performance, growth, and people are a relatively modest force in the market. Those states that have mandated public data have not encountered drastic shifts in market. Yet in the long run, places that achieve on these measures will be healthier and will spend less to stay healthy than places that do not. The best way to stimulate productive competition among providers in a single community is to focus that competition on measured performance of value to the community.

Index

Accountability, 5, 11–12, 75–76; CEO, 54–55; clinical outcomes as, 112; goal setting, 33–36; importance, 197; improvement goals, 76–77; measurement, 24, 29–37; public, 250–51; of service line administrators, 84; standards, 201–2

American Society for Training and Development, 224

Anderson, Jami: on CHAT, 134–35; on finance, 138

Aplin, Jill: on building cardiac services, 64–65; on service consolidations, 62–64

Ascension Health, 11

Audits, 27, 42. *See also* CHAN

Backstrom, Dean: on CHI consulting services, 47; on honesty, 26; on physician relations, 44–45

Balanced scorecard. *See* BSC

Batterer Intervention Prevention Program, 137

BCCHP, 129; contribution, 154; finance, 137–38; goals and achievements, 139–40; measures, 136–37; programs, 134–36, 156–57; results, 138–42; structure, 129, 133–34; workplace wellness program, 142–43

Beard, Joan, 108–9

Bechtle, Liz, 194

Benchmarks, 70, 247–48; CHI and, 85; importance of, 253

Bersante, Syd: on physician's role, 231–32; on resources, 220

Blanche, Sharon: on end-of-life program, 108; on quality improvement, 96–97

Board member training, 41–42

Board of Stewardship Trustees, 4

Bollwitt, Lesley, 155

Bowman, June, 211; on controversy, 215; on emergency services, 227; on future directions, 233; on nursing, 229–30; on quality of care, 225; on service excellence, 208; on worker satisfaction, 212

Bray, Steve, 176; on goals, 177; on internal listening, 184, 185

Brinkley, Ruth: on clinical excellence, 61; on core mission, 69; on culture of excellence, 83; on educational development, 74; on governing board support, 81–82

Brokel, Jane, 89; on community-based case management, 100

Brown, Diona, 65; on integrating clinical care, 66

Brown, Jeff, 158; on healthy lifestyles, 148–49

Brown, Sara, 210; on culture change, 214, 215–16; on service excellence structure, 211; on service recovery, 221

BSC: development of, 31–32; at FHS, 223; goal negotiation and, 35; importance of, 54, 253; publishing, 255; at St. John's Regional Medical Center, 28; service excellence and, 235; strategy and, 181; sustainability and, 52

Buffalo County Community Health Partners. *See* BCCHP

Burds, Ann, 98

Burkett, Lori, 178, 179

Bush, Bonnie: on celebration, rewards, 222; on service improvement, 226

Capital management, 186–87

Caretracs, 71

Carlberg, Kim, 105–6

Carlton, Stephen, 20; on board meeting, 48–49; on board member training, 41–42; on CHI involvement, 39, 53; on governance, 23; on honesty, 26; on physician relations, 43; on skill building, 50

Carondelet St. Mary's Hospital, 99

Case management, *ix*, 2; access to, 112; accountability for outcomes, 112; advantages, 95–97; community-based, 99–102; behavior motivation, 112; defined, 93–102; framework, 113–14; hospital-based, 97–99; lessons, 113–17; models, 102–9; professional collaboration in, 111; reimbursement for, 112; results, 109–11

"Case Management Guidebook," 114

Catholic Healthcare Audit Network. *See* CHAN

Catholic Health Initiatives. *See* CHI

"Caught in the Act" award, 221, 234, 236

Celebrations, 254. *See also* Rewards

CEO, 208; accountability, 54–55; appointment, 11; CHI and, 12, 14, 38, 49–50, 242; compensation program for, 14; at FHS, 207; at GSHS, 125; incentive plan for, 188; interactions with, 24; at MHN, 89; and operations council, 174; performance measurement, 77; physician relations, 43, 44–45; results and, 199; at St. Elizabeth Health System, 161–64; at St. John's Regional Medical Center, 20; and service on

board of trustees, 4; skills of, 49; and turnover, 8

CFO: audit services and, 42; and board meeting, 48–49; and operations council, 174

Champion groups, 84, 113, 170, 171

CHAN, 235, 253; audit by, 27, 239, 241; audit results of, 199; audit services of, 42

CHAT, 134–35

Chattanooga Heart Institute, 64, 75

CHI, *ix*; accountability, 11–12, 29, 31, 250–51; action plan, 160, 165; and adequate healthcare, 243–45; advantage of, 38, 243; BSC of, 223; benchmarking and, 85, 247–48; and board member training, 41–42; business model, 39–40; capital caps, 187; centralized services, 241–42, 250; clinical service lines, 61, 70; and competitive environment, 246–47, 252; consulting services programs, 45–47, 79; core values of, 9–10, 15–18, 71–72, 212, 213, 235–36, 238–39; corporate strategy, 31; educational programs, 73, 74; and emergency services, 227; and employee retention, 166; and existing systems, 249; focus development, 181–84; goal setting, 33; grants from 137; healthcare environment and, 1–3; healthy community concept, 154; holding company conversion to operating company, 249; honesty and, 27, 28; hospitalist program, 193; HR issues, 184, 245; initiatives, 3–4; and integrated healthcare, 147; involvement, 39; and leadership, 75, 110; lessons, 54–55, 252–55; "Living the Mission: Key Indicators," 51; MACBETH, 191; measurement and, 36, 239–40; mission, 71–72, 94–95; model extension, 248–52; and new systems, 251–52; operating model, 5, 8; orientation by, 169; outsourcing and, 193–94, 195–96; performance measurement and, 6–7, 32, 77; physician relations, 44; prevention and, 126–27; quality measurement and, 197–98; reinforcement from, 53;

results and, 199; scalable model of, 237; stewardship and, 14–15; stimulating improvement, 237–38; strategy of, 240, 246, 250; support of, 12–14, 124; surveys, 188; systematization in, 4–5, 8–18; worker satisfaction, 211
Chief executive officer. See CEO
Chief financial officer. See CFO
Chief nursing officer. See CNO
Child Health Improvement Program, 141
Clinical comanagement model, 65
CNO: role of, 82; and service line administration, 65–66
Cole, Marie, 100–101
Community-based case management, 99–102
Community Health Access Team. See CHAT
Community health development, 127–29
Compassion, 10, 11, 239
Competitive bids, 193–96
"Complaint as a Gift," 173
Continuous quality improvement. See CQI
Cooley, Dr., 44
Core values. See CHI: core values of
Cost management, 196–97, 201
CQI, 178
Critical Access Network, 150
Crocker, Karen: on screening, 144; on workplace wellness, 142
Culture of excellence, 83–84

Daniell, Malcolm, 61
DeBakey, Dr., 44
DeFreece, Randy, 155
DeHaven, Jr., Dean, 27; on consulting services, 48
Delegation: managed, 24, 37–49
Diagnosis-related group. See DRG
Diagnostic screening, 144–45
Dierkhising, Judy: on leadership focus, 75; on service line expansion, 67
Disease-specific case management: heart failure, 103–4
Donohoe, Sean, 77
"Door-to-doctor time," 212
Dowling, Jean, 177; on goals, 178
DRG, 68, 71, 110

Dumonceaux, John G., 174; on incentive plan, 188–89; on internal listening, 184; on outside searches, 167; on productive teamwork, 175, 176; on recruitment, 165; on retention, 166

Eagleton, Beth, 27; on goal setting, 35
Electronic patient record. See EPR
"Embrace the Spirit," 169, 170, 172, 181, 185
End-of-life case management, 106–9
Environmental assessment, 182–84
EPR, 71
Erickson, Lois, 211
Evidence, ix-x
Evidence-based medicine, 28
Evidence-based protocols, 115, 116–17
Excellence, 10,11, 239
Executive team: motivated, 24, 49–52

Family Advocacy Network, 152
FHS: applicant selection, 216–17; background, 203, 207; celebration, rewards of, 221–22; CHI success with, 244; costs of, 223–25; and culture change, 212–16; ED at, 227–28; and employee training, 217–20; future directions for, 232–33; lessons, 233–36; and nursing, 229–31; performance measures at, 204–6; physician's role at, 231–32; and quality of care, 225–26; resources of, 220; results of, 223–32; service excellence components, 208–9; service excellence measures, 211–12; service excellence reason, 207–9; service excellence structure, 209–11; service improvement at, 226; service recovery at, 220–21; workforce reduction at, 226–27
501(c)(3) tax exempt, nonprofit status, 9
Fortune 300 companies, 4
Franciscan Health System. See FHS
Freeman, Vance, 68

George, Barbara, 178
Gilles, Pat, 174; on outsourcing, 194, 195; on position control, 190; on productive teamwork, 175
Gillespie, Greg: on promotions, 167; on recruitment, 165–66; on retention, 166

Glover, Dave, 150–51
Good Samaritan Health Systems. *See*
    GSHS
Good Samaritan Hospital Foundation, 155
Goode, David, 52
Governance, *ix*, 2; board member train-
    ing, 41–42; goal setting, 33–36;
    internal consulting services, 45–49;
    lessons, 54–55; managed delegation,
    37–49; measured accountability, 29–
    37; medical staff support, 42–45;
    ministry/business model, 39–40; per-
    formance measurement commitment,
    20–22, 36–37; sustainability, 52–53;
    transparent honesty, 24, 25–29; and
    values, 24–25, 30, 50–52
Governing board support, 81–82
GSHS, 248; background, 119, 124;
    BCCHP programs of, 129–43; beyond
    acute care, 143–46; community health
    commitment, 127–29; diagnostic
    screening at, 144–45; hospice program,
    146; integrative health strategy, 147–
    50; lessons, 156–58; performance
    measures, 120–23; and post-acute care,
    145; prevention outreach at, 124–27,
    152–55; rehabilitation program, 146;
    seminar by, 135

Hamilton, Marilyn, 102
Hantho, Leigh, 181
Hatlelid, R. Robert, 23–24; on physician
    relations, 43
Health Development Center, 145–46
Health Partners, 133, 136
Heart failure case management, 103–4
Heart Hospital, 106, 109–11
Hickman, David: on case management, 95;
    on leadership, 93
Honey, Debbi, 74
Hopkins, Mike, 184
Hospice of Siouxland, 106–8
Hospital-based case management, 97–99
Hospitalist program, 192–93
Hoyer, Geraldine, 27, 242, 244–45

Idea Mill, 220, 223, 232, 234
Incentive compensation, 52, 79, 188–89,
    235, 242–43

Information systems, 85, 115
Infusion services, 105–6
Institute of Medicine, 10, 124–25
Integrative care, 147–50
Integrity, 10, 11, 27, 238
Interfaith Ministries of Nebraska, 136

Johnson, Allen, 124: on community
    health development, 128; on workplace
    wellness, 142
Johnson & Johnson, 8; Credo, 15, 28, 50
Johnson, Allen, 124
Jones, Clint, 158: on health partners, 134;
    on screening, 144–45

Kaskie, James, 24, 50; on operating model,
    53
Kearney Area Community Foundation,
    137
Kern, Brenda, 101
Kids Connection, 141
Koesterer, Curt: on environmental assess-
    ment, 182; on outsourcing, 194

Lanik, Robert: action plan of, 160, 165; on
    capital management, 186; on culture,
    168; on importance of focus, 181;
    on losing money, 160; on Physician
    Network, 190–91; on productive
    teamwork, 175; on strategic plan,
    181–82
"Learning Journeys," 147–49
Lee-Eddie, Deborah, 233–34
Liggett, Charlotte, 174; on environmental
    assessment, 182–84; on internal
    listening, 184, 185; on outsourcing,
    194, 195; on productive teamwork, 176
Lindenstein, Joan, 134; on community
    health development, 128; on surveys,
    136–37
"Living the Mission: Key Indicators," 51
Locum tenens service, 151
Luke, Bill, 155

MACBETH, 13, 191–92
"Make It Right," 172–73
Management Assistance Clinic Break Even
    Team. *See* MACBETH
Market-based organization. *See* MBO

Market-driven healthcare, 54
Martinez, Donell, 169
MBO: benchmarking and, 85; CHI and, 39; CHI contact with, 12; CHI empowerment of, 237–43; CHI model and, 5, 8, 39–40, 237; CHI support to, 12–14; CHI values and, 9, 50–52; divestiture of, 15; expertise, 47; explained, 4; incentive program, 52; interactions with, 24; leadership and, 75; outsourcing and, 193–94, 195–96; and prevention, 126–27; proposals from, 11; service excellence in, 233–34; skill building, 49–50; and stewardship, 14–15; systemization and, 4–5; value and, 16–18
Measurement, ix-x
Medical staff: relations, 202; support, 42–45
Med-Mobile program, 37
Memorial Health Care System, 248; accountability, 75–77; background, 57, 61–62; building services, 64–65; challenges, 79–81; clinical excellence blueprint, 62–65; employee retention/promotion, 73–75; leadership partners, 75; lessons, 81–85; performance measures, 58–60; quality of service, 69–71; results, 77–79; service line expansions, 67–69; service line management blueprint, 65–69; service line organization, 65–66; service tradition, 71–72
Memorial Home Health, 57
Memorial North Park Hospital, 64
Mercy-Clinton, 101
Mercy-Des Moines, 87, 89, 108–9, 110
Mercy-Dubuque, 98
Mercy Health Network. See MHN
Mercy Health Services, 89; case management definition, 94
Mercy-North Iowa, 89, 99–100
Mercy-Sioux City, 106–7
MHN 248; access to case management, 112; accountability for clinical outcomes, 112; background, 87–93; case management advantages for, 95–97; case management defined, 93–102; case management lessons, 113–17; case management models, 102–9; case management results, 109–11; community-based case management and, 99–102; dual system membership by, 113; hospital-based case management and, 97–99; incentive misalignment and, 112; Management Council, 89; motivation for behaviors, 112; performance measures, 90–92; and professional collaboration, 111; reimbursement, 112; telemanagement program, 105
Mid-Nebraska Community Action, 134
Mid-Nebraska Telemedicine Network, 119
Ministry/business model, 38, 39–40
Ministry Network "Health Ministry 101," 136
Mission, 9, 54; effectiveness, 201; at St. John's Regional Medical Center, 30
Moore, Deb: on cardiac care, 64; on CHI mission, values, 71–72; on educational development, 73
Moore, Kim S., 186; on capital management, 187; on goals, 177, 178; on hiring, 167–68; on performance improvement, 178, 179; on productive teamwork, 174–75, 176; on promoting excellence, 169, 172, 174; on recruitment, 166
Morrow, Shawn, 67–68
Morten, Lisa: on celebration, rewards, 222; on employee training, 219; on hiring goals, 217; on HR costs, 224; on nurse recruitment, 230; on workforce reduction, 226
Mueller, John: on costs, 224; on employee training, 217–20; on nursing, 230–31; on service improvement, 226

National Quality Forum, 198
National Retirement Foundation, 105
Nebraska Association for the Mentally Ill, 134
Nebraska State Health Department, 138
Networking, 254
"New Civilization—A Healthy Community" 128

Newton, Carol: on improvement goals, 77; on results orientation, 77–78
Nichols, Laure, 225
Nnanji, Chinma, 102
Noronha, Sr., Augusto (Tony), 29, 48; on audit services, 42; on CHI consulting services, 45, 47; on goal setting, 34, 35
North Park Hospital, 57
Nurse management, 115–16
Nursing, 229–31
Nursing support, 254–55

O'Bryant, Mark: on clinical service line organization, 68–69; patient care and, 83
Outreach program/services, 124–27, 130–32; benefits, 152–55; celebration, 157
Outsourcing, 193–96

Palliative care case management, 106–9
"Pass a Smile," 214
Patient-based care, 82–83, 124–25
Patient-oriented teams, 2
Patient satisfaction, 228
Payne, Nan, 70; on educational development, 73, 74
Pence, Mike, 23; on CHI involvement, 39; on honesty, 25; on performance measurement, 32
Performance improvement, 55, 198, 254; council, 235; initiation of, 5
Performance improvement team. See PIT
Performance measurement, 31–33, 77; at FHS, 204–6; at GSHS, 120–23; at Memorial Health Care System, 58–60; at MHN, 90–92; at St. Elizabeth Health System, 161–64; at St. John's Regional Medical Center, 20–22
Performance reviews, 52
Personnel recruitment, 245
Physician Network, 185, 190–92
Physician partners, 84
Physician relations, 37
Physician support, 254–55
PIT, 166, 179
Position control, 189–90
"Prairie pride," 135

Prevention, x, 2; BCCHP programs, 129–43; benefits, 143–46, 152–55; celebration, 157; community health commitment, 127–29; diagnostic screening and, 144–45; hospice program and, 146; integrative health strategy, 147–50; lessons, 156–58; performance measures, 120–23; and post-acute care, 145; outreach and, 124–27, 152–55; rehabilitation program, 146
Productive teams, 174–75
Professional boundaries, 80
Progress reports, 78–79, 187–88
Protocols, 3
Pruitt, Michelle, 210; on culture change, 214, 216; on nursing, 231; on service excellence structure, 211; on service recovery, 221

Quality of care, 225–26
Quality initiatives, 37
Quality measurement, 197–98
Quality of service, 69–71, 201

Raetz, Libby, 169, 171–74
Recognition Tool Kit, 222
Region III Behavioral Health Services, 134
Religious-lay partnership, 4, 9
Renner, Carol, 136
Reserved powers, 11
Reverence, 10, 11, 238
Rewards, 28, 198–99, 242–43, 254
Roden, Melissa, 65; on clinical guidelines, 70, 71; on service line fine-tuning, 66
Rowe, Gary L., 20; on accountability, 30–31; on audit services, 42; on CHI, 29; on goal setting, 33–35; hiring of, 23; on honesty, 26; incentive program, 52; on physician relations, 43–44; on values, 51
Rural support, 150–52

Safe Center, 137
St. Clare Hospital, 223
St. Elizabeth Health System, 248; background, 159–65; capital management, 186–87; culture, 168–69; environmental assessment, 182–84; improvement

goals, 176–78; incentives, 188–89; internal listening, 184–86; lessons, 196–200; outsourcing, competitive bids, 193–96; performance improvement teams, 178–79; performance measures, 161–64; and Physician Network, 190–92; and position control, 189–90; productive teams, 174–76; progress reports, 187–88; promoting excellence, 169–74; results, 187–96, strategy focus, 179–87; talent base, 165–68; team building, 168–79

St. Francis Hospital, 223, 231–32

St. John's Regional Medical Center, 199, 248; background, 19, 23; board member training, 41–42; goal setting, 33–36; governance, 23–25; internal consulting services, 45–49; lessons, 54–55; managed delegation, 37–49; measured accountability, 29–37; medical staff support, 42–45; ministry/business model, 39–40; mission, 30; performance measurement, 20–22, 36–37; skill building, 49–50; sustainability, 52–53; transparent honesty, 24, 25–29; values, 24–25, 30, 50–52; vision, 30

St. Joseph Hospital, 208, 216, 223, 229, 233

Satisfaction surveys, 11–12

Schultz, Cindy, 148–49

Schumacher, Larry: on case management action plans, 89; leadership and, 93

Service excellence: applicant selection/orientation, 216–17; celebration/rewards, 221–22; CHI success with, 244; components, 208–9; costs, 223–25; and culture change, 212–16; ED and, 227–28; and employee training, 217–20; future directions, 232–33; lessons, 233–36; measures, 211–12; and nursing, 229–31; performance measures, 204–6; physician's role, 231–32; and quality of care, 225–26; reason for, 207–9; resources, 220; results, 223–32; service improvement and, 226; service recovery and, 220–21; structure, 209–11; workforce reduction and, 226–27

Service improvement, 226

Service lines, ix, x, 3; accountability and, 75–77; blueprint for, 63–65; building, 64–65; challenges, 79–81; employee retention/promotion, 73–75; expansions, 67–69; leadership partners, 75; lessons, 81–85; management blueprint, 65–69; organization, 65–66; performance measures, 58–60; quality of service, 69–71

Service value chain, 207

"Show the Way," 214

Siouxland Palliative Care, 106–8

Sisters of Charity, 57, 156

Sisters of Charity Health Care Systems, 127

Sisters of Charity of Nazareth, 71, 82

Smith, Marshall, 35

Sommerfeld, Rev. Russell, 133–34, 135–36

Spangler, Patti, 70, 71

Specialist physicians, 245–46

Speck, Mary Ellen, 96

Spider diagram, 180

"Spirit at Work," 212–16, 221, 224, 231, 233, 235

Stephen Ministries, 135

Stewardship, 5, 14–15

"Strengthening Hospital Nursing Programs," 89

Support, 5, 12–14

Support services, x, 3; capital management and, 186–87; culture and, 168–69; environmental assessment, 182–84; improvement goals, 176–78; incentives, 188–89; internal listening and, 184–86; lessons, 196–200; outsourcing, competitive bids and, 193–96; performance improvement teams, 178–79; performance measures, 161–64; and Physician Network, 190–92; and position control, 189–90; productive teams, 174–76; progress reports, 187–88; promoting excellence, 169–74; results, 187–96; strategy focus, 179–87; talent base, 165–68; team building, 168–79

Swanson, Lori, 97

SWOT analysis, 182

Takes, Kay, 98
Telemanagement, 105, 110–11
Telemedicine, 153
Thomas de Sales, Sister, 61; on service consolidations, 62, 67
Todd, Linda, 106–8
Tomlon, Ken, 125
Tozzio, Mark: on business model, 40; on CHI consulting services, 48; on physician relations, 45; on strategic plan, 49
Transparent Honesty, 24–29, 32, 53–54
Trinity Community Health Fund, 110
Trinity Health, 87, 89, 113; case management definition, 94, 95
Turning Point, 138, 141

U.S. Preventive Services Task Force, 144
University of Nebraska, 151

Values, 5, 10–11, 15–18: CHI, core, 9–10, 50–52; and managed delegation, 24, 37–49; measured accountability for, 24, 29–37; motivated executive team for, 24, 49–52; review of, 253; at St. John's Regional Medical Center, 30; and transparent honesty, 24, 25–29
Vanderbilt triad model, 98
Vellinga, David, 89
Vision, 9, 10–11; St. John's Regional Medical Center, 30; GSHS, 128
"Vision Element Committees," 133
Vocational Rehabilitation, 134
Vosik, Bill, 144–45

Wachter, Terry, 51
Wadell, Jan: on internal listening, 184; on outsourcing, 194

Waibel-Rycek, Denise, 146
Ward, Cary: on hospitalist program, 192–93; on internal listening, 185–86
Weekley, Wanda, 151–52
Weems, Jim, 190, 191–92
Weight Management Center, 68
Weissert, Jeff, 184, 185
Welch, Jack, 14
"Well City USA," 129
Wellness, x
Wellness Works, 156–57
Wickemeyer, William, 103–4, 105
Wilczek, Joseph, 236; on bonuses, 222–23; on controversy, 215; on employee selection, 216; on employee training, 217; on future directions, 232–33; motto of, 207; on physician's role, 231, 232; on quality of care, 225–26; on results, 223; on service excellence, 208, 209, 210; on worker satisfaction, 212; workforce reduction, 227
Willyard, Deb, 104
Winchester, David, 77
"Women and Heart Disease," 144
Workforce reduction, 226–27
Workplace wellness program, 142–43, 153
"Work in Progress, A," 160, 165
Wojtalewicz, Jeanette, 174, 186; on capital management, 187; on goals, 177; on outsourcing, 196; on position control, 190; on productive teamwork, 175
Wright, Kinsman: on cardiac care, 61–62, 63; on leadership focus, 75

Zwiener, Denise: on BCCHP programs, 133; on goal measurement, 137; on workplace wellness, 143

About the Authors

John R. Griffith, M.B.A., FACHE, is the Andrew Pattullo Collegiate Professor in the Department of Health Management and Policy, School of Public Health, The University of Michigan, Ann Arbor. A graduate of Johns Hopkins University and the University of Chicago, he was director of the program and Bureau of Hospital Administration at The University of Michigan from 1970 to 1982 and chair of his department from 1987 to 1991.

Professor Griffith has been at Michigan since 1960. He is an educator of graduate students and practicing healthcare executives. He has served as chair of the Association of University Programs in Health Administration (AUPHA) and as a commissioner for the Accrediting Commission on Education in Health Services Administration. He is senior adviser to the National Center for Healthcare Leadership.

He is the author of numerous publications on best practices and performance measurement for healthcare organizations. The first edition of *The Well-Managed Healthcare Organization* won the ACHE Hamilton Prize for book of the year in 1987, and the fourth was named Book of the Year by the Health Information Management Systems Society.

Professor Griffith was awarded the Gold Medal of the American College of Healthcare Executives (ACHE) in 1992 and the Filerman Prize for Excellence in Teaching by AUPHA in 2002. He has also been recognized with the John Mannix Award of the Cleveland Hospital Council, the Edgar C. Hayhow (the most recent of which is in 2002) and Dean Conley Awards of ACHE, and citations from the Michigan Hospital Association and the Governor of Michigan. Professor Griffith has been a director of The Allegiance Corporation, a physician-hospital organization serving Ann Arbor. He was an examiner for the Malcolm Baldrige National Quality Award from 1997 to 1998. He speaks and consults widely on the development of voluntary healthcare systems.

Kenneth R. White, Ph.D., FACHE, is an associate professor and director of the graduate program in health administration at the Medical College of Virginia Campus of Virginia Commonwealth University (VCU). Dr. White received a Ph.D. in health services organization and research from VCU, a M.P.H. in health administration from the University of Oklahoma, and a M.S. in nursing from VCU.

Dr. White has extensive experience in hospital administration and consulting, particularly in the areas of leadership development, marketing, medical staff development, operations management, and facility planning and design. Dr. White is a registered nurse and a Fellow and Regent at Large (District 3) of the American College of Healthcare Executives.

Dr. White is a contributing author in the books *Human Resources in Healthcare: Managing for Success* (Health Administration Press 2001) and *Advances in Health Care Organization Theory* (Jossey-Bass 2003). He is the chair of the AUPHA editorial board of the American College of Healthcare Executives.

Patricia A. Cahill, J.D., is president and CEO of Catholic Health Initiatives (CHI), one of the largest not-for-profit healthcare systems in the country. CHI, based in Denver, Colorado, sponsors over 110 hospitals, nursing homes, and assisted living facilities in 19 states and has annual operating revenues of $6 billion. Prior to assuming this position in 1996, Ms. Cahill was director of Health & Hospitals for the Archdiocese of New York. She has also served as president and CEO of Calvary Hospital in the Bronx, the only acute care hospital in the country that is devoted solely to the care of advanced cancer patients. Ms. Cahill served as vice president of Governmental Services of the Catholic Health Association. She substantially expanded its activities in Washington, D.C., representing the association with both the legislative and administrative branches of government. She was educated at Emmanuel College in Boston and earned her law degree from George Washington University in Washington, D.C. Additionally, Ms. Cahill is the recipient of additional honors, including four honorary doctorates in humane letters and one honorary doctorate of law.